Nutshell Series
Hornbook Series
and
Black Letter Series
of
WEST PUBLISHING COMPANY
P.O. Box 64526
St. Paul, Minnesota 55164–0526

Accounting

FARIS' ACCOUNTING AND LAW IN A NUTSHELL, 377 pages, 1984. Softcover. (Text)

Administrative Law

GELLHORN AND LEVIN'S ADMINISTRATIVE LAW AND PROCESS IN A NUTSHELL, Third Edition, 479 pages, 1990. Softcover. (Text)

Admiralty

MARAIST'S ADMIRALTY IN A NUTSHELL, Second Edition, 379 pages, 1988. Softcover. (Text)

SCHOENBAUM'S HORNBOOK ON ADMIRALTY AND MARITIME LAW, Student Edition, 692 pages, 1987 with 1989 pocket part. (Text)

Agency—Partnership

REUSCHLEIN AND GREGORY'S HORNBOOK ON THE LAW OF AGENCY AND PARTNERSHIP, Second Edition, 683 pages, 1990. (Text)

STEFFEN'S AGENCY-PARTNERSHIP IN A NUTSHELL, 364 pages, 1977. Softcover. (Text)

American Indian Law

CANBY'S AMERICAN INDIAN LAW IN A NUTSHELL, Second Edition, 336 pages, 1988. Softcover. (Text)

Antitrust—see also Regulated Industries, Trade Regulation

GELLHORN'S ANTITRUST LAW AND ECONOMICS IN A NUTSHELL, Third Edition, 472 pages,

Antitrust—Continued

1986. Softcover. (Text)

HOVENKAMP'S BLACK LETTER ON ANTITRUST, 323 pages, 1986. Softcover. (Review)

HOVENKAMP'S HORNBOOK ON ECONOMICS AND FEDERAL ANTITRUST LAW, Student Edition, 414 pages, 1985. (Text)

SULLIVAN'S HORNBOOK OF THE LAW OF ANTITRUST, 886 pages, 1977. (Text)

Appellate Advocacy—see Trial and Appellate Advocacy

Art Law

DUBOFF'S ART LAW IN A NUTSHELL, 335 pages, 1984. Softcover. (Text)

Banking Law

BANKING LAW: SELECTED STATUTES AND REGULATIONS. Softcover. 263 pages, 1991.

LOVETT'S BANKING AND FINANCIAL INSTITUTIONS LAW IN A NUTSHELL, Second Edition, 464 pages, 1988. Softcover. (Text)

Civil Procedure—see also Federal Jurisdiction and Procedure

CLERMONT'S BLACK LETTER ON CIVIL PROCEDURE, Second Edition, 332 pages, 1988. Softcover. (Review)

FRIEDENTHAL, KANE AND MILLER'S HORNBOOK ON CIVIL PROCEDURE, 876 pages, 1985. (Text)

KANE'S CIVIL PROCEDURE IN A NUTSHELL, Third Edition, 303 pages, 1991. Softcover. (Text)

KOFFLER AND REPPY'S HORNBOOK ON COMMON LAW PLEADING, 663 pages, 1969. (Text)

SIEGEL'S HORNBOOK ON NEW YORK PRACTICE, Second Edition, Student Edition, 1068 pages, 1991. Softcover. (Text)

Commercial Law

BAILEY AND HAGEDORN'S SECURED TRANSACTIONS IN A NUTSHELL, Third Edition, 390 pages, 1988. Softcover. (Text)

HENSON'S HORNBOOK ON SECURED TRANSACTIONS UNDER THE U.C.C., Second Edition, 504 pages, 1979, with 1979 pocket part. (Text)

NICKLES' BLACK LETTER ON COMMERCIAL PAPER, 450 pages, 1988. Softcover. (Review)

SPEIDEL'S BLACK LETTER ON SALES AND SALES FINANCING, 363 pages, 1984. Softcover. (Review)

STOCKTON'S SALES IN A NUT-

Commercial Law—Continued

SHELL, Second Edition, 370 pages, 1981. Softcover. (Text)

STONE'S UNIFORM COMMERCIAL CODE IN A NUTSHELL, Third Edition, 580 pages, 1989. Softcover. (Text)

WEBER AND SPEIDEL'S COMMERCIAL PAPER IN A NUTSHELL, Third Edition, 404 pages, 1982. Softcover. (Text)

WHITE AND SUMMERS' HORNBOOK ON THE UNIFORM COMMERCIAL CODE, Third Edition, Student Edition, 1386 pages, 1988. (Text)

Community Property

MENNELL AND BOYKOFF'S COMMUNITY PROPERTY IN A NUTSHELL, Second Edition, 432 pages, 1988. Softcover. (Text)

Comparative Law

GLENDON, GORDON AND OSAKWE'S COMPARATIVE LEGAL TRADITIONS IN A NUTSHELL. 402 pages, 1982. Softcover. (Text)

Conflict of Laws

HAY'S BLACK LETTER ON CONFLICT OF LAWS, 330 pages, 1989. Softcover. (Review)

SCOLES AND HAY'S HORNBOOK ON CONFLICT OF LAWS, Student Edition, approximately 1100 pages, November 1991 Pub. (Text)

SIEGEL'S CONFLICTS IN A NUTSHELL, 470 pages, 1982. Softcover. (Text)

Constitutional Law—Civil Rights

BARRON AND DIENES' BLACK LETTER ON CONSTITUTIONAL LAW, Third Edition, 440 pages, 1991. Softcover. (Review)

BARRON AND DIENES' CONSTITUTIONAL LAW IN A NUTSHELL, Second Edition, 483 pages, 1991. Softcover. (Text)

ENGDAHL'S CONSTITUTIONAL FEDERALISM IN A NUTSHELL, Second Edition, 411 pages, 1987. Softcover. (Text)

MARKS AND COOPER'S STATE CONSTITUTIONAL LAW IN A NUTSHELL, 329 pages, 1988. Softcover. (Text)

NOWAK AND ROTUNDA'S HORNBOOK ON CONSTITUTIONAL LAW, Fourth Edition, approximately 1275 pages, August, 1991 Pub. (Text)

VIEIRA'S CONSTITUTIONAL CIVIL RIGHTS IN A NUTSHELL, Second Edition, 322 pages, 1990. Softcover. (Text)

Constitutional Law—Civil Rights—Continued

WILLIAMS' CONSTITUTIONAL ANALYSIS IN A NUTSHELL, 388 pages, 1979. Softcover. (Text)

Consumer Law—see also Commercial Law

EPSTEIN AND NICKLES' CONSUMER LAW IN A NUTSHELL, Second Edition, 418 pages, 1981. Softcover. (Text)

Contracts

CALAMARI AND PERILLO'S BLACK LETTER ON CONTRACTS, Second Edition, 462 pages, 1990. Softcover. (Review)

CALAMARI AND PERILLO'S HORNBOOK ON CONTRACTS, Third Edition, 1049 pages, 1987. (Text)

CORBIN'S TEXT ON CONTRACTS, One Volume Student Edition, 1224 pages, 1952. (Text)

FRIEDMAN'S CONTRACT REMEDIES IN A NUTSHELL, 323 pages, 1981. Softcover. (Text)

KEYES' GOVERNMENT CONTRACTS IN A NUTSHELL, Second Edition, 557 pages, 1990. Softcover. (Text)

SCHABER AND ROHWER'S CONTRACTS IN A NUTSHELL, Third Edition, 457 pages, 1990. Softcover. (Text)

Copyright—see Patent and Copyright Law

Corporations

HAMILTON'S BLACK LETTER ON CORPORATIONS, Second Edition, 513 pages, 1986. Softcover. (Review)

HAMILTON'S THE LAW OF CORPORATIONS IN A NUTSHELL, Third Edition, 518 pages, 1991. Softcover. (Text)

HENN AND ALEXANDER'S HORNBOOK ON LAWS OF CORPORATIONS, Third Edition, Student Edition, 1371 pages, 1983, with 1986 pocket part. (Text)

Corrections

KRANTZ' THE LAW OF CORRECTIONS AND PRISONERS' RIGHTS IN A NUTSHELL, Third Edition, 407 pages, 1988. Softcover. (Text)

Creditors' Rights

EPSTEIN'S DEBTOR-CREDITOR LAW IN A NUTSHELL, Fourth Edition, 401 pages, 1991. Softcover. (Text)

NICKLES AND EPSTEIN'S BLACK LETTER ON CREDITORS' RIGHTS AND BANKRUPTCY, 576 pages, 1989. (Review)

Criminal Law and Criminal Procedure—see also Corrections, Juvenile Justice

ISRAEL AND LAFAVE'S CRIMINAL PROCEDURE—CONSTITUTIONAL LIMITATIONS IN A NUTSHELL, Fourth Edition, 461 pages, 1988. Softcover. (Text)

LAFAVE AND ISRAEL'S HORNBOOK ON CRIMINAL PROCEDURE, Second Edition, Student Edition, approximately 1200 pages, December, 1991 Pub. (Text)

LAFAVE AND SCOTT'S HORNBOOK ON CRIMINAL LAW, Second Edition, 918 pages, 1986. (Text)

LOEWY'S CRIMINAL LAW IN A NUTSHELL, Second Edition, 321 pages, 1987. Softcover. (Text)

LOW'S BLACK LETTER ON CRIMINAL LAW, Revised First Edition, 443 pages, 1990. Softcover. (Review)

Domestic Relations

CLARK'S HORNBOOK ON DOMESTIC RELATIONS, Second Edition, Student Edition, 1050 pages, 1988. (Text)

KRAUSE'S BLACK LETTER ON FAMILY LAW, 314 pages, 1988. Softcover. (Review)

KRAUSE'S FAMILY LAW IN A NUTSHELL, Second Edition, 444 pages, 1986. Softcover. (Text)

MALLOY'S LAW AND ECONOMICS: A COMPARATIVE APPROACH TO THEORY AND PRACTICE, 166 pages, 1990. Softcover. (Text)

Education Law

ALEXANDER AND ALEXANDER'S THE LAW OF SCHOOLS, STUDENTS AND TEACHERS IN A NUTSHELL, 409 pages, 1984. Softcover. (Text)

Employment Discrimination—see also Gender Discrimination

PLAYER'S FEDERAL LAW OF EMPLOYMENT DISCRIMINATION IN A NUTSHELL, Second Edition, 402 pages, 1981. Softcover. (Text)

PLAYER'S HORNBOOK ON EMPLOYMENT DISCRIMINATION LAW, Student Edition, 708 pages, 1988. (Text)

Energy and Natural Resources Law—see also Oil and Gas

Environmental Law—see also Energy and Natural Resources Law; Sea, Law of

FINDLEY AND FARBER'S ENVIRONMENTAL LAW IN A NUTSHELL, Second Edition, 367

Environmental Law—Continued

pages, 1988. Softcover. (Text)

RODGERS' HORNBOOK ON ENVIRONMENTAL LAW, 956 pages, 1977, with 1984 pocket part. (Text)

Equity—see Remedies

Estate Planning—see also Trusts and Estates; Taxation—Estate and Gift

LYNN'S AN INTRODUCTION TO ESTATE PLANNING IN A NUTSHELL, Third Edition, 370 pages, 1983. Softcover. (Text)

Evidence

BROUN AND BLAKEY'S BLACK LETTER ON EVIDENCE, 269 pages, 1984. Softcover. (Review)

GRAHAM'S FEDERAL RULES OF EVIDENCE IN A NUTSHELL, Second Edition, 473 pages, 1987. Softcover. (Text)

LILLY'S AN INTRODUCTION TO THE LAW OF EVIDENCE, Second Edition, 585 pages, 1987. (Text)

MCCORMICK'S HORNBOOK ON EVIDENCE, Fourth Edition, Student Edition, approximately 1200 pages, January

1992 Pub. (Text)

ROTHSTEIN'S EVIDENCE IN A NUTSHELL: STATE AND FEDERAL RULES, Second Edition, 514 pages, 1981. Softcover. (Text)

Federal Jurisdiction and Procedure

CURRIE'S FEDERAL JURISDICTION IN A NUTSHELL, Third Edition, 242 pages, 1990. Softcover. (Text)

REDISH'S BLACK LETTER ON FEDERAL JURISDICTION, Second Edition, 234 pages, 1991. Softcover. (Review)

WRIGHT'S HORNBOOK ON FEDERAL COURTS, Fourth Edition, Student Edition, 870 pages, 1983. (Text)

First Amendment

Future Interests—see Trusts and Estates

Gender Discrimination—see also Employment Discrimination

THOMAS' SEX DISCRIMINATION IN A NUTSHELL, Second Edition, approximately 400 pages, 1991. Softcover. (Text)

Health Law—see Medicine, Law and

Human Rights—see International Law

Immigration Law

WEISSBRODT'S IMMIGRATION LAW AND PROCEDURE IN A NUTSHELL, Second Edition, 438 pages, 1989, Softcover. (Text)

Indian Law—see American Indian Law

Insurance Law

DOBBYN'S INSURANCE LAW IN A NUTSHELL, Second Edition, 316 pages, 1989. Softcover. (Text)

KEETON AND WIDISS' INSURANCE LAW, Student Edition, 1359 pages, 1988. (Text)

International Law—see also Sea, Law of

BUERGENTHAL'S INTERNATIONAL HUMAN RIGHTS IN A NUTSHELL, 283 pages, 1988. Softcover. (Text)

BUERGENTHAL AND MAIER'S PUBLIC INTERNATIONAL LAW IN A NUTSHELL, Second Edition, 275 pages, 1990. Softcover. (Text)

FOLSOM, GORDON AND SPANOGLE'S INTERNATIONAL BUSINESS TRANSACTIONS IN A NUTSHELL, Third Edition, 509 pages, 1988. Softcover. (Text)

Interviewing and Counseling

SHAFFER AND ELKINS' LEGAL INTERVIEWING AND COUNSELING IN A NUTSHELL, Second Edition, 487 pages, 1987. Softcover. (Text)

Introduction to Law—see Legal Method and Legal System

Introduction to Law Study

HEGLAND'S INTRODUCTION TO THE STUDY AND PRACTICE OF LAW IN A NUTSHELL, 418 pages, 1983. Softcover. (Text)

KINYON'S INTRODUCTION TO LAW STUDY AND LAW EXAMINATIONS IN A NUTSHELL, 389 pages, 1971. Softcover. (Text)

Judicial Process—see Legal Method and Legal System

Juvenile Justice

FOX'S JUVENILE COURTS IN A NUTSHELL, Third Edition, 291 pages, 1984. Softcover. (Text)

Labor and Employment Law—see also Employment Discrimination, Workers' Compensation

LESLIE'S LABOR LAW IN A NUTSHELL, Second Edition, 397 pages, 1986. Softcover. (Text)

Labor and Employment Law—
Continued

NOLAN'S LABOR ARBITRATION LAW AND PRACTICE IN A NUTSHELL, 358 pages, 1979. Softcover. (Text)

Land Finance—Property Security—see Real Estate Transactions

Land Use

HAGMAN AND JUERGENSMEYER'S HORNBOOK ON URBAN PLANNING AND LAND DEVELOPMENT CONTROL LAW, Second Edition, Student Edition, 680 pages, 1986. (Text)

WRIGHT AND WRIGHT'S LAND USE IN A NUTSHELL, Second Edition, 356 pages, 1985. Softcover. (Text)

Legal Method and Legal System—see also Legal Research, Legal Writing

KEMPIN'S HISTORICAL INTRODUCTION TO ANGLO-AMERICAN LAW IN A NUTSHELL, Third Edition, 323 pages, 1990. Softcover. (Text)

REYNOLDS' JUDICIAL PROCESS IN A NUTSHELL, Second Edition, approximately 310 pages, 1991. Softcover. (Text)

Legal Research

COHEN'S LEGAL RESEARCH IN A NUTSHELL, Fourth Edition, 452 pages, 1985. Softcover. (Text)

COHEN, BERRING AND OLSON'S HOW TO FIND THE LAW, Ninth Edition, 716 pages, 1989. (Text)

Legal Writing and Drafting

SQUIRES AND ROMBAUER'S LEGAL WRITING IN A NUTSHELL, 294 pages, 1982. Softcover. (Text)

Legislation—see also Legal Writing and Drafting

DAVIES' LEGISLATIVE LAW AND PROCESS IN A NUTSHELL, Second Edition, 346 pages, 1986. Softcover. (Text)

Local Government

MCCARTHY'S LOCAL GOVERNMENT LAW IN A NUTSHELL, Third Edition, 435 pages, 1990. Softcover. (Text)

REYNOLDS' HORNBOOK ON LOCAL GOVERNMENT LAW, 860 pages, 1982, with 1990 pocket part. (Text)

Mass Communication Law

ZUCKMAN, GAYNES, CARTER AND DEE'S MASS COMMUNICATIONS LAW IN A NUTSHELL, Third Edition, 538 pages, 1988. Softcover. (Text)

Medicine, Law and

HALL AND ELLMAN'S HEALTH CARE LAW AND ETHICS IN A NUTSHELL, 401 pages, 1990. Softcover (Text)

JARVIS, CLOSEN, HERMANN AND LEONARD'S AIDS LAW IN A NUTSHELL, 349 pages, 1991. Softcover. (Text)

KING'S THE LAW OF MEDICAL MALPRACTICE IN A NUTSHELL, Second Edition, 342 pages, 1986. Softcover. (Text)

Military Law

SHANOR AND TERRELL'S MILITARY LAW IN A NUTSHELL, 378 pages, 1980. Softcover. (Text)

Mortgages—see Real Estate Transactions

Natural Resources Law—see Energy and Natural Resources Law, Environmental Law

Office Practice—see also Computers and Law, Interviewing and Counseling, Negotiation

HEGLAND'S TRIAL AND PRACTICE SKILLS IN A NUTSHELL, 346 pages, 1978. Softcover (Text)

Oil and Gas—see also Energy and Natural Resources Law

HEMINGWAY'S HORNBOOK ON THE LAW OF OIL AND GAS, Third Edition, Student Edition, approximately 700 pages, Aug., 1991 Pub. (Text)

LOWE'S OIL AND GAS LAW IN A NUTSHELL, Second Edition, 465 pages, 1988. Softcover. (Text)

Partnership—see Agency— Partnership

Patent and Copyright Law

MILLER AND DAVIS' INTELLECTUAL PROPERTY—PATENTS, TRADEMARKS AND COPYRIGHT IN A NUTSHELL, Second Edition, 437 pages, 1990. Softcover. (Text)

Products Liability

PHILLIPS' PRODUCTS LIABILITY IN A NUTSHELL, Third Edition, 307 pages, 1988. Softcover. (Text)

Professional Responsibility

ARONSON AND WECKSTEIN'S PROFESSIONAL RESPONSIBILITY IN A NUTSHELL, Second Edition, approximately 500 pages, 1991. Softcover. (Text)

ROTUNDA'S BLACK LETTER ON PROFESSIONAL RESPONSIBILITY, Second Edition, 414 pages, 1988. Softcover. (Review)

WOLFRAM'S HORNBOOK ON

Professional Responsibility— Continued

MODERN LEGAL ETHICS, Student Edition, 1120 pages, 1986. (Text)

Property—see also Real Estate Transactions, Land Use, Trusts and Estates

BERNHARDT'S BLACK LETTER ON PROPERTY, Second Edition, approximately 375 pages, 1991. Softcover. (Review)

BERNHARDT'S REAL PROPERTY IN A NUTSHELL, Second Edition, 448 pages, 1981. Softcover. (Text)

BURKE'S PERSONAL PROPERTY IN A NUTSHELL, 322 pages, 1983. Softcover. (Text)

CUNNINGHAM, STOEBUCK AND WHITMAN'S HORNBOOK ON THE LAW OF PROPERTY, Student Edition, 916 pages, 1984, with 1987 pocket part. (Text)

HILL'S LANDLORD AND TENANT LAW IN A NUTSHELL, Second Edition, 311 pages, 1986. Softcover. (Text)

Real Estate Transactions

BRUCE'S REAL ESTATE FINANCE IN A NUTSHELL, Third Edition, approximately 270 pages, 1991. Softcover. (Text)

NELSON AND WHITMAN'S BLACK LETTER ON LAND TRANSACTIONS AND FINANCE, Second Edition, 466 pages, 1988. Softcover. (Review)

NELSON AND WHITMAN'S HORNBOOK ON REAL ESTATE FINANCE LAW, Second Edition, 941 pages, 1985 with 1989 pocket part. (Text)

Regulated Industries—see also Mass Communication Law, Banking Law

GELLHORN AND PIERCE'S REGULATED INDUSTRIES IN A NUTSHELL, Second Edition, 389 pages, 1987. Softcover. (Text)

Remedies

DOBBS' HORNBOOK ON REMEDIES, 1067 pages, 1973. (Text)

DOBBYN'S INJUNCTIONS IN A NUTSHELL, 264 pages, 1974. Softcover. (Text)

FRIEDMAN'S CONTRACT REMEDIES IN A NUTSHELL, 323 pages, 1981. Softcover. (Text)

O'CONNELL'S REMEDIES IN A NUTSHELL, Second Edition, 320 pages, 1985. Softcover. (Text)

Sea, Law of

SOHN AND GUSTAFSON'S THE LAW OF THE SEA IN A NUTSHELL, 264 pages, 1984. Softcover. (Text)

Securities Regulation

HAZEN'S HORNBOOK ON THE LAW OF SECURITIES REGULATION, Second Edition, Student Edition, 1082 pages, 1990. (Text)

RATNER'S SECURITIES REGULATION IN A NUTSHELL, Third Edition, 316 pages, 1988. Softcover. (Text)

SECURITIES REGULATION, SELECTED STATUTES, RULES, AND FORMS. Softcover. 1331 pages, 1991.

Sports Law

SCHUBERT, SMITH AND TRENTADUE'S SPORTS LAW, 395 pages, 1986. (Text)

Tax Practice and Procedure

MORGAN'S TAX PROCEDURE AND TAX FRAUD IN A NUTSHELL, 400 pages, 1990. Softcover. (Text)

Taxation—Corporate

SCHWARZ AND LATHROPE'S BLACK LETTER ON CORPORATE AND PARTNERSHIP TAXATION, Approximately 500 pages, September, 1991 Pub. Softcover. (Review)

WEIDENBRUCH AND BURKE'S FEDERAL INCOME TAXATION OF CORPORATIONS AND STOCKHOLDERS IN A NUTSHELL, Third Edition, 309 pages, 1989. Soft-

cover. (Text)

Taxation—Estate & Gift—see also Estate Planning, Trusts and Estates

MCNULTY'S FEDERAL ESTATE AND GIFT TAXATION IN A NUTSHELL, Fourth Edition, 496 pages, 1989. Softcover. (Text)

Taxation—Individual

HUDSON AND LIND'S BLACK LETTER ON FEDERAL INCOME TAXATION, Third Edition, 406 pages, 1990. Softcover. (Review)

MCNULTY'S FEDERAL INCOME TAXATION OF INDIVIDUALS IN A NUTSHELL, Fourth Edition, 503 pages, 1988. Softcover. (Text)

POSIN'S HORNBOOK ON FEDERAL INCOME TAXATION, Student Edition, 491 pages, 1983, with 1989 pocket part. (Text)

ROSE AND CHOMMIE'S HORNBOOK ON FEDERAL INCOME TAXATION, Third Edition, 923 pages, 1988, with 1989 pocket part. (Text)

Taxation—International

DOERNBERG'S INTERNATIONAL TAXATION IN A NUTSHELL, 325 pages, 1989. Softcover. (Text)

BISHOP AND BROOKS' FEDERAL

STUDY AIDS

Taxation—International—Continued

PARTNERSHIP TAXATION: A GUIDE TO THE LEADING CASES, STATUTES, AND REGULATIONS, 545 pages, 1990. Softcover. (Text)

SCHWARZ AND LATHROPE'S BLACK LETTER ON CORPORATE AND PARTNERSHIP TAXATION, Approximately 500 pages, September, 1991 Pub. Softcover. (Review)

Taxation—State & Local

GELFAND AND SALSICH'S STATE AND LOCAL TAXATION AND FINANCE IN A NUTSHELL, 309 pages, 1986. Softcover. (Text)

Torts—see also Products Liability

KIONKA'S BLACK LETTER ON TORTS, 339 pages, 1988. Softcover. (Review)

KIONKA'S TORTS IN A NUTSHELL: INJURIES TO PERSONS AND PROPERTY, 434 pages, 1977. Softcover. (Text)

MALONE'S TORTS IN A NUTSHELL: INJURIES TO FAMILY, SOCIAL AND TRADE RELATIONS, 358 pages, 1979. Softcover. (Text)

PROSSER AND KEETON'S HORNBOOK ON TORTS, Fifth Edition, Student Edition, 1286 pages, 1984 with 1988 pocket part. (Text)

Trade Regulation—see also Antitrust, Regulated Industries

MCMANIS' UNFAIR TRADE PRACTICES IN A NUTSHELL, Second Edition, 464 pages, 1988. Softcover. (Text)

SCHECHTER'S BLACK LETTER ON UNFAIR TRADE PRACTICES, 272 pages, 1986. Softcover. (Review)

Trial and Appellate Advocacy—see also Civil Procedure

BERGMAN'S TRIAL ADVOCACY IN A NUTSHELL, Second Edition, 354 pages, 1989. Softcover. (Text)

GOLDBERG'S THE FIRST TRIAL (WHERE DO I SIT? WHAT DO I SAY?) IN A NUTSHELL, 396 pages, 1982. Softcover. (Text)

HEGLAND'S TRIAL AND PRACTICE SKILLS IN A NUTSHELL, 346 pages, 1978. Softcover. (Text)

HORNSTEIN'S APPELLATE ADVOCACY IN A NUTSHELL, 325 pages, 1984. Softcover. (Text)

JEANS' HANDBOOK ON TRIAL ADVOCACY, Student Edition, 473 pages, 1975. Softcover.

Advisory Board

EUROPEAN COMMUNITY LAW
IN A NUTSHELL

By

RALPH H. FOLSOM
Professor of Law
University of San Diego

ST. PAUL, MINN.
WEST PUBLISHING CO.
1992

COPYRIGHT © 1992 By WEST PUBLISHING CO.

50 West Kellogg Boulevard
P.O. Box 64526
St. Paul, MN 55164–0526

Library of Congress Cataloging-in-Publication Data

Folsom, Ralph Haughwout.
    European Community law in a nutshell / by Ralph H. Folsom.
      p.   cm. — (Nutshell series)
    Includes index.
    ISBN 0–314–92781–6
    1. Law—European Economic Community countries. I. Title.
  II. Series.
  KJE949.F55   1992
  349.4—dc20
  [344]   91–31811
                                             CIP

ISBN 0–314–92781–6

Folsom, Eur.Comm.Law NS

Preface

It is difficult to capture in one small "nutshell" the vastness and excitement that accompanies European Community (EC) law. Truly, this is one of the great undertakings of modern times. I have tried to present not only the big picture, but also to analyze in more detail some of the most critical developments in EC law. This selectivity was undertaken primarily with North American and other audiences located outside the Community in mind. Thus, there is special emphasis throughout the book on the external impact of European Community law, e.g. in its 1992 campaign legislation, litigation procedures, trading rules and business competition law. It is important to bear in mind, however, that it is not just the externalities of EC law that command attention. The internal operations of the Community are significant not only for Europeans, but also to the many foreign investors flocking to the world's largest and most lucrative market.

Inevitably, I have made judgments about what to emphasize, what to exclude and the like. I have also taken a few liberties in characterizing EC law and procedures by using terminology that is familiar to Americans. It is my sincere hope that the final product will meet the needs of students, lawyers and people in business who seek an introduction to the European Community and its law. I take comfort that this is but a first edition. Your suggestions for the second edition are most welcome.

RALPH H. FOLSOM

October, 1991

Acknowledgments

Many colleagues and students have contributed over the years to my learning and understanding of European Community law. For me, it really all began in Britain from 1972–75 when I was an LL.M. student at the London School of Economics followed by two years as a Lecturer in Law at the University of Warwick. Those were formative times, not only for me, but also for Britain as it joined the Community in 1973. Since 1975 I have greatly benefited from teaching and professional contacts at the University of San Diego's summer legal studies program in Paris. This program is organized each year through the USD Institute on International and Comparative Law. It is co-sponsored by ESSEC, the law faculty at the University of Paris I and the Institute Catholique de Paris. Perhaps no other person has had a more profound influence on my European Community law interests than Professor Herbert Lazerow, the Director and Co-Founder of the Institute and its Paris program.

In recent years I have served as Director of USD's Master of Comparative Law program for foreign attorneys enrolled in San Diego. Many of these wonderful students have been Europeans, and some have kindly taken time out of their busy professional lives to read drafts of this Nutshell. To them, my most sincere thanks and warmest acknowledgment:

> Hanne Biltoff-Jensen (Professor of Law, University of Aarhus, Denmark)
>
> Simone Byrch (Clifford Chance, London)
>
> Alexander Ehrhardt (Blessing & Berweck, Rechtsanwälte, Germany)
>
> Danielle Flükiger (Avocat, Switzerland)
>
> Mogens Yde Knudsen (Lober & Lauritsen, Advokatfirma, Denmark)
>
> Michael Langer (Kniepkamp & Kirsch, Rechtsanwälte, Germany)
>
> Klas Lundgren (Advokat, Sweden)
>
> Leo Schmid, McKinsey, Inc. (Zurich)
>
> Babette G. M. Van Look (Advokaat, Belgium) (assisted by Jan Steenlant, Legal Advisor to the Fédération des Entreprises de Belgique)

I have also benefited from a review of the outlines of Professors Bermann, Davey, Fox and Goebel for their forthcoming coursebook on European Community Law by West Publishing Company.

European Community Law Resources

Many students and attorneys first encountering European Community law wonder if and how it can be researched in English in the United States. Since 1973, English is an official Community language and official translations of the treaties and much prior law have been completed. Language is not really a research barrier, access can be. The following is a list of basic resources that suggests how to proceed. This list also serves to identify the abbreviations used in this book.

1. *Depository Libraries.* Directives, regulations and other types of secondary EC law, including proposed legislation, are all published in the Official Journal of the European Communities (O.J.). A surprisingly large number of libraries in the United States have been designated "depository institutions" for EC documents. This means that they eventually receive almost every document (e.g. annual reports of the Commission) that a student or lawyer could want to locate. The University of California at San Diego, for example, is such a depository.

2. *Law Reports.* There is an official European Community Reports (Eur.Comm.Rep.) which reproduces all of the opinions of the European Court of Justice and Court of First Instance. Many also rely on private *selective* reporters. The two most useful are Common Market Law Reports (Common Mkt.L.Rep.) (Sweet & Maxwell, London) and CCH Common Market Reporter Decisions (CCH Common Mkt.Rep.Dec.) (Commerce Clearing House, Chicago). The Common Market Law Reports also cover EC cases of note in the national courts and selected draft legislation.

3. *Law Reviews.* Articles on European Community topics are increasingly appearing in North American law reviews. Some European reviews focus on EC matters. These include, in English, the Common Market Law Review (Common Mkt.L.Rev.) (Sitjhoff, The Netherlands), the European Law Review (Eur.L.Rev.) (Sweet & Maxwell, London), and the European Competition Law Review (Eur.Compt.L.Rev.) (ESC, Oxford).

4. *EC Information Service.* The Community operates a branch of its information service at 2100 M St., N.W., Suite 707, Washington, D.C. 20037. This office is often

most helpful when new or fast-breaking developments are involved.

5. *Legal Newsletters.* The Commerce Clearing House publishes a newsletter in connection with its Common Market Reporter service. Coverage of major EC developments is given in the Bureau of National Affairs (BNA) International Trade Reporter. Many American firms with offices in Brussels publish EC newsletters for their clients and others. The best is probably done by LeBoeuf, Lamb, Leiby & MacRae, with which this biased author was once associated.

6. *Treatises and Collections of Documents.* There are a large number of EC law treatises, some broad and others narrow in focus. See generally Smit and Herzog, *Law of the European Economic Community* (Matthew-Bender, current); *Encyclopedia of European Community Law* (Sweet & Maxwell, current) (collection of EC treaties and secondary law); Kapteyn and van Thematt, *Introduction to the Law of the European Communities* (Second Edition) (Kluwer, 1989); *Halsbury's Laws of England,* Volumes 51 and 52 (Butterworths, current); Brown, *The Court of Justice of the European Communities* (Sweet & Maxwell, 1989); Hartley, *The Foundations of*

XXIII

European Community Law (Second Edition) (Oxford, 1988).

7. *Commission and Other Reports.* Each year the Commission prepares a General Report on the activities of the Community in time for Parliament's first session in March. This report is discussed in open session by the Parliament. General reports are also prepared by the Council and the European Investment Bank. In addition, the Commission issues annual reports on agriculture, social affairs, competition policy, the Regional Development Fund, the environment and on consumer protection. These reports present useful summaries of proposed and current Community activities. They are available in EC depository libraries and from the EC information service.

8. *Computerized Resources.* * LEXIS has several libraries of primary significance for computer assisted research relating to the European Community. INTLAW is the name of one LEXIS library which contains four files that deal directly with the European Community. The ECLAW file has selected portions of the CELEX database, including an edited version of the Official Journal produced by the European Com-

---

* Prepared by Michael White, Reference Librarian, University of San Diego Legal Research Center (January 15, 1991).

munity. The ECLAW file has full text of Treaty Documents from 11/19/79, EC Legislation from 1/30/80, Commission Proposals from 1/84, Parliamentary Resolutions from 6/79, Parliamentary Questions from 1/89, and National Legislative References from 1/89.

The INTLAW library also contains the ECCASE file. ECCASE includes all decisions of the Court of Justice of the European Community since its foundation in 1954, as reported in the European Community Reports. ECCASE also contains transcripts of cases not yet reported in the European Community Reports, including not only the judgment of the Court but also the opinion delivered by the Advocate-General. ECCASE also encompasses the European Commercial Cases from 1978, the European Human Rights Reports from 1979, and the Common Market Law Reports from 1959.

The two other files in the INTLAW library of LEXIS are COMDEC and ECTY. COMDEC has decisions made by the European Commission applying the competition rules under Articles 85 and 86 of the Treaty of Rome, and parallel articles in other EC treaties. The COMDEC file has coverage from December 1972. The ECTY file has EC Treaties in Basic Documents of International Economic Law.

The other library in LEXIS which directly relates to European Community research is the EURCOM library. It repeats access to exactly the same files as does the IN-TLAW library. EURCOM has the CASES file which is identical in content to the ECCASES file in the INTLAW library. EURCOM also has the COMDEC file, once again identical to the COMDEC file in the INTLAW library.

LEXIS also has a library which covers English law generally, which is called ENGGEN. ENGGEN includes decisions of the European Court of Justice which are reported in standard law reports of the United Kingdom. European Community treaties, directives and regulations appended to relevant acts or statutory instruments may be available in full text in the ENGGEN library.

One French law library in LEXIS, INTNAT, contains the Official Journal, L series, in French, from 1952 to date. INTNAT also contains all decisions of the European Court of Justice, in French, from 1954 to date. INTNAT has EC related treaties, conventions and agreements from 1958, and agreements dated before 1958 that are effective today. The other

French law library in LEXIS, LOIREG, also has the Official Journal, in French, but only from 1955.

WESTLAW, by the end of 1991, will also have European Community legal materials available online. WESTLAW's International Law topic will contain CELEX materials in seven databases. CELEX will combine all European Community Law material from Context, Ltd., publishers of JUSTIS, a CD–ROM version of CELEX, the Official Legal Database of the European Communities.

CELEX–TRTY will contain Treaty Documents in force after 7/1/79 and subsequent treaties; CELEX–LEG will have EC secondary legislation in force after 7/1/79 and subsequent legislation; CELEX–PREP will have Commission Proposals from 1/1/84 and European Parliament resolutions from 6/79; CELEX–PQ will contain Parliamentary Questions from 7/79; and CELEX–NP will have references to national provisions implementing Community Directives beginning with 1989. In addition, CELEX–CS will include European Court of Justice judgements and orders from 1954 and Advocates-General opinions from 1965.

*

A Timeline of European Integration

1948 — Benelux Customs Union Treaty

1949 — COMECON Treaty (Eastern Europe, Soviet Union)

1951 — European Coal and Steel Community ("Treaty of Paris")

1957 — European Economic Community (EEC) ("Treaty of Rome"), European Atomic Energy Community Treaty (EURATOM)

1959 — European Free Trade Area Treaty (EFTA)

1968 — EEC Customs Union fully operative

1973 — Britain and Denmark switch from EFTA to EEC; Ireland joins EEC; Remaining EFTA states sign industrial free trade treaties with EEC

1979 — Direct elections to European Parliament

1981 — Greece joins EEC

1983 — Greenland "withdraws" from EEC

1986 — Spain and Portugal join EEC, Portugal leaves EFTA

1987 — Single European Act amends EEC Treaty to initiate 1992 campaign for a Community without internal frontiers

1990 — East Germany merged into EEC via reunification process

1991 — COMECON defunct; EEC trade relations with Eastern Europe developing rapidly

Dec. 31, 1992 — Target date for full implementation of EEC without internal frontiers and expanded trade relations with EFTA nations creating a European Economic Area (EEA)

Jan. 1, 1993 — Target date for amendment of Treaty of Rome to provide for greater economic, monetary and political union

Outline

Page

Appendices

Table of Cases

References are to Pages

TABLE OF CASES

TABLE OF CASES

TABLE OF CASES

TABLE OF CASES

TABLE OF CASES

TABLE OF CASES

EUROPEAN COMMUNITY LAW

IN A NUTSHELL

*

CHAPTER 1

THE HISTORY AND GROWTH OF THE EUROPEAN COMMUNITY

War, twice in the Twentieth Century and for ages previously, has plagued the European continent. The desire for peace after World War II helps explain the beginnings of European integration. As Allied control of West Germany declined in the late 1940s, the return of Germany's basic war industries became a prominent issue. Coal and steel in particular were seen as essential to war-making potential on the Continent. Many feared that if these basic industries were left in national hands, future wars between traditional enemies might emerge. Winston Churchill, in his famous Zurich speech of 1946, urged the establishment of a United States of Europe. He meant that there should be a partnership between France and Germany. The United Kingdom would simply act as a friend and sponsor of this partnership but would not participate. France was especially concerned about what it often called "the German problem." The solution that emerged in 1951 was the creation of the European Coal and Steel Community (ECSC).

Treaty of Paris (1951)

The Coal and Steel Community was the first of Western Europe's major treaties of integration. The basic theory behind this development was that war would be more difficult to pursue if European institutions empowered with substantial regulatory authority controlled the coal and steel industries. Known as the Schuman Plan after Robert Schuman, the Foreign Minister of France, the ECSC was opened for membership in 1950. Although addressed to much of Europe, only France, Germany, Italy and the three Benelux countries (Belgium, Luxembourg and The Netherlands) joined by signing the Treaty of Paris in April of 1951. West Germany and Italy, of course, were still politically weak from the aftermath from World War II. The Benelux countries, though often united in perspective, were not significantly influential to the development of the European Coal and Steel Community. Thus the Community essentially represented French ideas and these ideas permeated its founding treaty.

The Treaty of Paris is a complicated document. It is very detailed and legalistic, what the French call a "traité-loi." Its regulatory approaches to the coal and steel industries are diverse. On the one hand, there are provisions which permit substantial European control over prices, the level of subsidies, investment incentives, production levels, transportation rates, discriminatory and restrictive trade practices, employment and industrial structure. These controls represent a regime of French "dirigisme". At the same time, other provisions of the Treaty of Paris contemplate freer trade and more competitive coal and steel markets with only occasional governmental intervention. Over the years, regulation of the coal and steel industries in the ECSC has gone through different cycles but predominantly followed the French regime. The Treaty of Paris remains the legal basis for European Community law governing these two industries. However, it is often overlooked that the Treaty of Paris will expire near the end of the year 2002. At that time the coal and steel industries are likely to be subsumed under the much broader and more economically significant Treaty of Rome of 1957 which established the European Economic Community (EEC) for an "unlimited period" of time. Article 240.

The most critical features of the Treaty of Paris were those establishing regional institutions for the governance of coal and steel. Here the French perspective that new institutions were required, to which substantial power would be conveyed by national governments, prevailed. The willingness to transfer control over coal and steel to European institutions seems even more remarkable when the prevalence of government ownership of companies in those industries is taken into account. In contrast, the British at that time were of the view that governance of coal and steel in the pursuit in peace did not require the establishment of numerous powerful European institutions. Thus it is in the

Treaty of Paris that the four fundamental institutions of the European Community originate: The Council of Ministers, the Commission, the Court of Justice, and the Parliament.

These institutions are sometimes referred to as *supranational* in character although this term is no longer in fashion. They are neither national nor international (i.e. intergovernmental). Within the limits of the treaties empowering them, they exercise sovereignty. It is to the ECSC institutions that responsibility for the establishment and operation of a free trade area in and the regulation of coal and steel was given. Indeed, some powers granted the Commission (initially called the High Authority) by the Treaty of Paris are not to be found in the subsequent Treaty of Rome establishing the EEC. For example, the Commission is given the power to levy taxes directly on coal and steel enterprises. This is a power that is generally absent from the Treaty of Rome. Each of the four major institutions of the European Community will be reviewed subsequently. For now, it is worth noting that their origins strongly reflect the French view that only European institutions could solve "the German problem."

Treaty of Rome (1957), EFTA (1959), and COMECON

As the post-war economies of Europe revitalized, it became increasingly evident that France and Britain were vying for leadership of Western Eu-

rope. Each had its own vision of how to proceed
beyond the limited European Coal and Steel Community with which Britain became loosely "associated" in the mid–1950s. The British maintained
that a free trade area, as distinct from more advanced forms of integration such as a customs
union, a common market, an economic community
or an economic union, was all that was required for
economic integration in Western Europe. The major difference between a free trade area and a
customs union is the presence of a common external tariff in the latter. Common market treaties
additionally provide for the free movement of what
economists call the "factors of production": capital, labor, enterprise and technology. Economic
communities seek to coordinate or harmonize economic policies important to the functioning of the
common market, e.g. transport, taxation, monetary
matters and government subsidies. Economic unions embrace a more or less complete harmonization of national policies related to the economy of
the union. The difference between a treaty establishing an economic community and one creating
an economic union is in the number and importance of harmonized national policies.

Britain continued to believe regional integration
could be achieved with a minimum of European
governance and a maximum of retention of national sovereignty. France, on the other hand, generally envisioned a broader economic community
modeled and implemented on the basic design provided by the Treaty of Paris, although even it had

begun to express reservations about the degree of power vested in the ECSC. France had the support and could point to the successful integration of the Benelux countries. Belgium, Luxembourg and The Netherlands had signed a Customs Union Treaty in January of 1948. By the middle of the 1950s, the Benelux nations were close to agreement on a comprehensive economic union. Benelux integration was already providing substantial economic growth to its member nations. Though not as heavily ladened with European institutions as the Coal and Steel Community, the Benelux union served as a pacesetter for wider European economic integration. To a limited degree this remains true. The Treaty of Rome expressly permits the existence and completion of the Benelux Union to the extent that its objectives are not attained through the EEC. Article 233.

In June of 1955 a conference of the foreign ministers of the European Coal and Steel Community, responding to a Benelux memorandum, authorized an intergovernmental committee to study and report on the prospects for a Western European common market and peaceful use of atomic energy. This committee, still heavily influenced by French perspectives but increasingly subject to a resurgent West Germany, laid the foundations for the Treaty of Rome establishing the European Economic Community in 1957. The Committee was led by a dynamic Belgian, Paul–Henri Spaak. Its report is sometimes referred to as the Spaak Plan and focuses on the fusion of markets. Adoption of the Committee's report and its embodiment in the Treaty of Rome was influenced by an equally dynamic Frenchman long an advocate of European integration. Jean Monnet organized a pressure group known as the Action Committee for the United States of Europe.

At the same time, by separate treaty in 1957, the third European Community was created. This is the European Atomic Energy Community (EURATOM). EURATOM is a very specialized community focused on joint research and peaceful development of atomic energy. Its Supply Agency owns all fissionable materials located within the member states not intended for defense requirements. About 35 percent of all electricity, and 14 percent of all EC energy needs, are now supplied by nuclear plants. EURATOM has joined the Treaty on the Non–Proliferation of Nuclear Weapons. In the Chernobyl aftermath, renewed attention has been paid to EURATOM safety standards and the Court of Justice has held that the Commission's advisory opinion must be obtained prior to approval of the final plans for radioactive effluent disposal. *Saarland v. Minister for Industry, Posts and Telecommunications and Tourism* (1988) Eur.Comm.Rep. 5013. Nevertheless, it is the least significant of the three European Communities.

The Treaty of Rome and the EURATOM Treaty follow the institutional pattern of the Treaty of Paris. Each of these three treaties empowers a Council of Ministers, a Commission (called High

Authority in the ECSC Treaty), an Assembly (Parliament) and a Court of Justice. This led to an unnecessary and confusing institutional structure which was remedied in part by merging the Court and Parliament in 1957 and later the Council and Commission by the so-called "Merger Treaty" of 1967. Since then, there has been one Council, one Commission, one Parliament and one Court, all staffed by the same people. Each of these European Community institutions, however, derives its power and authority from the terms and conditions of whatever treaty it is acting under. In other words, the treaties were not merged, only their institutions. Thus when the Commission acts on coal and steel matters, the legality of its actions is measured by the Treaty of Paris. When the Council legislates on atomic energy, the EURATOM treaty controls, and so forth. See Article 232 of the Treaty of Rome (ECSC and EURATOM treaties not affected by EEC). Given the scope of the Treaty of Rome establishing the EEC, the institutions of the Community most often operate under its terms and implementing protocols and legislation.

The Treaty of Rome establishing the European Economic Community in 1957 is the penultimate source of EEC law. Some have analogized this Treaty to a constitution. Certainly it is the founding document of the EEC. Unlike the Coal and Steel Treaty, the Treaty of Rome is open-ended in much of its language, a "traité-cadre" or "traité de procedure" in French terms. It provides the framework and process upon which to build the European Community. The Treaty as amended through 1991 is divided into six parts and over 250 articles. When compared with the narrowness of the Treaty of Paris establishing the European Coal and Steel Community in 1951, the Treaty of Rome is breathtaking in scope.

It commences in Part I with some fundamental principles. These principles elaborate upon the goal of establishing a common market throughout the member states and list the activities of the Community to achieve that objective. This listing is found in Article 3 and includes the elimination of customs duties and quotas on internal EEC trade, the establishment of a common external tariff and trade policy towards third countries, the free movement of persons, services and capital, the adoption of common policies on agricultural and transportation, the institution of a "system" of non-distorted competition within the Common Market, the use of procedures to coordinate the economic policies of member states and remedy disequilibria in their balance of payments, the "approximation" of member state laws "to the extent required" for the proper functioning of the Common Market, the creation of a European Social Fund to promote employment and raise standards of living, a European Investment Bank to foster economic growth, and the "association" of overseas countries and territories (e.g. former colonies) with the EEC.

Though the Treaty of Rome is much less dirigiste than the Coal and Steel Treaty, Britain once again abstained from membership because of the nature and extent of the European controls over the economy of the Community. Britain, too, was still preoccupied with its empire-based trade relations. Europe was important, but it had not yet become critical to British trading interests.

Early American support for European integration came through the Marshall Plan which was distributed through the Organization for European Economic Cooperation. This organization had no real political power, but successfully mediated some differences in national economic policies prevalent during the late 1940s. By 1957, the cold war between the United States and the Soviet Union was evident. This caused the United States to be generally supportive of the EEC initiative under the theory that a united Europe would present a stronger defense to Soviet aggression.

The Soviets, in turn, increasingly emphasized Eastern European integration through the Council for Mutual Economic Assistance (COMECON). This effort, commenced in 1949, was basically seen as a counterweight to the developments in Western European integration. Locked behind the Iron Curtain, the countries of Eastern Europe found themselves producing whatever the Soviet economic plans required. In exchange, they mostly received subsidized oil and other basic resources.

The fragmentation of Europe's economy during the 1950s became even more accentuated by the emergence of another competing organization. Led by Britain, many of the fringe or traditionally neutral nations of Western Europe organized themselves into the European Free Trade Association (EFTA) in 1959. Austria, Denmark, Iceland, Norway, Portugal, Sweden and Switzerland joined this undertaking. With eight nations essentially surrounding the core six nations who created the EEC in 1957, Britain felt that it had contained French influence and ideas in the economic sphere. True to British philosophy, the EFTA Treaty was very limited in scope. It applied only to free trade in industrial goods, omitting coverage of agriculture, transport, labor, capital, technology and services to mention only a few areas fully incorporated into the Treaty of Rome. Moreover, the British view on the nature of the governmental institutions required to achieve industrial free trade prevailed. A single institution, the EFTA Council, was created. Since it normally followed a unanimous voting principle, each of the member states retained a veto over new policy developments within the EFTA group. The surrender of national sovereignties to EFTA was minimized.

Thus, by 1960, Europe was economically divided into three major trade blocks. France and an increasingly powerful West Germany led Italy and the Benelux states in the European Coal and Steel and Economic Communities. Britain and its partners were loosely integrated through the European

Free Trade Association. And the whole of Eastern Europe came under the sway of Soviet dominance through COMECON. In addition, Finland became associated with EFTA and Greece and Turkey were associated with the EEC. Only Spain under Franco remained an economic outcast. More than a decade passed before these divisions began to seriously erode.

The Treaty of Rome and the GATT

The General Agreement on Tariffs and Trade ("GATT"), adopted in 1948 and much amended and interpreted since then, governs many features of the free world trading system. Approximately 100 nations, including those of the EEC, now adhere to the GATT. In 1957, when the Treaty of Rome was signed, the United States, Britain and other GATT members protested that the Treaty was not in accord with the terms of Article 24 of the GATT.

Article 24 permits contracting parties to enter into free trade area and customs union agreements of a fixed or evolutionary character. The premise here is that regional economic groups can be viewed as gradual steps (second-best alternatives) along the road to freer, less discriminatory *world* trade. At the same time, Article 24 attempts to manage the internal trade-creating and external trade-diverting effects of regional economic groups. These effects are known in economic literature as "the customs union dilemma." See Viner, *The Customs Union Issue* (1950).

Free trade area and custom union proposals must run the gauntlet of a formal GATT approval procedure during which "binding" recommendations are possible to bring the proposals into conformity with Article 24. Such recommendations might deal with Article 24 requirements for the elimination of internal tariffs and other restrictive regulations of commerce on "substantially all" products originating in a customs union or free trade area. Or they might deal with Article 24 requirements that common external tariffs not be "on the whole higher or more restrictive" in effect than the general incidence of prior existing national tariffs. The broad purpose of Article 24, acknowledged therein, is to facilitate trade among the GATT contracting parties and not to raise trade barriers.

It is under these treaty terms and through this GATT approval mechanism that most regional economic treaties, including those of Western Europe, have passed *without* substantial modification. Only the EFTA Treaty seems to have come genuinely close to meeting the terms of Article 24. The GATT, not the regional economic treaties, most often has given way. With the European Coal and Steel Community only two products were involved. Clearly no case could be made for its compliance with the requirement of elimination of internal trade barriers on "substantially all" products. Hence, the GATT members, passing over Article 24's own waiver proviso for proposals leading to a customs union or a free trade area "in the sense of

Article 24," reverted to Article 25. That article allows a two-thirds vote by the contracting parties to waive any GATT obligation.

During passage through the GATT of the Treaty of Rome, many "violations" of the letter and spirit of Article 24 were cited by nonmembers. The derivation of the EEC common customs tariff by arithmetically averaging existing national tariffs was challenged as more restrictive of trade than previous arrangements. Such averaging on a given product fails to take account of differing national import volumes. If a product was faced originally with a lower than average national tariff and a larger than average national demand, the new average EEC tariff is clearly more "restrictive" of imports than before. Averaging in high tariffs of countries of low demand quite plausibly created more restrictions on third-party trade with the EEC. If so, the letter and spirit of Article 24 were breached.

The economic association of Overseas Territories (mainly former French, Dutch, and Belgian colonies) with the EEC also raised considerable difficulty under Article 24. The Community argued that these "association" agreements were free trade areas in the long run, while the GATT officials viewed them as rather open efforts at purely preferential tariff status. Similar problems arose later in the GATT review of the multitude of EC "evolving" free trade area treaties with Mediterranean nations. Finally, in 1975, the openly preferential and discriminatory Lomé Convention negotiated between the European Community and forty-six African, Pacific, and Caribbean nations (including many former colonies) laid to rest any doubts as to the evolutionary character of EEC "free trade areas" with developing states. Once again it was the GATT and not the European Community that gave way.

Despite these and other arguments, the Treaty of Rome passed through the GATT study and review committees without final resolution of its legal status under Article 24. Postponement of these issues became permanent. GATT attempts— through the lawyer-like conditions of Article 24 to maximize trade creation and minimize trade diversion—must be seen in the EEC context as generally inadequate. Treaty terms became negotiable demands that were not accepted.

EFTA and the EEC Reconciled (1973)

During the 1960s, Britain began to come to grips with the loss of its empire. Although special trading relations were often preserved with former colonies through the Commonwealth network, it became increasingly apparent that Britain's economic future lay more in Europe than Africa, Asia or the Caribbean. Moreover, the EEC had helped to spur a phenomenal economic recovery on the Continent at a time when many were questioning the competitiveness of British industry. For these reasons, and others, Britain began to seek membership in the EEC as early as 1961 (only two years after the formation of EFTA). France under the leadership of Charles De Gaulle would have none of it. Since the Treaty of Rome provided (as it still does) that all new memberships in the EEC require a unanimous Council vote, France was effectively able to veto the British application. It was not until the resignation of De Gaulle in 1969 that the British were able in due course to secure membership in the EEC.

Agreement on the terms of British accession (including withdrawal from EFTA and the elimination of trade preferences with major Commonwealth nations) was reached in 1971, with an effective date of January, 1973. The switch from EFTA to the EEC by Britain under Conservative Party leadership was undertaken with an ambivalence that continues to be evident. It was only with reluctance that the British accepted the surrenders of sovereignty inherent in the Treaty of Rome. From 1973 onwards, more and more of the economic life of the United Kingdom would be governed by the four institutions of the European Community. British reluctance to join the Common Market was replayed in a 1975 national referendum under a Labor Party government. Approximately 60 percent of the populace voted to remain a member of the EC.

Denmark also switched sides in 1973. Norway was scheduled to become a member of the EEC at that time, and the terms of its membership had been negotiated, but the people of Norway rejected the Community in a national referendum. The rejection had a lot to do with the requirements of the Common Fisheries Policy which would have unacceptably opened Norwegian waters to fishermen from the Continent, Britain and Ireland (which followed the British lead into the Community in 1973). This Policy also regulates the type and number of fish that can be caught in EC waters, significantly subsidizes the fishing industry and protects it from foreign competition.

In addition to the expansion of the EEC to nine members, 1973 brought an even greater degree of European economic integration. Although EFTA remained intact, each of the six remaining EFTA nations signed bilateral trade treaties with the expanded EEC. These treaties continue to govern trade relations between EFTA nations and the EEC. They essentially provide for industrial free trade. Thus the 1973 enlargement of the European Economic Community was the catalyst for the most wide-scale and comprehensive effort at Western European integration yet to take place, the reconciliation of the EFTA and EEC trading blocks. This was an historic watershed in European economic integration.

The Community's Membership Into the 1990s

During the 1980s there was a strong trend toward increased membership in and expansion of the European Community. The only exception to this trend was the "withdrawal" of Greenland in 1983. Greenland had been admitted with Denmark in 1973, but voted in a home rule referendum (essentially rejecting the Common Fisheries Policy) to withdraw. It is now associated with the EC as an overseas territory of Denmark. In 1981, Greece joined the Community. Portugal and Spain became members in 1986. Portugal left the EFTA group, and Spain finally overcame the yoke of General Franco.

It has always been a rule, at times unwritten, that EC members and applicants must support democratic governments. This principle was applied to Greece during the coup by the colonels in the late 1960s and early 1970s. The Community suspended trade relations with Greece during this period and the coup certainly delayed admission of that country to the EC. The commitment of the Community to governance by representative democracy, the rule of law, social justice and respect for human rights was formalized in 1977 under a Declaration on Democracy by the heads of all the member state governments. At the same time, the Council, Commission and Parliament issued a Joint Declaration on Fundamental Rights to much the same effect.

With 12 member states, the EC in 1991 is a powerful and lucrative economic market. Its aggregate population and gross community product exceed that of the United States and Canada, which implemented a Free Trade Agreement in

1989. Free trade negotiations with Mexico, and the possible emergence of a North American Common Market, are just some of the continuing repercussions of the need to compete with the European Community.

With the Community committed since 1986 to full internal economic integration by the end of 1992, Austria, Cyprus and Malta have formally applied to join. Austria's application raises prominent questions as to the suitability of "neutral" nations as EC members in the face of ever increasing EC political union and foreign policy cooperation. There is talk of the inevitability of membership in the EC by Norway, Sweden and most of the rest of Western Europe. Sweden was expected to apply for membership in the summer of 1991. Indeed, in the newly liberated environment of Eastern Europe, a number of politicians are running on platforms which promise membership in the EC for Hungary, Poland, Czechoslovakia and the like. Some Eastern European nations may first seek EFTA membership as a stepping stone to full EC participation.

Politics will of course play a role in future membership decisions. Turkey, for example, has been associated with the EC as a trade ally since 1963. Relations were suspended during the military takeover of Turkey from 1981 to 1986. Turkey formally applied for EC membership in 1987 but has been kept under study since then. Apart from concerns about the stability of democracy in Turkey, Greek membership in the Community would seem to make admission unlikely. Furthermore, membership is limited by the Treaty of Rome to "European states". Article 237. Morocco's application was rejected because it is not a European nation. Turkey's application presents difficult questions about its status in Europe and the meaning of the Treaty. Does "European" only have geographic implications or is there an expectation that members must also be culturally or religiously European?

The Community, for its part, is not entirely sure that it wishes to expand membership rapidly. Many speak of the need for "deepening before enlargement" of the EC. Already there has been an incorporation of what was East Germany into the Community through the reunification process. By the end of 1992, nearly all EC law will apply to it, including EC environmental and agricultural subsidy rules. The accession of East Germany to the EC has renewed concerns over the role of Germany in Europe. Instead of four large member states (France, West Germany, Italy and the United Kingdom) of roughly equal populations, united Germany has substantially more people and potentially much more economic clout than any other member of the Community. This has caused anxieties about keeping that country well anchored by European institutions.

European leaders speak with caution of expanded relations between the Community and the remaining EFTA states and Eastern Europe. Negotiations for closer economic relations with EFTA countries short of membership are underway. These envision a linkage of the two groups in what is called a European Economic Area (EEA) or European Economic Space (EES). The EEA would include free movement of goods, services, persons and capital. Decision-making and dispute settlement remain issues, but the hope is that the EEA will come into existence at the end of 1992 concurrently with the EC campaign for a Europe without internal frontiers (infra). A variation on this theme would be "affiliate memberships" for EFTA and East European nations. One reason for the Community's reluctance to accept new members is its intensive focus on the 1992 campaign for a fully integrated common market. Other reasons involve the practical problems associated with governance of a community with substantial numbers of nations. Already, with 12 member states, the EC finds it difficult to arrive at a consensus and move forward towards further integration without substantially overriding national interests. A community with 20 members would presumably be all that more difficult to govern.

Europe Without Internal Frontiers

The 1992 campaign for a European Community without internal frontiers was the product of Commission studies in the mid–1980s which concluded that a hardening of the trade arteries of Europe had occurred. The Community was perceived to be stagnating relative to the advancing economies of North America and East Asia. Various projections of the wealth that could be generated from a truly common market for Western Europe suggested the need to revitalize the EC. A "white paper" drafted under the leadership of Lord Cockfield of Britain and issued by the Commission in 1985 has since become the blueprint for the 1992 campaign.

The Commission's white paper identified three types of barriers to a Europe without internal frontiers—physical, technical and fiscal. Physical barriers occur at the borders and for goods include national trade quotas (mostly authorized by Article 115 of the Treaty of Rome), health checks, agricultural monetary compensation amount (MCA) charges, statistical collections and transport controls. For people, physical barriers involve clearing immigrations, security checks and customs. Technical barriers mostly involve national standards and rules for goods, services, capital and labor which operate to inhibit trade among the member states. Boilers, railway, medical and surgical equipment, and pharmaceuticals provide good examples of markets restrained by technical trade barriers. Fiscal barriers center on different value-added and excise taxation levels within the Community and the corresponding need for tax collections at the border. There are, for example, very wide VAT differences on auto sales within the Common Market.

The Commission (Cecchini Report) estimates that removal of all of these barriers could save the

Community upwards of 100 billion ECUs (European Currency Units) in direct costs. In addition, another roughly 100 billion ECUs may be gained as price reductions and increased efficiency and competition take hold. Overall, the Commission projects an increase in the Community's gross domestic product (GDP) of between 4.5 to 7 percent, a reduction in consumer prices of between 6 to 4.5 percent, 1.75 to 5 million new jobs, and enhanced public sector and external trade balances. These figures are thus said to represent "the costs of non-Europe."

Major amendments to the Treaty of Rome were undertaken in the Single European Act (SEA) which became effective in 1987. Amendments to the Treaty can occur by Commission or member state proposal to the Council which calls an intergovernmental conference to unanimously determine their content. The amendments are not effective until ratified by all the member states in accordance with their respective constitutional requirements. Article 236. Proposals originating in the Commission's 1985 white paper on a Europe without internal frontiers were embodied in the Single European Act. The SEA amendments not only expanded the competence of the European Community institutions, but also sought to accelerate the speed of integration by relying more heavily on qualified majority (not unanimous) voting principles in Council decision-making. The Single European Act envisions the adoption of 282 new legislative measures designed to fully integrate the

Common Market. See "1992 at a Glance" in the Appendix. As of 1991, proposals for all of these measures have been drafted by the Commission and roughly three-quarters of them adopted by the Council. Implementation at the national level has proceeded much more slowly and is of concern. Italy and Greece appear particularly behind schedule. Denmark and the United Kingdom rank first on implementation of 1992 legislation.

CHAPTER 2

LAW–MAKING IN THE
EUROPEAN COMMUNITY

The focus in this chapter is on the Community's law-making institutions and procedures. Without an understanding of these areas, it is almost impossible to function as a lawyer on EC matters.

The treaties of the three European communities (the ECSC, the EEC and EURATOM) as amended are the "primary" sources of Community law. The EC treaties have had a common set of institutions since 1967. These are the Council of Ministers, the Commission, the Parliament and the Court of Justice (to which the Court of First Instance was attached in 1989). These institutions, supplemented by national legislatures, courts and tribunals, have been busy generating a remarkably vast and complex body of "secondary" Community law. Regarding legislation, some of this law is adopted directly at the EC level, but much of it is enacted by national governments under the "direction" of the Community. Similarly, some (and the most important) of the secondary case law of the EC is created by decisions of the European Court of Justice or Court of First Instance, but much development of Community law also occurs in the national courts acting in many instances with "advisory rulings" from the Court of Justice. Community secondary law also includes international obligations, often undertaken through "mixed" EC and national negotiations and ratifications.

The starting point for a basic understanding of Community law-making is, as always, the founding treaties. The Treaty of Rome is premised upon the idea of a Community government of limited or derived powers (compétence d'attribution). That is to say, the Treaty does not convey a general power to create Community law. Community law-making is either specifically authorized (including the many authorizations found in the 1987 Single European Act amendments to the Treaty of Rome) or dependent upon the terms of Article 235. That article permits action if "necessary to attain, in the course of the operation of the common market, one of the objectives of the Community and this Treaty has not provided the necessary powers." Article 235 has been used rather extensively, and in ways which suggest that there are relatively few limits upon what the Community can legislate or negotiate by way of international agreements once a political consensus has been reached to move forward. For example, Article 235 was widely used as the legal basis of the Community's environmental programs well prior to the Single European Act amendments that specifically authorize Community action in this field. Furthermore, the Court of Justice has slowly been fashioning a doctrine of *implied* powers under the Treaty of Rome, most notably concerning the Community's external relations' powers. Although variations do occur from treaty to treaty, the Community's legislative, administrative and judicial processes are generally similar. Unless otherwise indicated, the analysis in this chapter is drawn from the Treaty of Rome establishing the EEC.

Legislation—Directives and Regulations

The Community has two primary types of legislative acts, directives and regulations (ECSC recommendations and general decisions). These should be distinguished from declarations, resolutions, notices, policy statements, EEC recommendations, opinions and individual decisions which rarely involve legislative acts. These can, however, be used to interpret related national or Community law. Article 189 of the Treaty of Rome clarifies the powers of the Council of Ministers and the Commission, in accordance with the Treaty, to make regulations and issue directives. EEC regulations are similar in form to administrative regulations commonly found in North America. EEC directives, on the other hand, have no obvious parallel.

A directive establishes Community policy. It is then left to the member states to implement the directive in whatever way is appropriate to their national legal system. This may require a new statute, a Presidential decree, an administrative act or even a constitutional amendment. Sometimes it may require no action at all. As Article 189 indicates, a directive is "binding as to the result to be achieved" but "leave[s] to the national authorities the choice of form and methods." The vast majority of the legislative acts of the 1992 campaign are directives. All EEC directives contain time limits for national implementation. The more controversial the EEC policy, the longer the likely allotment of time.

The Commission's civil servants initiate the process of legislation by drafting proposals which the Council of Ministers (from the governments of the member states) has the power to adopt into law. Although the Council may request the Commission to submit legislative proposals (Article 152), it cannot force the Commission to do so except by way of litigation before the Court of Justice nor draft legislative proposals itself. This makes the Commission the focal point of EC lobbying activities. The Commission's legislative proposals are always influenced by what it believes the Council will accept. The Council, however, has the right to amend legislative proposals by unanimous vote. Readers will immediately note that the European Parliament does not have the power to propose legislation, nor the power to enact it! Parliament's role is primarily consultative. Secondarily, it is the source of proposed amendments when the so-called "cooperation" procedure (infra) applies. These absences of Parliamentary power are so fundamental that many observers now decry a "democratic deficit" in the European Community.

The Council does not always act through directives and regulations. At times, especially when the heads of state and government meet in the European Council (infra), it issues "declarations" or "resolutions." Council resolutions and declarations are used when a political but not necessarily a legislative consensus has been reached. For example, the 1981 Council resolution on the adoption of Community passports with uniform characteristics fits this mold. Official Journal C241/1 (1981). This symbolic resolution has been fully implemented, adding significantly to the consciousness of the Community among its citizens. Another example is the Council's Declaration on Democracy (1977), which "codifies" the longstanding tradition that no European state can join or remain associated with the EC without a pluralistic democratic form of government. A third example is the formulation of foreign policy resolutions by the European Council (see Chapter 8).

The Parliament

The European Parliament (first called the Assembly in the treaties) was originally composed of representatives appointed by member state governments. In other words, the people's representation was indirect, although the members of the European Parliament (MEPs) had to be serving in their national parliaments. Since 1979, universal suffrage is employed to directly elect the 518 representatives of the citizens of the Community to their Parliament. There are 81 MEPs from Britain, Germany, France and Italy, 60 from Spain, 25 from Holland, 24 from Belgium, Greece and Portugal, 16 from Denmark, 15 from Ireland and 6 from Luxembourg. Article 138. These numbers correspond roughly to the populations of each country except united Germany. MEPs serve 5–year terms, and are presently divided into transnational political groups.

The European Parliament is a kaleidoscope of European politics. As of Jan. 1, 1990, there were 180 Socialists, 121 European People's Party, 49 in the European Democratic Group, 34 Greens, 28 European Unitarian Left, 22 European Democratic Alliance, 17 in the Technical Group of the European Right, 14 of the Left Unity Group, 14 Rainbow Group and 10 non-affiliated MEPs. Even these groupings fail to capture the full picture of diversity as the Socialists often realize once they start talking to each other. Since it takes 260 votes to pass a measure in Parliament, alliances are essential. There are 18 standing Parliamentary Committees. Each is responsible for reviewing and reporting on legislative proposals within its expertise, e.g. agriculture, external relations, etc. In addition, unofficially allied groups of MEPs with special interests in particular areas of Community development (e.g. the European Monetary System and the internal market) have been formed. These groups are quite influential in proposing legislative amendments under the cooperation procedure (infra).

The member states have fulfilled their obligations for direct elections under Article 137 of the Treaty of Rome. The Community is supposed to enact "uniform procedures" for these elections. It has not done so. Thus member states draw up the electoral rules for the European Parliament. All member states save Britain basically use proportional representation systems via party lists. Britain employs single-ballot majority voting by constituency. European Community MPs need not, and these days typically are not, representatives in their national parliaments. Some commentators have suggested that this leads to an estrangement between European Community and national politicians.

Another member state failure in connection with the Parliament is to locate its seat. Parliament's plenary sessions are held in Strasbourg, its committee meetings in Brussels and its secretariat is in Luxembourg. Each nation has vied for a permanent assignment of Parliament to it. And the member states have sued to protect their existing allocations. See *Luxembourg v. Parliament* (1983) Eur.Comm.Rep. 255 (Parliament may hold all plenary sessions in Strasbourg); *France v. Parliament* (1988) Eur.Comm.Rep. 4821 (Parliament may hold exceptional plenary sessions in Brussels); *Luxembourg v. Parliament* (1984) Eur.Comm.Rep. 1945 (Parliament could not transfer secretariat from

Luxembourg). One suspects that this litigation reflects the economic more than the political value associated with Parliament and its expense account spending members.

With direct elections, the impetus toward greater Parliamentary input into the legislative process has magnified. Traditionally, the Parliament has a right to be consulted and to give an "opinion" as part of the Community's legislative process. That opinion is not binding upon the Commission or Council, but it can prove increasingly awkward if it is disregarded. For example, in 1980 the Court of Justice held that the Council acts illegally if it legislates without waiting for the Parliament's opinion. *Roquette Frères SA v. Council* (1980) Eur. Comm.Rep. 3333. Left unanswered is how long Parliament may delay giving an opinion. If the Council amends the Commission's legislative proposal substantively, the Parliament has the right to be consulted and issue a second opinion. *ACF Chemiefarma v. Commission* (1970) Eur.Comm.Rep. 661. Since 1977, a "conciliation procedure" may be used whenever the Council departs from an opinion of the Parliament on proposed legislation of importance to the Community's income or expenses. This procedure was instituted by a Joint Declaration of the Parliament, Council and Commission. Official Journal C98/1 (1975).

An important step forward towards democratic governance of the Community was taken in the Single European Act of 1987. Article 149 of the

Treaty of Rome creates a "cooperation procedure" which gives the Parliament more of a voice on selected legislation. See "EC Legislation From Start to Finish" in the Appendix. Basically, when the Treaty requires adherence to this procedure, the Parliament may reject or seek to amend the Council's "common position" on a legislative proposal from the Commission. The formation of a common position by qualified majority vote in the Council of Ministers and use of the cooperation procedure is not needed if on the traditional "first reading" the Council decides to follow the opinion of Parliament on the legislative proposal. Since this does not often happen, the "second reading" commences with the communication of the common position by the Council to the Parliament. If Parliament fails to act within three months, the Council may adopt the proposal into law. If the Parliament rejects the common position, the legislation may still be adopted by a unanimous vote in the Council.

If the Parliament proposes amendments (the most common practice) by an absolute majority, the Commission reexamines the legislative draft in their light. If the Commission's civil servants agree with the Parliament, the amendments are then included in the legislative proposal which is sent to the Council of Ministers a second time. If the Commission rejects the amendments suggested by the Parliament, they are excluded from the legislative proposal but transmitted to the Council with the Commission's opinion on them. In either case, unanimity within the Council is required to alter the legislative proposal. Again, in either case, a qualified majority vote in the Council will in most cases adopt the measure into law. One 1989 study indicates that Parliament introduced nearly 1,000 amendments after the cooperation procedure was adopted in 1987. Of these, 72 percent were accepted by the Commission and 42 percent ultimately adopted by the Council.

The "cooperation procedure" applies selectively. Most significantly, it applies to nearly all 1992 internal market measures. See Articles 100A, 100B. It also applies under Article 7 (non-discrimination on grounds of nationality), Article 49 (free movement of workers), Article 54(2) (right of establishment), Article 56(2) (public security exceptions to free movement), Article 57 (mutual recognition of diplomas), Article 118A (occupational safety), Article 130E (Regional Development Fund) and Article 130Q(2) (research and development). With the development of the cooperation procedure, and success in persuading the Commission and Council to adopt its amendments, Parliament has become a second center of legislative lobbying in the EC. Even so, the Parliament as a legislative institution has not really come of age.

Other powers of the European Parliament should be noted. First, it can put written and oral questions to the Council and the Commission on virtually any Community matter, legislative or otherwise. This prerogative mostly has a nuisance and information gathering value. Absent forceful persuasion, it is not terribly influential. Second, Article 144 of the Treaty of Rome gives the Parliament the power to "censure" the Commission by a two-thirds vote. A motion of censure would require all 17 Commissioners to resign, but the member states acting in common accord (not the Parliament) get to choose the new Commissioners. These could conceivably be the very persons just censured. Parliament cannot selectively censure one Commissioner, nor can it censure the Council of Ministers at all. A motion of censure has at times been threatened by Parliament, but never adopted. Third, the Parliament can initiate a lawsuit against the Council or Commission under Article 175 of the Treaty of Rome for failure to act. Parliament did exactly this when it sued the Council over the failure to implement a Common Transport Policy as required by the Treaty. The Court of Justice ruled that the Council had failed to act, but denied the Parliament a remedy given the imprecise nature of the Council's obligation to act. *European Parliament v. Council* (1985) Eur.Comm. Rep. 1513. Nevertheless, the Council has since undertaken a number of reforms in the transport sector. See Chapter 4.

The Parliament has selected other litigation alternatives. It can intervene as an interested party in cases pending before the Court, which it did quite successfully when challenging a regulation enacted by the Council without its consultation and opinion. *Roquette Frères SA v. Council* (1980)

Eur.Comm.Rep. 3333. But it does not appear to have a right to file briefs in Article 177 litigation (see Chapter 3). As a rule, it cannot litigate the legality of acts of the Commission or Council under Article 173. *European Parliament v. Council* (1988) Eur.Comm.Rep. 5615 (comitology procedures). This is a major omission which further insulates Parliament's influence over Community legislation. But see *European Parliament v. Council* (1990) Eur.Comm.Rep. ___ (Case 70/88) (Parliament may invoke Article 173 when its cooperation prerogatives are at stake).

Budgetary Legislation

The Coal and Steel Community is financed exclusively by taxes levied against producers. The European Economic Community was originally financed by contributions from the member states. This created a fiscally dependent relationship. Since 1971, the Community is funded through its "own resources," but still dependent upon the member states for their collection and transfer. The Community's income is now principally derived from the common external tariff, agricultural levies on imports, a small but growing portion of the value-added tax (VAT) collected in every state, and an assessment based upon the gross domestic product (GDP) of the member states.

Article 199 of the Treaty of Rome requires a balanced Community budget. This requirement has been met by increasing the level of Community revenues and, occasionally, reducing (agricultural) expenditures. Revenue-raising decisions are undertaken by the heads of state and government meeting in the European Council. In other words, Parliament lacks the power to tax. Control over the spending of these resources, however, is another area where the Parliament has sought to acquire power.

The Community's budgetary process is outlined in Article 203 of the Treaty of Rome. The Commission creates a preliminary draft budget which it forwards to the Council of Ministers. The Council revises it and then sends a draft budget to the Parliament. The Parliament can reject the draft budget in its entirety, something it did in 1979 and 1984. Article 203 gives the Parliament the power to propose changes in the budget regarding matters "necessarily resulting from this Treaty or from acts adopted in accordance therewith." This has increased Parliamentary influence over "compulsory expenditures" (mostly agricultural subsidies), but the Council has the final word.

Since 1975, Parliament has had ultimate control by way of amendment over "non-compulsory" EEC expenditures, about 25 percent of the EEC budget. As a practical matter, this gives the Parliament influence over expenditures in many of the new and important policy areas of the Community. See "EC 1989 Budget By Main Area of Expenditure" in the Appendix. However, Parliamentary amendments to the Council's draft budget cannot exceed the maximum rate of increase allowed under Article 203(9). *Council v. European Parliament* (1986) Eur.Comm.Rep. 288. This maximum involves a complex calculation by the Commission of EC inflation and gross domestic product (GDP) rates as well as national budget variations. Parliament, at the end of a laborious process with multiple communications to the Council, adopts the final budget.

Parliament and the Council of Ministers often quarrel over creation of the budget, with Parliament prevailing more and more. Parliament and the Council review how the Commission has implemented the budget. The Court of Justice has indicated that the Commission's power to implement the budget does not include making decisions which are legislative in character. *Commission v. Council* (1989) Eur.Comm.Rep. ___ (Case 16/88). Upon Council recommendation, Parliament gives the Commission a "discharge" of its budgetary duties. Articles 205A, 206B. The EC Court of Auditors assists the Parliament and Council in these tasks, which are reasonably routine. In 1982, however, Parliament refused to discharge the Commission, resulting in tighter controls thereafter. Parliament's power over the purse is increasing and its President reportedly remarked: "As long as Parliament does not have more power in other fields, there will be conflicts on the budget."

Which Council?

The foregoing analysis of the Community's legislative process illustrates the dominant role given by the Treaty of Rome to "the Council" in EC affairs. The Council as an institution is a bit of a moving target. The Council of Ministers consists of representatives of the governments of the member states. Thus there are twelve Council members. However, the people who comprise the Council of Ministers change according to the topic at hand. The national ministers of foreign affairs, agriculture, economy and finance ("ecofin"), social affairs, environment, etc. are sent to Brussels to confer and vote on EC matters within their competence. Several different Council meetings can take place at once. Some refer to the Ecofin Council, the Environment Council, the Agriculture Council and so forth in order to differentiate the various Councils of Ministers. The Presidency of these Councils rotates among the member states every six months and a certain amount of competition has emerged to see who can achieve the most under their Presidency. It is from all these meetings that the legislation of the Community pours forth.

The Council of Ministers are greatly assisted in their work by a Committee of Permanent Representatives known as COREPER. The Committee is comprised of high-ranking national civil servants and based in Brussels. COREPER in turn consults extensively with a large number of "working groups" composed of other national civil servants with expertise in areas of Community concern. Thus, by the time a legislative proposal from the Commission reaches the Council for a vote, the proposal has been thoroughly reviewed by CORE-PER and the appropriate working groups. If there is no controversy, the proposal is scheduled as an "A point" on the Council's agenda and virtually certain to be adopted. If no agreement is reached within COREPER, the proposal becomes a "B point" on the agenda which means that the Council of Ministers will discuss and debate its merits.

Then there is the "European Council." The Community has grown and its legislative and other decisions have inevitably become more political and thus more difficult. A new institution has emerged to keep the EC moving, mostly forward but arguably (at times) backward. The "European Council" consists of the heads of the state or government of the member nations, a kind of ultimate Council of Ministers. The heads of state have met twice a year since 1974 to formulate broad policy guidelines or initiatives for the Community. For example, the European Council has shown leadership on direct elections to Parliament, the European Monetary System, new memberships and innovative legislative agendas. Its meetings are sometimes called "summits," and Article 2 of the Single European Act of 1987 formally recognizes their existence.

European Council summits (though sometimes fractious) have generally proved to be quite successful. They have greatly facilitated the development of common foreign policy positions. Although these meetings are undertaken in close consultation with the EC Commission and Parliament, they are not subject to the procedural rules of the Treaty of Rome. For example, whereas the Council of Ministers must seek the opinion or cooperate with the Parliament on Community legislative acts (supra), the European Council need not do so. Whether the European Council can be subjected to judicial review by the Court of Justice is most unclear. This is the case despite the fact that European Council pronouncements (e.g. the Social Charter in 1989, see Chapter 5) may have important legal implications for the Community. Some fear that the European Council's ability to operate outside the Treaty of Rome may exacerbate the Community's "democratic deficit."

Voting Procedures of the Council

The voting procedures of the Council of Ministers and the European Council are critical to an understanding of law-making in the European Community. The Treaty of Rome provides for simple majority voting unless otherwise specified. Article 148(1). However, nearly all the voting rules of the Treaty do specify otherwise. The exceptions thus become the rule. The point of contention is always whether unanimous or "qualified majority" voting is required. Unanimous voting has the practical effect of giving each member state a veto over Community legislation and policy developments. If a consensus cannot be reached, the minority always seeks shelter under the Treaty of Rome for unanimous voting. The Treaty, however, has only a limited number of such mandates. This is especially true since the Single European Act amendments of 1987. A partial list of the Treaty of Rome's unanimous voting requirements is provided below.

Much of the voting in the Council of Ministers and the European Council now takes place on a "qualified majority" basis. The rules that define this procedure are given in Article 148. There are a total of 76 votes, with Germany, France, Italy and Britain having 10 each. Prior to German reunification, this reflected the roughly equal populations of the Community's largest nations. Spain has 8 votes, and Belgium, Greece, The Netherlands and Portugal all have 5 qualified majority votes. Denmark and Ireland have 3 votes, Luxembourg 2 votes. To adopt legislation or otherwise proceed by qualified majority vote, at least 54 votes must be cast in favor. When the Council is not acting upon a Commission proposal, eight member states must participate in the majority. This means that the "Big Four" and even (with Spain) the "Big Five" cannot prevail without some support from smaller nations. Put conversely, if the little nations stick together, they can block anything. Over the years, as the Community has grown from 6 to 9 to 10 to 12 members, these political dynamics have always been preserved in the qualified majority voting rules. Other "block-ing minorities" can emerge on North–South lines within the Community. Italy, Spain and either Greece or Portugal can deny a qualified majority vote. Germany, the Benelux nations and Denmark can do likewise.

Treaty of Rome terms notwithstanding, a special agreement known as the "Luxembourg accord" sometimes leads to unanimous voting. In 1965, France under General de Gaulle walked out of a Council meeting in a dispute over agricultural poli-cy. Many believe that the real reason for the dispute was the fact that qualified majority voting was due to come into force in 1966. This was the major crisis of the early years of the Community of six. A compromise agreement was reached, which when "very important interests" are at stake, com-mits the Council to reaching solutions by consensus if at all possible. This "Luxembourg accord" then proceeds to express disagreement over what is to be done if a consensus cannot be reached. The French delegation took the view that discussions must continue until unanimity is achieved. The five other delegations took the position that the Treaty rules apply and a decision by qualified majority vote must follow.

For many years, the Luxembourg accord was followed under the French perspective. Qualified majority voting was almost non-existent. Surpris-ingly, there was no challenge by the Commission before the Court of Justice to this breach of the

Treaty's terms. Arguably, the Council was not acting in accordance with an essential procedural requirement of the Treaty. If so, the Commission could have brought suit under Article 173. As the Community grew to twelve member states, it became more and more difficult for the Council to arrive at a consensus. New legislation and new policy initiatives floundered, the Community's institutional and trade arteries hardened.

The Commission, recognizing the economic costs involved (especially vis-a-vis the Community's competitive position with North America and Japan), proposed in its "white paper" of 1985 a return and indeed expansion of qualified majority voting. These proposals bore fruit in the Single European Act of 1987. The Act amends the Treaty of Rome extensively. It is the authority for all 1992 campaign legislation, and much of that legislation can be adopted by qualified majority vote. Article 100A. Moreover, the Act amended the Treaty in a few instances to change unanimous voting requirements to a qualified majority. The net result, operationally speaking, has been the demise of the French perspective to the Luxembourg accord. Unanimity is still sought, sometimes at great lengths, but qualified majority voting prevails. A partial list of the Treaty of Rome provisions specifying qualified majority voting follows.

Unanimous Vote Required *
Article 45(3)   — agricultural subsidies to buy
                         from EC sources

Article 51	— social security for workers who move
Article 57(2)	— professionals (training and access)
Article 76	— discriminatory transport exceptions
Article 93(2)	— state subsidy exceptions
Article 99	— taxation
Article 100	— harmonization of national laws
Article 126(b)	— new uses for Social Fund
Article 130D **	— coordination of Social, Regional and Agricultural Funds
Article 130S **	— environment
Article 138(3)	— Parliamentary election rules
Article 145 **	— delegation of powers to Commission
Article 149(1), (2)(d) and (e) **	— adoption of amendments to legislation, override Parliamentary rejection of common position
Article 168(A) (1) and (4) **	— creation of Court of First Instance, rules of procedure
Article 188	— Court of Justice rules of procedure
Article 200(3)	— contributions to Funds
Article 223	— military material free trade exceptions list
Article 227(2)	— application of specific Treaty articles to French overseas departments
Article 235	— general power to act when necessary to EC objectives
Article 237	— new members
Article 238	— association agreements (trade treaties)

* Transitional (now elapsed) unanimous voting rules excluded.

** Indicates Single European Act of 1987 is source of voting rule.

Qualified Majority Vote Suffices *

Article 7	— nondiscrimination on grounds of nationality
Article 14(5)	— removal of customs duties
Articles 20, 21, 28	— creation of common external tariff
Article 33	— removal of quotas
Articles 38, 42–44	— agriculture
Article 49	— free movement of workers
Articles 54–56	— right of establishment
Article 57	— mutual recognition of diplomas
Articles 59,** 63(2)	— freedom to provide services
Articles 69, 70, ** 73(1) *	— free movement of capital
Articles 75, 79	— road and rail transport
Article 84(2) **	— sea and air transport
Article 87	— competition law
Articles 92, 94	— state subsidies
Articles 100A 100B **	— 1992 legislation except taxation, free movement of persons and employment
Article 101	— distortions of competition
Articles 106–109 *	— balance of payments problems
Articles 111–115 *	— common external commercial policy
Article 118A **	— occupational safety
Article 127	— Social Fund policies
Article 130E **	— Regional Development Fund policies

Article 130Q ** — research and development (se-
                              lected)
Article 149(2)   — adoption of common position
   (a) and (e) **   on legislative proposals, adop-
                              tion of re-examined proposals
Article 203   — budget proposals

   * Indicates 8 member states must join in qualified majority when Council is not acting upon a
Commission proposal.

   ** Indicates Single European Act of 1987 is
source of voting rule.

Which Voting Procedure?

   With the revival of qualified majority voting in
the Council, one critical question is the source of
authority under the Treaty of Rome for legislative
action. For example, when nontariff trade barriers (NTBs) are removed via the traditional harmonization process, Article 100 mandates a unanimous vote. But if an NTB can be dealt with as
part of the 1992 campaign for an internal market
without frontiers, Article 100A stipulates a qualified majority vote in most cases. Naturally, the
Council (composed of government representatives)
and the member states favor interpretations that
result in unanimous voting and greater retention
of national sovereignty. See *United Kingdom v.
Council* (1988) Eur.Comm.Rep. 855 (beef hormones
directive validly adopted by qualified majority vote
under Article 43, unanimous vote under Article
100 not required.) Naturally, the Parliament favors interpretations that require use of the cooperation procedure and its power to propose amend-

ments. Most of these areas correspond with qualified majority voting rules.

The Commission, as the independent "guardian of the treaties," favors interpretations that promote integration and particularly the 1992 campaign. It thus tends to side with Parliament in disputes over the source of power for EC legislative enactments. But it did not do this when proposing post–Chernobyl safety legislation under EURATOM instead of Article 100A of the Treaty of Rome. This had the effect of avoiding Parliamentary cooperation procedures. The Parliament sued the Council before the European Court, which has ruled the suit admissible under Article 173. *European Parliament v. Council* (1990) Eur.Comm.Rep. ___ (Case 70/88).

Legislative authority issues came to a head in a Commission prosecution against the Council initiated on the very day that the Single European Act was signed. *Commission v. Council* (1987) Eur. Comm.Rep. 1493. In this decision, the Court of Justice ruled that the Council violated Article 190 by failing to clearly state the legal basis for regulations implementing the Community's generalized system of tariff preferences (GSP) for goods originating in the developing world. More importantly, the Court held that the Council enacted the regulations on the wrong legal basis. Both of these violations, which were longstanding Council practices, amounted to unlawful failures to act in accordance with the Treaty of Rome.

The Commission had proposed adoption of the GSP regulations under the common external commercial policy provisions, specifically Article 113 which employs qualified majority voting. The Council replaced this proposal with vague language simply referring to "the Treaty" as the legal basis for its acts. In court, the Council explained that this reference was really to Article 113 *and* Article 235. Article 235 authorizes legislation necessary to achieve EC objectives for which specific enabling powers are otherwise not found in the Treaty. Article 235 had been previously used by the Council as the legal basis for a number of innovative Community programs and laws, including the Monetary Cooperation Fund, the Center for Development of Vocational Training, the Foundation for the Improvement of Living and Working Conditions, and environmental, research and development and energy legislation. It has also been used in areas where the Treaty had other provisions, including agriculture, the customs union, services, the right of establishment and (as in the GSP case) external commercial policy.

Article 235 legislation must be enacted by a unanimous Council vote and does not require cooperation with Parliament. By ruling that Article 113 alone was the proper legal basis for GSP regulations, the Court nullified the Council's unanimous decision and reaffirmed its power to subject Council actions to judicial review. The Commission now has more leeway when proposing legislation for which the Treaty stipulates qualified majority voting. And the Council is clearly limited in its use of Article 235 to situations where no other authority to act is found in the Treaty of Rome as amended by the Single European Act.

The Commission as an Institution and Law–Maker

The pivotal role of the Commission in the law-making process of the European Community should be evident. It alone drafts legislative proposals. As the GSP litigation makes clear, the Commission can also prosecute when proper legislative procedures are not followed. Furthermore, in certain areas (notably agriculture and competition law) the Commission has been delegated by the Council the authority to issue implementing regulations and decisions that establish EEC law. Articles 145, 155. These acts detail administrative rules rather than create new or broad policies. Thus the Council establishes the Community's "target prices" for agriculture, but the Commission issues thousands of regulations aimed at actually realizing these goals. The Commission has also promulgated an important series of "group exemption" regulations under EEC competition law. See Chapter 7. These cover franchising, patent licensing, exclusive dealing and a variety of other business agreements. Lastly, the Commission is authorized by Article 90 of the Treaty of Rome to issue (on its own initiative) *directives* addressed to member states regarding public enterprises. Id. This authority avoids the usual Community legislative process.

When exercising law-making powers conferred upon it by the Council, the Commission must first consult various committees. These requirements are known as the "comitology" rules of the Council. Council Decision No. 87/373, Official Journal L197/33 (1987). These rules, in essence, allow the Council to actively monitor the Commission as a law-maker. In most cases, they vest a power of reversal or modification in the Council.

Who and what is the Commission? There are 17 EC Commissioners; two from Germany, France, Italy, Britain and Spain and one each from the remaining seven states. Commissioners are appointed by the member states acting in common accord for four-year renewable terms. The President of the Commission is similarly appointed. Great pains are taken to ensure the independence of Commissioners from their home governments. Article 157 (now Article 10 of the Merger Treaty) stipulates that Commissioners must be chosen on the basis of competence and their independence must be "beyond doubt." Any breach of this trust by Commissioners could lead to compulsory retirement. Unlike the Ministers of the Council, Commissioners are not supposed to function as representatives of their nations. Over the years, in large measure, this has been true. Indeed, Prime Minister Thatcher once failed to renew a British Commissioner's appointment because he had "gone native." Sent over to Brussels in a stormy period when the Prime Minister was quite hostile to Community developments, this Commissioner proceeded to act independently, too independently as it turned out. His non-renewal, however, broke with a longstanding tradition of regular reappointments for competent Commissioners. Renewal decisions have thus become more politicized in recent years and Commissioners no doubt look over their shoulders towards home as their four-year terms begin to expire.

Each Commissioner supervises one or more "Directorate–Generals" or departments of the Commission. These "portfolios" are determined by the President of the Commission. Each Directorate–General (DG) has a Director–General of a nationality different than that of its supervising Commissioner. Each DG has a specific allocation of administrative, legislative drafting and law enforcement duties. Each DG has a staff of highly paid Eurocrats selected in part to ensure national diversity. The staff regulations officially refer to a "geographical distribution" (quotas) of employees based upon the populations of the various member states. Acts performed by Commissioners and their staff in an official capacity are immune from legal proceedings in national courts. *Sayag v. Leduc* (1968) Eur.Comm.Rep. 395. Community employees are also exempt from national income taxation, although they pay a nominal tax to the EC. *Hamblet v. Belgium* (1960) Eur.Comm.Rep. 559 (official's salary cannot be used when calculating income of spouse). There are presently 24 DGs which correspond roughly to the main divisions of the three EC treaties. Many consider this to be an excessive and inefficient number of governmental departments. And some DGs, like environment and external relations, are seriously understaffed while others (especially personnel and information) seem grossly overstaffed.

At the beginning of 1990, there were the following Directorates–General:

DG I   : External Relations,
DG II   : Economic and Financial Affairs,
DG III   : Internal Market and Industrial Affairs,
DG IV   : Competition,
DG V   : Employment, Social Affairs and Education,
DG VI   : Agriculture,
DG VII   : Transport,
DG VIII   : Development,
DG IX   : Personnel and Administration,
DG X   : Information, Communication and Culture,
DG XI   : Environment and Nuclear Safety,
DG XII   : Science, Research and Development, Joint Research Centre,
DG XIII   : Telecommunications, Information Industry and Innovation,
DG XIV   : Fisheries,
DG XV   : Financial Institutions and Company Law,
DG XVI   : Regional Policy,
DG XVII   : Energy,
DG XVIII   : Credit and Investment,
DG XIX   : Budgets,

DG XX : Financial Control,
DG XXI : Customs Union and Indirect Taxation,
DG XXII : Coordination of Structural Instruments, and
DG XXIII : Enterprise Policy, Tourism and Social Economy.

Each Commissioner also supervises a personal staff, known as a cabinet. Critics maintain that there has been excessive growth in the size and power of cabinets. These staff members have been known to override the advice of the various Directors–General and generally isolate their Commissioners from professional civil servant input. Defenders of these trends maintain that some of the DGs have been less than competent, and that the Commissioners need another, less bureaucratic perspective. The truth no doubt lies somewhere in between. Just as there are energetic and effective Commissioners, Directors–General and cabinets, none of these offices is immune from the deadwood syndrome.

The Treaty of Rome also establishes voting rules for the Commission. Simple majority votes prevail with at least 9 Commissioners present. As a matter of custom, considerable deference is usually given to the Commissioner in charge of a DG when legislative or other proposals are being reviewed by the Commission as a whole. This is sometimes achieved by circulating files with proposed actions which are implemented unless objections are shortly received. Individual Commissioners can be delegated authority to act for the whole on routine matters. For example, when the Commissioner on Agriculture adopts new regulations, these are likely to involve such delegation.

The Commission performs a number of functions in addition to those concerning Community lawmaking. The most important of these include its prosecutorial powers against individuals and enterprises for breach of selected EC law, and against member states for failure to adhere to their treaty obligations. See Chapters 2 and 7. The Commission negotiates the Community's international trade and other agreements. See Chapter 6. It also administers the EC budget and publishes a general and a series of specific annual reports (e.g. on competition policy), all of which are a good way to survey Community affairs.

The Court of Justice as a Law–Maker

United States students of law and attorneys are familiar (if not always comfortable) with the lawmaking role of American courts. This perspective is a product of the common-law tradition inherited from Britain made explicit by the teachings of American realists. Such awareness is less present in European legal communities for a variety of reasons. One important factor is the pre-dominance of the civil law tradition on the Continent. This tradition, with its heavy reliance upon abstract inductive (not deductive) reasoning, tends to obscure rather than illuminate the way in which judges on the Continent do in fact make law. Like their common-law counterparts, European judges must often fill in legislative gaps and arrive at conclusions based upon broadly worded legal language. Anyone who has ever read a "Code" knows that it invites, indeed often requires, law-making by judges. Nevertheless, the mystique that judges can only apply the law, not create it, weighs heavily in the minds of many Europeans.

It is against this background that the law-making achievements of the European Court of Justice take on a truly remarkable significance. There are 13 justices on the Court, one from each member nation plus a rotating thirteenth justice. Thus only two or perhaps three are trained in the common law. All are prominent jurists who serve six-year terms by appointment of the member states acting in common accord. The Court was created by the Treaty of Paris in 1951 establishing the Coal and Steel Community. At that time neither Britain nor Ireland was a member. Its procedures and methods (but not its mentality) remain solidly based upon civil law, especially French law, traditions. See Chapter 3.

The Court of Justice emerged in the earliest years as a powerful law-maker. In part, this role was thrust upon it by the open-ended, constitutional language of the EEC Treaty. This is noticeably less true of the ECSC and EURATOM treaties. In part, also, the Court simply embraced the role, drawing power and influence to it while constantly pushing the Community forward through its "integrationist jurisprudence." The supremacy doctrine (*infra*) and the "doctrine of direct effect" (see Chapter 3) have been called the twin pillars of this jurisprudence. No less potentially significant are the general principles of Community law articulated by the Court.

General Principles of Community Law—Fundamental Rights

The law-making role of the Court of Justice is evident when it recognizes general principles of EC law, a kind of common law of the Common Market. This is similar to what occurs when the Court finds the general principles of non-contractual liability common to the member states as required by Article 215. See Chapter 3. However, there is no other express Treaty authorization for the development by the Court of general principles of EC law. Article 164 does oblige the Court to ensure that "the law" is observed when interpreting and applying the Treaty of Rome. In different contexts, as part of "the law," the Court has recognized a right of legitimate expectation (*Töpfer v. Commission* (1978) Eur.Comm.Rep. 1019), a right to be heard (*Transocean Marine Paint Association v. Commission* (1974) Eur.Comm.Rep. 1063), the duty to respect fundamental human rights (*Rutuli v. Minister for the Interior* (1975) Eur.Comm.Rep. 1219), a right to equality of treatment (*Louwage v. Commission* (1974) Eur.Comm.Rep. 81) and a duty to employ means that are proportional (not excessive) to the end sought (*Buitoni SA v. FORMA* (1979) Eur. Comm.Rep. 677).

Other general principles of EC law recognized by the Court of Justice include contractual certainty (*Brasserie de Haecht v. Wilkin–Janssen* (1973) Eur. Comm.Rep. 77), legal certainty (*Openbaar Ministerie v. Bout* (1982) Eur.Comm.Rep. 381), and the right to engage in trade union activities (*Union Syndicale, Massa and Kortner v. Council* (1974) Eur. Comm.Rep. 917). A limited attorney-client privilege of confidentiality has been recognized by the Court of Justice as a general principle of Community law applicable to Community proceedings. This right, however, only applies to external EC-licensed counsel. *AM & S v. Commission* (1982) Eur.Comm.Rep. 1575. A limited doctor-patient right of confidentiality has also been acknowledged by the Court. *M v. Commission* (1980) Eur.Comm. Rep. 1797.

A good example of the way in which ECJ-recognized general principles of law can permeate Community affairs is presented by the principle of legal certainty. This principle means that Community acts must be clear, precise and predictable to those subject to them. *Ireland v. Commission* (1987) Eur.Comm.Rep. 5041. Legal certainty has been invoked in connection with Community competition, agricultural, customs, and social security law so as to protect individuals and their rights. For example, social security notices to workers in other member states must be in a language the worker can understand. *Re Farrauto* (1975) Eur.Comm. Rep. 157. In general, legal certainty bars the adoption of retroactive legislation. *Re Racke* (1979) Eur.Comm.Rep. 69. And ECJ decisions can, in the name of legal certainty, apply only prospectively. *Defrenne v. Sabena* (1976) Eur.Comm.Rep. 455.

In the *Rutuli* decision, the Court recognized the relevance and drew upon the European Convention for the Protection of Human Rights and Fundamental Freedoms (1950). This Convention has been ratified by every EC member state. The Commission has proposed that European Community accede to the Human Rights Convention. This would mean that the Community itself would be bound by the catalogue of human rights enumerated in it. These include property, privacy, fair trial, equal treatment, religious, associational and trade or professional rights. If the Community acceded to the Convention's "right of individual petition," EC citizens would be able to file complaints with the European Commission on Human Rights in Strasbourg, France against acts of the Community's institutions. The European Court of Human Rights in Strasbourg ultimately decides upon such complaints. Neither the Commission nor the Court of Human Rights are Community institutions. They operate in a broader European sphere. Americans should particularly note the ruling of the Human Rights Court that extradition of criminals who face a possible death sentence and the "death row phenomenon" in the United States amounts to torture or an inhuman or degrading treatment or punishment in breach of the Convention. *Re Soering* (1989) Eur.Ct.Hum.Rgts. 161.

The Court's decisions in the field of fundamental rights also draw upon the different constitutional traditions of the member states. *Stauder v. City of Ulm* (1969) Eur.Comm.Rep. 419. The Court, in this respect, does not see itself as merely replicating human rights found in common at the national levels. It is instead "inspired" by these traditions to create of its own accord a European Community law of fundamental human rights and freedoms. *Internationale Handelsgesellschaft GmbH v. Einfuhr-und Vorratsstelle für Getreide und Futtermittel* (1970) Eur.Comm.Rep. 1125. EC human rights are not absolute and public interest exceptions not disturbing "the substance" of those rights may be allowed. *Nold v. Commission* (1974) Eur.Comm. Rep. 491. One interesting and sensitive issue is the possible supremacy of EC law on fundamental rights over national rights.

Finally, the Treaty of Rome is not completely devoid of human rights protections. Article 7, for example, establishes the fundamental principle of non-discrimination on grounds of nationality, including corporate nationality. This principle has been frequently invoked in Community law litigation, very often to set aside national rules embodying such discrimination. See *Patrick v. Ministre des Affaires Culturelles* (1977) Eur.Comm.Rep.

1199; *Knoors v. Secretary of State for Economic Affairs* (1979) Eur.Comm.Rep. 339; *Cowan v. Trésor Public* (1989) Eur.Comm.Rep. 195. Discrimination on grounds of nationality by private parties acting within the scope of the Treaty of Rome is also prohibited. *Walrave and Koch v. Association Union Cycliste Internationale* (1974) Eur.Comm. Rep. 1405. Furthermore, Article 7 applies to the Community and its institutions. *Italy v. Commission* (1963) Eur.Comm.Rep. 165. The principle of nondiscrimination on grounds of nationality applies to covert activities. *Sotgiu v. Deutsche Bundespost* (1974) Eur.Comm.Rep. 153. Speaking generally, the Court of Justice has ruled that Article 7 requires comparable situations not to be treated differently and different situations not to be treated in the same way, unless such treatment is objectively justified (permissible differentiation). *Sermide v. Cassa Conguaglio Zucchero* (1984) Eur. Comm.Rep. 4209.

Other provisions of the Treaty of Rome also touch upon fundamental human rights. These include the right to challenge Council or Commission action taken in breach of essential procedural requirements (see Chapter 3) and equal pay for equal work (see Chapter 5). In addition, Article 222 provides that the Treaty shall not prejudice the rules of the member states governing property ownership. However, this has not stopped the Commission and Council from extensively regulating agricultural land. *Hauer v. Land Rheinland–Pfalz* (1979) Eur.Comm.Rep. 3727 (planting of new wine grapes barred). And the Court of Justice has significantly limited the exercise of intellectual property rights when they inhibit Community trade. See Chapter 4.

Supremacy Doctrine

None of the three EC treaties addresses the question of what to do when national and EC law are in conflict. There is no supremacy clause analogous to that found in the United States constitution. The issue is absolutely critical to the success or failure of Community law in all its manifestations; the founding treaties, directives, regulations, ECJ and CFI decisions, international obligations, the general principles of Community law, etc. Its omission from the treaties was perhaps necessary to secure their passage through various national parliaments. But the issue did not disappear, it was merely left to the European Court to resolve.

In a very famous 1964 decision, the Court ruled that it simply had to be the case that Community law is supreme. *Costa v. ENEL* (1964) Eur.Comm. Rep. 585. The Court reasoned that the whole of the Common Market edifice would be at risk if national laws at variance with EC law could be retained or enacted:

> "The transfer by the states from their domestic legal systems to the Community legal system of the rights and obligations arising under the Treaty carries with it a permanent limitation of

their sovereign rights, against which a subsequent unilateral act incompatible with the concept of the Community cannot prevail."

Under its supremacy doctrine, the European Court of Justice has (effectively speaking) invalidated countless national laws as in conflict with EC law. However, such laws may retain validity for purely internal member state affairs that are not subject to EC jurisdiction. Repeal or amendment of conflicting national law is a duty of the member states that can be reviewed by the Court of Justice in further legal proceedings. *Commission v. France* (1981) Eur.Comm.Rep. 2299. An alternative growing in use and encouraged by the European Court is creative judicial interpretation by national courts so as to incorporate Community law requirements and avoid conflicts. *Von Colson and Kamann v. Land Nordrhein–Westfalen* (1984) Eur.Comm.Rep. 1891. For quite some time after *Costa v. ENEL,* and even somewhat today, national courts, legislatures and executives have resented the supremacy doctrine. They adhere, in the end, to this judge-made law because of their mutual interest in the success of the Community enterprise and their respect for the rule of law by its prestigious Court.

One especially sensitive point has been the conflict of national constitutional rights and EC law. Unlike Britain, many Continental states have written constitutions and some have specialized courts or tribunals vested with exclusive powers of constitutional interpretation. Both Germany and Italy, for example, have such "constitutional courts." The Court of Justice has explicitly ruled that *every* national court or tribunal must apply EC law in its entirety so as to set aside *any* conflicting provision of national law. This duty arises out of EC law. *Nold v. Commission* (1974) Eur.Comm.Rep. 491; *Amministrazione delle Finanze v. Simmenthal Spa* (1978) Eur.Comm.Rep. 629. In France, implementation of this duty by its highest courts has been mixed. The Conseil d'Etat (but not the Cour de Cassation) ordinarily has not invalidated French law when in conflict with EC law because it (under French law) is not empowered to review the constitutionality of administrative acts. The Conseil d'Etat does not acknowledge EC law as a source of review power and duty. *Re Syndicat Général de Fabricants de Semoules de France* (1970) Common Mkt.L.Rep. 395 (Conseil d'Etat): Compare *Administration de Douanes v. Société Café Jacques Vabre* (1975) Common Mkt.L.Rep. 367 (Cour de Cassation adheres to EC law supremacy). But there are signs that the Conseil d'Etat may be coming in from the cold. See *Re Application of R. Nicolo* (1990) 1 Common Mkt.L.Rep. 173 (supremacy of EC law acknowledged when Conseil d'Etat functions as an electoral court). See generally Cohen, "The Conseil d'Etat: Continuing Convergence with the Court of Justice," 16 Eur.L.Rev. 144 (April, 1991).

The German and Italian constitutional courts also initially refused to strike down inconsistent national law. See *Frontini et al v. Ministero delle*

Finanze (1974) 2 Common Mkt.L.Rep. 386; *Solange I* (1974) 2 Common Mkt.L.Rep. 551. Indeed, the Bundesverfassungsgericht went so far as to review and find EC law deficient as against German constitutional protections for human rights. Both courts have retreated from their initial positions. Practically speaking, they have accepted the supremacy doctrine of the European Court and their duty to set aside contrary national law. See *Solange II* (1988) 25 Common Mkt.L.Rep. 201; *Granital Spa v. Administrazione delle Finanze* (1984) translated in 21 Common Mkt.L.Rev. 756. In the human rights area, however, neither has fully given up its review powers when EC law is challenged. *Solange II,* supra; *Fragd Spa v. Amministrazione delle Finanze* (1989) reported in Caja, 27 Common Mkt.L.Rev. 83. Recently, in a case where Irish constitutional restraints on the advertising of the availability of abortion services in Britain were challenged as incompatible with the Treaty of Rome, there were signs within the Irish Supreme Court that supremacy might not prevail. See *Society for the Protection of Unborn Children (Ireland) Ltd. v. Grogan* (1990) Common Mkt.L.Rep. 689.

The collision and reconciliation of the European Court's supremacy doctrine with national constitutions illustrates an essential feature of the EC legal system. The efficacy of the system depends heavily upon the willingness of national judges to acknowledge and adhere to EC law, in particular to adhere to the European Court's interpretation of that law. This dependency has meant that the outer limits of the Court's authority and credibility are really to be found amongst the national judiciaries. On supremacy, the European Court has largely prevailed. In other areas, notably the question of giving "direct effect" to EC directives (see Chapter 3), the process of education and persuasion continues.

CHAPTER 3

LITIGATING EUROPEAN COMMUNITY LAW

There has been an explosive growth in litigation of European Community law. The bulk of this growth has taken place in national courts and tribunals. These bodies are vested with wide (but not final) authority to resolve EC legal issues. For example, contracts disputes can raise a host of Community law questions. Is an exclusive dealing distribution contract enforceable as a matter of competition law? Can goods to which a sales contract applies be freely traded in the Common Market? Is payment for sales across borders protected by EC law? Does an employment contract fail to provide equal pay for equal work? Can employees be terminated because of their nationality? May patent licensing agreements contain grant-back clauses? Can franchisees be limited to certain geographic markets? What joint ventures can be established for research and development purposes?

Administrative decisions present another fertile field of EC law litigation. When can customs officers seize goods in transit between member states? When can they collect money in such situations? When can immigrations authorities keep workers

from other EC states out? When can they deport
them? When can professional licensing boards
deny the applications of citizens of Community
nations? Can national authorities deny EC nationals the right to establish a restaurant? Can they
require residency or work permits? What about
the families of all these persons? What about
pensions, social security, health insurance and other job-related benefits for resident EC workers?
These listings only scratch the surface of EC law
litigation in national courts and tribunals.

Direct Effects Doctrine

The right to commence litigation in national
forums must be given to the plaintiff by national
law. In other words, EC law has not (as yet) been
interpreted to create national causes of action.
What it does do, according to the "direct effects
doctrine," is give litigants the right to raise many
EC law issues ("Euro-defenses" and "Euro-
offenses") in national courts and tribunals. In
doing so, individuals often function as guardians of
the treaty (like the Commission). Americans
might analogize this role to that of "private attorneys general," a law enforcement technique
adopted in a number of United States statutes.
The Court of Justice has noted that the vigilance of
private litigants enforcing their EC law rights is an
important element in the Community's legal system. *Van Gend en Loos v. Nederlandse Administratie der Belastingen* (1963) Eur.Comm.Rep. 585.

The direct effects doctrine is, to a very large degree, a product of the jurisprudence of the European Court of Justice. It can apply to EC treaties, directives (ECSC recommendations), regulations (ECSC general decisions), decisions and international agreements. When any of these measures are of direct effect, this impact generally commences from the date of its entry into force. *Amministrazione delle Finanz v. Salumi* (1980) Eur. Comm.Rep. 1237. But the direct effects doctrine is not automatically applied. For example, although the General Agreement on Tariffs and Trade (GATT) is binding upon the Community and its member states, it has typically been construed by the Court not to have direct legal effects. See *International Fruit Company Produktschap voor Groenten en Fruit* (1972) Eur.Comm.Rep. 1219; *FEDIOL v. Commission* (1989) Eur.Comm.Rep. ___ (Case 70/87). Compare *Bresciani v. Amministrazione delle Finanze* (1976) Eur.Comm.Rep. 129 (Yaoundé Convention trade agreements directly effective and thus override conflicting national law); *Hauptzollamt Mainz v. Kupferberg* (1982) Eur. Comm.Rep. 3641 (EC–Portugal Free Trade Agreement has direct effect). Both the Council of Ministers and the European Council tend to issue resolutions or declarations when there is a political consensus but no desire to adopt legislation. For the most part, the Court of Justice has held such acts incapable of creating direct legal effects in the member states. *Pubblico Ministero v. Manghera*

(1976) Eur.Comm.Rep. 91; *Schülter v. Hauptzollamt Lörrach* (1973) Eur.Comm.Rep. 1135.

The legal effects of regulations are the easiest to understand. Article 189 of the Treaty of Rome provides that EEC regulations are "directly applicable in all member states." In other words, EEC regulations have immediate unconditional legal effect. They are law in the member states from the moment of issuance, binding upon all individuals, business organizations and governments. See, e.g., *Politi SAS v. Ministry of Finance of the Italian Republic* (1971) Eur.Comm.Rep. 1039; *Fratelli Zerbone SNC v. Amministrazione delle Finanze* (1978) Eur.Comm.Rep. 99. For litigants, when EEC regulations are applicable, they control the outcome. This is true under the supremacy doctrine even in the face of contrary national law. See Chapter 2.

Directives are more difficult to understand. Article 189 does *not* specify that they shall have "direct applicability." In part, their design prohibits this. Directives are addressed to member states, instructing them to implement (in whatever way is required) certain Community policies within a fixed timetable. These policies do not become law in the member states until implemented or, if timely implementation does not follow, until the European Court rules that the directive is of "direct effect." Some national courts have opposed the doctrine. See especially *In re Cohn–Bendit* (1978) 1979 Common Mkt.L.Rep. 702 (French Conseil d'Etat); German Federal Tax Court (Bundesfinanzhof) V.B. 51/80 (July 16, 1980) (reversed on appeal).

Not all directives of the Community have direct effect. The Court of Justice has selectively ruled that only those directives that establish clear and unconditional legal norms and do not leave normative discretion to the member states are of direct effect. *Van Duyn v. Home Office* (1974) Eur. Comm.Rep. 1337. Once a directive has direct effect, litigants can rely on it to the full extent of its application to member states. Litigants can challenge contrary national law, including defective implementing measures if required. But, unlike regulations, directives cannot be used to challenge private activities. Thus it is said that directives are incapable of "horizontal" direct effects. *Marshall v. Southampton and South West Hampshire Area Health Authority (teaching)* (1986) Eur.Comm. Rep. 723.

Directly Effective Treaty Provisions

The third major category of directly effective law originates in the treaties establishing the Coal and Steel, EURATOM and EEC communities. The Court of Justice has ruled that parts of these treaties are capable of having immediate, binding legal effect in the member states. Here again the Court has been selective, sorting out which treaty provisions establish clear, unconditional and nondiscretionary legal norms. Those many articles of the treaties that are largely aspirational, procedural or written as guidelines for the exercise of member state discretion are unlikely to have direct effect. See *Spa Salgoil v. Italian Ministry for Foreign Trade* (1968) Eur.Comm.Rep. 453 (Articles 33(1) and (2) discretionary and not directly effective).

The Court of Justice has consistently refused to view the EC treaties as merely creating obligations among the contracting states. Citing Article 177 (infra), the Court finds acknowledgment that the Treaty of Rome was intended to have effect in national legal regimes.

"The conclusion to be drawn ... is that the Community constitutes a new legal order of international law for the benefit of which the States have limited their sovereign rights, albeit within limited fields, and the subjects of which comprise not only Member States but also their nationals. Independently of the legislation of Member States, Community law therefore not only imposes obligations on individuals but is also intended to confer upon them rights which become part of their legal heritage. These rights arise not only where they are expressly granted by the Treaty, but also by reason of obligations which the Treaty imposes in a clearly defined way upon individuals as well as upon the Member States and the institutions of the Community." *Van Gend en Loos v. Nederlandse Administratie der Belastingen* (1963) Eur.Comm.Rep. 1.

Once the Court has held a Treaty term directly effective in the member states, litigants before national courts and tribunals can rely fully upon it. They can, under the supremacy doctrine, use it to set aside contradictory national law. Like regulations, directly effective Treaty of Rome provisions can apply horizontally to private parties. *Defrenne v. Sabena* (1976) Eur.Comm.Rep. 455. This follows, in the court's view, because national courts are an arm of the states that signed the Treaty and therefore bound to apply the law in all cases. The same logic has not been carried over to directives. *Marshall v. Southampton,* supra.

The following is a partial list of the articles of the Treaty of Rome that have been held directly effective by the European Court of Justice. Many of these decisions are qualified.

Article 7 — no discrimination on grounds of nationality

Articles 9–10 — customs union free trade rules

Articles 12, 13(2), 16 — no internal customs duties or measures of equivalent effect

Article 30 — no internal trade quotas or measures of equivalent effect

Article 36 — no disguised restraints on internal trade

Article 37 — state trading monopolies cannot discriminate between EC nationals

Article 48 — free movement and employment of workers without nationality discriminations

Articles 52, 53 — right of establishment for self-employed

Articles 59(1), 62	— freedom to provide services across borders
Article 60(3)	— national treatment of cross-border service providers
Articles 67, 106	— current payments for goods, services and capital transfers
Articles 76, 79, 80	— transport discriminations prohibited
Articles 85, 86, 90	— competition law prohibitions
Articles 92(1), 93(3)	— state subsidies cannot distort competition without Commission approval
Article 95	— national treatment on taxation of EC goods
Article 96	— no excessive tax rebates upon EC exports
Article 119	— equal pay for equal work
Article 221	— no discrimination on capital participation in companies

The following Treaty of Rome provisions have generally been held *not* to have direct legal effect. Again, many of these ECJ decisions are qualified.

Articles 2, 3	— general Community tasks and objectives
Article 5	— member state obligations to facilitate and not jeopardize Treaty of Rome
Articles 32(2), 33	— elimination of internal quotas
Articles 67(1), 71	— free movement of capital
Article 93	— state subsidies
Article 97	— discriminatory or protective taxation

Article 102 — harmonization of laws
Article 107 — balance of payments
Article 220 — negotiation of certain conventions

National Legal Remedies for Directly Effective EC Law

Directly effective Community law conveys at the national level immediate legal rights and obligations. What remedies can be secured in national courts and tribunals when Community law has these effects? The Treaty of Rome does not provide a ready answer. In general, the Court of Justice has held that directly effective Community rights must be enforceable in the national courts by means of remedies that are real, effective and non-discriminatory. *Rewe Zentralfinanz v. Landwirtschaftskammer Saarland* (1976) Eur.Comm. Rep. 1989; *Amministrazione delle Finanze v. San Giorgio* (1983) Eur.Comm.Rep. 3595. Interim or preliminary judicial and administrative remedies may be required to protect directly effective EC rights. *Regina v. Secretary of State for Transport* (1990) Eur.Comm.Rep. ___ (Case C–213/89); *Zukerfabrik Süderithmarschen v. Hauptzollamt Itzehoe* (1991) Eur.Comm.Rep. ___ (Cases 143/88 and C–92/89). The precise determination of those remedies is a matter for the national courts to decide.

In Britain, the Court of Appeal has ruled that a failure on the part of the government to adhere to Treaty of Rome obligations does *not* give rise to an action for damages even when directly effective rights are involved. *Bourgoin SA v. Ministry of Agriculture, Fisheries and Food* (1985) 3 All Eng. Rep. 585, (1986) 1 Common Mkt.L.Rep. 267. This litigation was commenced by French turkey producers who lost sales when Britain imposed import restraints, allegedly for animal health reasons. The Court of Justice had previously ruled that the restraints were unlawful under Article 31 as measures of equivalent effect to quotas. The British restraints were not subject to the animal health exception created by Article 36 because they were economically motivated, i.e. they were disguised restraints on internal free trade. *Commission v. United Kingdom* (1982) Eur.Comm.Rep. 2793. The plaintiffs in *Bourgoin* apparently could have obtained injunctive relief had Britain continued to impose its restrictions after the European Court's decision. Accord, *Regina v. Secretary of State for Transport* (1990) 3 Common Mkt.L.Rep. 375 (House of Lords).

There is some question whether *Bourgoin* meets the general criteria of the Court of Justice for real, effective and non-discriminatory national legal remedies when directly effective EC rights are at stake. The case was settled before reaching the House of Lords by payment to Bourgoin of 3.5 million Pounds Sterling for damages, costs and interest by the UK government. Similar remedial issues have been litigated in Britain concerning directly effective EEC competition law (Articles 85 and 86, *infra* Chapter 7). In contrast, the French Conseil d'Etat has awarded damages against the

French government for harm caused by a breach of Community law. *Ministre du Commerce Extérieur v. Alivar* (March 23, 1984). Dutch law also permits such recoveries. *Roussel Laboratories* (Hague District Court, July 18, 1984).

In the absence of precise Community rules on remedies for directly effective legal rights, the results vary from country to country and context to context. Many cases involve the question of repayment of custom duties, customs charges and taxes paid to governments under national laws that are invalidated by Community law. Some concern national laws implementing Community law which is subsequently invalidated by the Court of Justice. See, e.g. *Haegeman v. Commission* (1972) Eur. Comm.Rep. 1005; *Amministrazione delle Finanze v. Denkavit Italiana Srl* (1980) Eur.Comm.Rep. 1205. The Court has reiterated in these decisions that the means of recovery for monies unlawfully paid to governments are controlled by national law. Thus, statutes of limitations, the forum, interest on the amounts paid and related issues are national legal questions. The Court has also reiterated that procedural hurdles which discriminate against recoveries based upon EC rights when measured against procedures for similar domestic recoveries do not satisfy the requirements of the Treaty of Rome. *Deville v. Administration des Impôts* (1988) Eur.Comm.Rep. 3513. And, in general, national rules on recovery of unlawful payments to governments cannot have the practical result of making it impossible to recover such sums. *Express Dairy Foods Ltd. v. Intervention Board for Agricultural Produce* (1980) Eur.Comm. Rep. 1887.

Article 177—Referrals By National Courts and Preliminary ECJ Rulings

The European Court of Justice derived its doctrine of directly effective Community law partly from Article 177 of the Treaty of Rome. This article is the linchpin that joins the national legal systems of the member states to the European Court.

Article 177 vests jurisdiction in the European Court to give "preliminary rulings" (sometimes called "advisory rulings") on the interpretation of the Treaty, the validity and interpretation of acts by the Community's institutions and other EEC matters. These rulings occur when national courts or tribunals (faced with an issue of Community law) request them. Professional bodies may or may not constitute "tribunals of a member state" for these purposes. Compare *Re Jules Borker* (1980) Eur.Comm.Rep. 1975 (Bar Council of Cour de Paris not a tribunal; preliminary ruling request rejected); with *Broekmeulen v. Huisgarts Registratie Commissie* (1981) Eur.Comm.Rep. 2311 (Dutch Appeals Committee for General Medicine is a tribunal of the state; request accepted).

Article 177 requests or "references" are discretionary with the judges of the lower-level courts and tribunals of the member states. They cannot be initiated as a matter of right by litigants, nor by arbitrators designated by contract to resolve a dispute when those arbitrators are not functioning as a court or tribunal of a member state. *Nordsee v. Reederei Mond* (1982) Eur.Comm.Rep. 1095 (German arbitration court reference rejected). Whenever a national court considers a reference necessary to enable judgment, it may seek the advice of the European Court by posing questions to it. It may do so even when the European Court or a higher national court has already ruled on the question of EC law at hand. In other words, the common law doctrine of binding precedent does not remove the discretion of lower courts to invoke Article 177. *Rheinmülen–Düsseldorf v. Einfuhr- und Vorratsselle für Getreide und Futtermittel* (1974) Eur.Comm.Rep. 33. But see to the contrary *Duke v. GEC Reliance Systems Ltd.* (1987) 2 Common Mkt.L.Rep. 24 (English Court of Appeal).

Assuming the request comes from a proper national court or tribunal, the European Court of Justice cannot refuse the reference, even when it has already ruled on the EC legal issue. *Re Da Costa en Schaake* (1963) Eur.Comm.Rep. 11. Once underway, the Commission almost always files a written brief expressing its opinion in Article 177 proceedings. The government of the member state whose court or tribunal is the source of the reference typically does so as well. Once a preliminary ruling of the European Court is secured, the national court is obliged to implement that ruling in its final judgment. *Rewe Zentralfinanz v. Land-*

wirtschaftskammer Saarland (1976) Eur.Comm. Rep. 1989. The ruling is also binding on appeal of that judgment, and (at a minimum) persuasive in courts of other nations. *International Chemical Corp. v. Amministrazione delle Finanze* (1983) Eur. Comm.Rep. 1191.

The discretion of national courts to refer EC law questions to the European Court is largely removed whenever the question is one of the *invalidity* (not interpretation) of Community law. The Court of Justice has ruled that national courts cannot determine the invalidity of an EC legal measure. *Foto–Frost v. Hauptzollamt Lübeck–Ost* (1987) Eur. Comm.Rep. 4199. The Court reasoned that divergent invalidity determinations could place the unity of the Community legal order in jeopardy and detract from the general principle of legal certainty. However, national courts can declare EC legislation valid and proceed accordingly. Id.

There is a dispute as to whether the European Court can pronounce without request upon the effects of an invalid Community measure, e.g. whether monies paid previously can be recovered. The Court asserts the power to spell out the consequences of its invalidity rulings under Article 177. *Roquette v. French Customs* (1980) Eur.Comm.Rep. 2917. It draws upon the analogy to Article 174 which conveys to the ECJ the power to determine the effects of its decisions made in the context of Article 173 challenges to Council or Commission action (infra). The highest French courts are split as to the duty to follow the Court's Article 177 rulings on the consequences of invalid Community law. The Cour de Cassation adheres, while the Conseil d'Etat rejects. The Conseil d'Etat limits adherence to ECJ rulings to the scope of the questions posed by the national courts. The Court's rulings on repayment in *Roquette* were treated as gratuitous and uncontrolling since not requested. Conseil d'Etat (1985) Rec. des Décisions 233. This dispute illustrates, more generally, the distinct tendency on the part of the European Court not to see itself confined by the limits of the questions posed by national forums under Article 177. Rarely, however, has such a hostile national response been received upon delivery of the ruling.

On questions of the validity of *national* laws (including apparently the laws of other member states) under the EC legal regime, the lower courts retain complete discretion to use the Article 177 reference procedures, or to immediately set aside national laws under the EC supremacy doctrine (See Chapter 2). Nevertheless, the Court's preliminary ruling jurisdiction cannot be invoked through "sham litigation" where there is no genuine dispute before the national court, only a desire to challenge the validity of national law. *Foglia v. Novello* (1980) Eur.Comm.Rep. 745; (1981) Eur. Comm.Rep. 3045.

In the early years of the European Community, lower courts and tribunals in the member states hesitated to invoke the preliminary ruling procedure of Article 177. In some cases, this was a matter of ignorance, in others a matter of national pride. Over the years, Article 177 references of EEC law issues have risen dramatically. By 1987, they amounted to nearly half of the Court's caseload. This is done not only out of need for advice, but also a growing sense of judicial cooperation in the Community. Absent such cooperation, there is a great risk that different interpretations of Community law would proliferate among member state forums.

For the lower courts, Article 177 references are discretionary. For courts of last resort (no appeal as a matter of right), Article 177 *requires* a reference to the European Court except in interlocutory proceedings. *Hoffmann-La Roche v. Centrafarm* (1977) Eur.Comm.Rep. 957. This requirement insures that the European Court will have the last and supreme word on EEC legal issues. Thus, if a litigant is willing to exhaust his or her national judicial remedies, access to the European Court is supposed to be guaranteed. In many instances, this is exactly what happens. In others, the doctrine of "acte clair" has been invoked so as to avoid mandatory Article 177 references.

Acte Clair

"Acte clair" originates in the French law. It posits that appeals need not be taken whenever the law and result in the case at hand are clear. Appeals in such circumstances are wasteful of judicial and litigant time and energy. The problem in the European Community context, of course, is that differences of opinion as to the clarity of EC law will often exist. If abused by national courts of last resort, acte clair could break rather than occasionally remove the linchpin of Article 177.

The *Enterprises Garoche* case provides a good example of French invocation of acte clair so as to totally avoid an Article 177 reference. A Dutch boat builder entered into a three-year exclusive dealing agreement with a French agent concerning France, Belgium, Switzerland, Monaco, and Corsica. The Dutch builder undertook to refrain from selling in these territories directly or indirectly through agents. Shortly thereafter he sold two boats through an Italian dealer to two customers domiciled in Monaco. The French agent sued for breach of the exclusive dealing contract. The Tribunal de Commerce de Paris awarded him damages.

The Cour d'Appel de Paris and then the Cour de Cassation held that the contract was void under Articles 85(1) and (2) and not subject (for lack of notification to the Commission) to individual exemption under Article 85(3). Furthermore, the contract was outside the protection afforded by group exemption Regulation 67/67 because the isolation of national markets from other distributors resulted in high prices being charged by the French agent and hence did not allow consumers "a fair share of the resulting benefit". Thus the principle of the illegality under Article 85(1) of absolute territorial protection clauses prevailed. See Chapter 7. Moreover, the direct effect of EEC competition law in the French courts was not in doubt. The Dutch builder could rely on it as a matter of right.

None of these three French courts found it necessary to refer any of the issues in *Enterprises Garoche* to the European Court of Justice. Both the Tribunal de Commerce and the Cour d'Appel invoked the acte clair doctrine while noting that their decisions were subject to appeal and hence not mandatorily referable. The Cour de Cassation, from which no appeal lies under the French legal system, agreed that the dispute was fundamentally centered on an interpretation of Article 3 of Regulation 67/67. That Regulation was clear to the highest French court in light of a 1971 Court of Justice opinion dealing with it. Consequently a "fresh interpretation" by way of reference in 1973 to the European Court was not required. *Enterprises Garoche v. Société Striker Boats* (1973) 1974 Common Mkt.L.Rep. 469. Although it is difficult to criticize the actual results of the *Garoche* case in the French courts, their application of acte clair illustrates how dependent European Community law is on national courts and national legal principles.

Despite an initial annoyance at French invocations of acte clair (see especially *Re Société des Pétroles Shell–Barre* (1964) Common Mkt.L.Rep.

462 (Conseil d'Etat)), courts in other member states soon became converts. By 1982, when the European Court ruled definitively on the validity under EC law of this practice, it was faced with widespread but not particularly abusive utilization of acte clair. In *CILFIT*, the Italian Corte Suprema di Cassazione made a mandatory referral of the acte clair issue to the European Court. That is to say, the question it posed to the European Court was whether it was absolutely obliged to refer all issues of interpretation of EC law to the Court. The European Court deferentially incorporated acte clair into Community law as a gloss on the otherwise straightforward language of Article 177. In doing so, however, it was able to spell out the terms and conditions for its invocation:

"The correct application of Community law may be so obvious as to leave no scope for any reasonable doubt as to the manner in which the question raised is to be resolved. Before it comes to the conclusion that such is the case, the national court or tribunal must be convinced that the matter is equally obvious to the courts of the other Member States and to the Court of Justice. Only if those conditions are satisfied may the national court or tribunal refrain from submitting the question to the Court of Justice and take upon itself the responsibility for resolving it. . . .

It must be borne in mind that Community legislation is drafted in several languages and that the different language versions are all equally authentic. An interpretation of a provision of Community law thus involves a comparison of the different language versions.... Even where the different language versions are entirely in accord with one another, Community law uses terminology which is peculiar to it. Furthermore, it must be emphasized that legal concepts do not necessarily have the same meaning in Community law and in the law of the various Member States." *CILFIT v. Ministro della Santa* (1982) Eur.Comm.Rep. 3415.

Ten Official and Nine Working Languages

In *CILFIT,* the European Court issues a reminder of the problems of language in interpreting EC law. The Coal and Steel Treaty sought to avoid these problems by making French the only official language of that treaty. Article 100 of the Treaty of Paris. There are presently ten official and (less Irish) nine working languages within the Common Market. Each working language can be consulted on questions of interpretation. However, with Treaty of Rome terms (such as Article 177) it is important to remember that English was *not* an official language of the Community prior to 1973 when the British joined. Thus, with reference to older legal documents *and* the Treaty of Rome, French, German, Dutch or Italian versions are arguably more authoritative. The French version is considered the most authoritative of all because the Treaty of Rome was originally drafted in

French. At a minimum, reference to different versions will promote greater understanding of Community law. Attorneys practicing EC law routinely consult different language versions of Community regulations, directives, decisions and treaties.

The European Court of Justice, when confronted with linguistic difficulties, has stressed the need to reconcile different official texts without giving preference to any one language. *Regina v. Bouchereau* (1977) Eur.Comm.Rep. 425. Difficulties of this kind are minimized in the foreign policy arena (which operates outside the Treaty of Rome, see Chapter 8) by using only English and French in the European Council. To the same effect, in Court of Justice or Court of First Instance proceedings, the plaintiff generally gets to choose the official language of the case unless the defendant is from or is a member state (in which case the language of that member state prevails). When Article 177 proceedings are involved, the language of the nation whose court or tribunal is making the reference is official.

The Court's decision will be published in all nine working Community languages but only the language of the case is authentic. By custom, French is the internal working language of the Court of Justice. This means that judgments are debated and drafted in French. All other versions are translations, even when French is not the language of the case. Parliament, the Commission and the

Court in public session, on the other hand, are a veritable babble of languages with simultaneous translations occurring. There are 72 different possible pairs of official Community languages.

Articles 173 and 175—Challenging The Council or Commission

In *CILFIT,* the Court of Justice also warned against the transferability of legal concepts within the Community. Article 173 provides a good example of these kinds of problems.

Article 173 gives the Court the power to review the legality of acts of the Council of Ministers or Commission. In unusual circumstances, acts of Parliament may also be challenged. *Les Verts v. Parliament* (1986) Eur.Comm.Rep. 1339. Acts which are merely preparatory, such as the commencement of a competition law investigation by the Commission, cannot be challenged. *IBM Corp. v. Commission* (1981) Eur.Comm.Rep. 2639. To be challengeable, the "legal interests" of those under investigation must have been affected. Id. Member states, the Commission or Council, and directly concerned individuals may challenge Council or Commission regulations, directives or enforcement decisions on specified grounds. Parliament has no express authority to challenge Council or Commission action under Article 173. No challenges may be brought against Council or Commission recommendations or opinions.

There are four grounds for challenging (often called "appealing") Council or Commission acts. These are specified in Article 173 and originate in French administrative law. These grounds do not apply to challenges under Article 175, which concerns failures of the Council or Commission to act as required by the Treaty of Rome. The four grounds are:

(1) lack of competence (i.e. *ultra vires,* or lack of jurisdiction or authority to act);

(2) infringement of an essential procedure (e.g. failure to provide reasons for Community acts, see Article 190);

(3) infringement of the Treaty or any related rule of law (including general principles of EC law and international law); and

(4) misuse of powers.

Each of these grounds for challenging Commission or Council acts or failures to act has been extensively and uniquely developed in the jurisprudence of the European Court. For example, the term "misuse of powers" in Article 173 originated in the French administrative law concept of *détournement de pouvoir.* Research on and an understanding of French administrative law thus becomes important to Article 173. See *ASSIDER v. High Authority* (1954–56) Eur.Comm.Rep. 63 (Advocate–General's opinion). Misuse of powers is a term of art in British administrative law which is narrower than the U.S. concept of abuse of administrative discretion. The original French concept is limited to situations in which public institutions or personnel use their powers for personal benefit, such as to favor a relative or for financial gain. Thus the concept of détournement de pouvoir does not transfer easily from French into British or American law. Moreover, as *CILFIT* suggests, the Court of Justice is entirely free to develop its own doctrine in this area independent of its French origins. See *Guiffrida v. Council* (1976) Eur.Comm.Rep. 1395 (sham competition for EC job is misuse of power).

Article 173 litigation must be brought within two months of the publication of the act that is being challenged or its notification to the appellant (in the absence of notice, two months from the day when that person had knowledge of it). Article 174 authorizes the Court to declare acts of the Council or Commission null and void if the appeal is well founded. This explains why Article 173 litigation is sometimes referred to as "actions for annulment." Regulations may be partially or fully annulled, or retain validity until replaced, at the Court's discretion. Article 174(2); *Commission v. Council* (1989) Eur.Comm.Rep. 259.

Challenges for failure to act under Article 175 can only be brought if the Council or Commission has first been called upon to act, and only if either fails to "define its position" within two months thereafter. This definition is not necessarily an act that can itself be challenged under Article 173. *GEMA v. Commission* (1979) Eur.Comm.Rep. 3173. The challenge for failure to act may then be

brought in two additional months. If an Article
175 challenge is well founded, Article 176 in essence authorizes the Court to order action by the
Council or Commission. In both Article 173 and
175 litigation, Article 176 imposes a duty on the
Council or Commission, as appropriate, to "take
the necessary measures to comply with the judgment of the Court of Justice."

Standing to Challenge the Council or Commission, Pleas of Illegality

One limitation on Article 173 actions before the
Court concerns the appeal rights of natural and
legal persons. Such persons may only challenge
decisions addressed to them, or regulations or decisions addressed to others which are of "direct and
individual concern" to them. The Court has nar-
rowly construed the concept of "directly concerned
individuals" so as to effectively limit the number of
private challenges capable of being raised under
Article 173. See, e.g. *Confédération Nationale des
Producteurs de Fruits et Legumes* (1962) Eur.
Comm.Rep. 471. But see *Les Verts v. Parliament*
(1986) Eur.Comm.Rep. 1339 (political group has
standing to challenge electoral budget decision).
However, in the competition law area where private interests are at stake when individual exemptions are issued by the Commission (see Chapter 7),
the Court has been more liberal in its allowance of
challenges by concerned third parties. *Metro SB–
Grossmärkte GmbH & Co. KG v. Commission* (1977)

Eur.Comm.Rep. 1875 (complainant allowed to challenge). Jurisdiction to hear competition law challenges by private parties to Commission actions in the competition field has been transferred since 1989 to the Court of First Instance (infra).

The selectively liberal approach to Article 173 standing has also been followed regarding Commission decisions on antidumping duties, internal state aids, countervailable subsidies applicable to Community imports, and illicit commercial practices of non-member nations. *COFAZ SA v. Commission* (1986) Eur.Comm.Rep. 391 (complainant allowed to challenge aid authorization by Commission); *Allied Corp. v. Commission* (1984) Eur. Comm.Rep. 1005 (named exporters may challenge imposition of dumping duties); *Timex Corp. v. Council and Commission* (1985) Eur.Comm.Rep. 849 (complainant may challenge antidumping decisions); *FEDIOL v. Commission* (1983) Eur.Comm. Rep. 2913 (complainant may challenge countervailing duties decision); *FEDIOL v. Commission* (1989) Eur.Comm.Rep. ___ (Case 70/87) (complainant may challenge illicit commercial practices decision).

Article 175 governs the failure of the Council or Commission to undertake actions required by the Treaty or other Community law. Actions by individuals and enterprises under Article 175 challenge the failure of the Council or Commission to address an act to the appellant. They cannot be used to compel discretionary Commission acts, such as Article 169 prosecutions of member states or competition law prosecutions of anticompetitive airline practices. *Alfons Lütticke GmbH v. Commission* (1966) Eur.Comm.Rep. 19; *Lord Bethell v. Commission* (1982) Eur.Comm.Rep. 2277.

The expiration of the two months period for challenges to Council or Commission acts under Article 173 is not a firm statute of limitations. Article 184 allows any party to a proceeding where a Council or Commission regulation is in issue to plead the grounds for challenge specified in Article 173 in order to claim its inapplicability before the Court of Justice. This means, as a practical matter, that EC regulations can be challenged at any time by what is called a "plea of illegality." Moreover, the European Court has extended this plea to directives, decisions and other acts of the Council or Commission. *Simmenthal v. Commission* (1979) Eur.Comm.Rep. 777. Private parties may thus wait until the implementation of Community law is of immediate concern to them without losing an ability to test the legality of that law. Pleas of illegality are frequently made in Community torts and contracts litigation (infra).

Articles 173 and 175 have spawned an interesting series of EC institutional litigations. In these cases, the Council, Commission and Parliament end up suing each before the European Court of Justice. These suits reflect the struggle for power and influence among the Community's institutions. One major limitation upon them is the general absence of authority for Parliamentary suits under Article 173 against Council or Commission acts. *European Parliament v. Council* (1988) Eur.Comm. Rep. 5615. Such suits can be filed when Parliamentary legislative prerogatives are at stake. *European Parliament v. Council* (1990) Eur.Comm. Rep. ___ (Case 70/88).

The Parliament is authorized by the Treaty of Rome to file Article 175 suits when the Council or Commission has failed to act. Thus the Parliament has successfully sued the Council over its failure to act in accordance with Treaty obligations to implement a Common Transport Policy. *Parliament v. Council* (1985) Eur.Comm.Rep. 1513. The Council in turn has successfully sued the Parliament for excessive budgetary allocations. *Council v. Parliament* (1986) Eur.Comm.Rep. 288. The Commission has challenged the Council frequently before the European Court. Some of its most important victories concern the proper "legal basis" for Community legislation and international agreements. *Commission v. Council* (1989) Eur.Comm. Rep. 1493 (GSP preferences); (1971) Eur.Comm. Rep. 263 (the *ERTA* decision).

Articles 173 and 175 also provide the member states with the means to challenge the Commission. This is the reverse of the type of litigation that flows from Article 169 prosecutions of member states by the Commission (infra). See, e.g. *Germany v. Commission* (1987) Eur.Comm.Rep. 3203 (lack of competence to act); *Ireland v. Commission*

(1987) Eur.Comm.Rep. 5041 (violation of EC law); *Netherlands v. Commission* (1971) Eur.Comm.Rep. 639 (failure to act). The Council can likewise be challenged by the member states under Articles 173 and 175. *United Kingdom v. Council* (1988) Eur.Comm.Rep. 855 (infringement of essential procedural requirement). Member state challenges of legislative acts by the Council seem likely to rise as more qualified majority voting occurs and the minority seeks legal redress. See Chapter 2.

Article 169—Commission Prosecutions of Member States

Article 169 authorizes the Commission (alone) to bring an action before the Court of Justice against member states that have failed to fulfill their obligations under the Treaty of Rome. This authority is reinforced by Part I of the Treaty which includes some basic normative rules. In Article 5 the member states undertake to adopt "all appropriate measures" to ensure the fulfillment of obligations arising out of the Treaty of Rome or resulting from action taken by the institutions of the Community. They "shall facilitate" achievement of its tasks and "shall abstain" from jeopardizing its objectives. These fundamental principles have frequently been the subject of litigation as the Commission seeks to enforce member state duties under EC law.

The Commission's prosecutorial powers under Article 169 must be distinguished from its ability in selected other circumstances to "directly" file actions against member states before the Court of Justice. Such direct actions do not involve the lengthy procedures described below in connection with Article 169 prosecutions. The Commission is authorized to sue the member states "directly" when they infringe Community rules on government subsidies to enterprises (see Chapter 5). This can also be done when the member states "improperly" invoke Article 36 exceptions to 1992 campaign legislation adopted by qualified majority voting in the Council of Ministers (see Chapter 4).

Prior to commencing any Article 169 prosecutions before the Court of Justice, the Commission first delivers notice and the member state may submit a reply. Hundreds of such infringement notices are issued annually. The next stage involves issuance by the Commission of a reasoned opinion setting time limits for compliance. These time limits must be reasonable. *Commission v. Belgium* (1988) Eur.Comm.Rep. 305. The member state can submit a reply if it wishes. When a member state claims to have conformed to the opinion within the stipulated time limits, the burden of proof shifts to the Commission to prove otherwise. *Commission v. Italy* (1987) 3 Common Mkt.L.Rep. 483. Negotiations may ensue at any time, and settlements frequently result. If no settlement is reached, the Commission commences suit before the Court of Justice. Compliance after this point does not moot or remove the suit. *Commission v. Italy* (1988) 2 Common Mkt.L.Rep. 951.

The most common type of Article 169 enforcement action actually filed with the Court of Justice concerns member state failures to implement EEC directives. Constitutional, political or legal problems are unacceptable excuses for such failures. *Commission v. Italy* (1979) Eur.Comm.Rep. 771. All Article 169 prosecutions are discretionary with the Commission and cannot be forced by individual complaints. *Alfons Lütticke GmbH v. Commission* (1966) Eur.Comm.Rep. 19.

Article 171 specifically requires member states to take the measures necessary to remedy failures identified by the Court in Article 169 proceedings. There are no obvious means by which the Court may enforce its judgments under Article 169 against member states. This contrasts with the power of the Court and the Commission in some areas of Community law to levy fines and penalties against individuals and corporations. Such fines and penalties can be collected in judgments enforced in the national courts. Article 192. To compel a member state to follow EC law, the Commission has little alternative but to bring yet another enforcement proceeding for determination before the Court. It has actually done this on occasion. *Commission v. Italy* (1972) Eur.Comm. Rep. 527; *Commission v. France* (1979) Eur.Comm. Rep. 2729. Private litigants may also remedy member state failures, functioning in effect as attorneys general of Community law. See *Minister for Fisheries v. Schoenenberg* (1978) Eur.Comm. Rep. 473 (Irish law invalid); *Meijer v. Department of Trade* (1979) Eur.Comm.Rep. 1387 (British law declared invalid).

The unwillingness of member states to carry out Court rulings under Article 169 is a growing problem. It could test the very fabric of the Rome Treaty. One enforcement option would be to allow the Court to authorize the withholding of EC subsidies and benefits from non-conforming states. Sanctions of this kind are possible at present only under the Coal and Steel Treaty by joint Commission and Council action. See Article 88 of Treaty of Paris. Another option would be to permit the Court or Commission to levy fines and penalties against member state governments.

Article 182 allows member states to submit (by special agreement) disputes concerning the Treaty of Rome to the European Court. In Article 219, the member states have agreed not to submit such disputes to any method of settlement other than those of the Treaty. Article 170 authorizes member states to prosecute each other before the European Court for failure to fulfill Treaty obligations. For diplomatic and institutional reasons, these options are almost never pursued. But see *Ireland v. France* (1977) Case 58/77 (withdrawn); *France v. United Kingdom* (1979) Eur.Comm.Rep. 2923 (fisheries dispute). The preferred approach is to persuasively complain to the Commission and then allow it to commence an Article 169 prosecution. Article 170 supports this approach by mandating a cooling off period of three months during which the Commission considers the arguments of both member states and issues a reasoned opinion.

Contract and Tort Litigation—Court of First Instance

Article 210 of the Treaty of Rome provides that the European Community is a legal person. As such, it can sue and be sued like most corporations or governments. These disputes can involve employees of the Community, parties with whom the EC has contracted and those who are victims of its negligence or other tortious behavior.

The Treaty of Rome conveys exclusive jurisdiction to the Court of Justice over employment and non-contractual liability disputes involving the Community. Articles 178 and 179. It also can function as an arbitrator pursuant to dispute settlement clauses of Community contracts. Article 181. Contract disputes in the Community may otherwise be entertained in the national courts. Article 183. The contractual liability of the Community is governed by the law applicable to the contract in question. Article 215.

Much of the work of the Court of Justice in employment and non-contractual liability litigation is now handled by the European Court of First Instance (CFI). This court was authorized by 1987 Single European Act amendments to the Treaty of Rome found in Article 168A. The CFI is "attached" to the European Court of Justice and its jurisdiction is limited to actions or proceedings by individuals or legal persons. Thus the Court of First Instance cannot hear Article 169 prosecutions of member states by the Commission, Article 177 references of EC legal issues from national courts, nor Article 173 or 175 challenges of Council or Commission acts or failures to act when these are initiated by member states or Community institutions. It can hear such challenges and related "pleas of illegality" when they are privately initiated in the business competition law area (see Chapter 7), coal and steel regulatory matters and in staff cases. Additional grants of jurisdiction to the CFI may occur in the dumping and external subsidies law fields.

The purpose, in general, behind creation of the Court of First Instance (CFI) was to relieve the Court of Justice of some of its caseload. It commenced doing this in November of 1989. However, there is a right of appeal on points of law from the CFI to the Court of Justice. Article 51 of the Council Decision establishing the CFI indicates that such appeals lie on the grounds of lack of competence, procedural failures that adversely affect the appellants' interests, and infringement of Community law by the CFI. Any failure by the CFI to follow prior ECJ decisions could amount to such an infringement. To distinguish between the judgments of these European Community courts, the law reporters now prefix Court of Justice case numbers with a "C" (Case C–213/89) (Court) and Court of First Instance cases with a "T" (Case T–81/90) (Tribunal).

The Court of First Instance is partially heir to an interesting body of EC law on non-contractual liability created by the Court of Justice. In this area, the Court's role as a lawmaker was fully anticipated by the Treaty of Rome. Article 215 provides that the non-contractual liability of the Community is governed by the "general principles common to the laws of the member states." Under these principles, the Community is obliged to "make good any damage caused by its institutions or servants in the performance of their duties." For example, the negligent disclosure by the Commission of the identity of an informant who was a former employee of a company subject to Community competition law sanctions was an actionable tort. *Adams v. Commission* (1985) Eur.Comm.Rep. 3539. See Article 214 creating an EC duty of confidentiality. In this case, a Swiss informant was arrested, held in solitary confinement, interrogated and convicted under Swiss law for economic espionage. While in prison, his wife was interrogated by Swiss police officers and then committed suicide.

The European Court of Justice, and now the Court of First Instance when damages are sought in litigation properly before it, has had to determine just what general principles of non-contractual liability are common to the laws of the member states. At first, of course, there were only six civil law states to consider. Now there are twelve, including two common law jurisdictions. The Court of Justice has ruled that Article 215 does not require adherence to the highest common denominator of liability law in the member states. Rather, the Court's duty is to track down in the national laws the elements or measures necessary to create *Community* liability principles which are fair and viable. *Plaumann & Co. v. Commission* (1963) Eur.Comm.Rep. 95. Such principles can include no-fault under the EEC and EURATOM treaties, but not the ECSC treaty which contains language derived from French law mandating a finding of fault. See Article 40 of the Treaty of Paris. It is now generally recognized that the Community is liable in non-contractual cases when unlawful EC conduct causes actual damages. *Alfons Lütticke GmbH v. Commission* (1971) Eur.Comm.Rep. 325.

Unlawful EC conduct includes unlawful legal measures, e.g. Community regulations, and unlawful failures to adopt such measures. The "plea of illegality" (supra) is used to challenge such activities. At first, the Court of Justice held that damages actions on these bases could only be pursued if successful challenges had been previously undertaken under Article 173 or 175. *Plaumann*, supra. In a good demonstration of its willingness to reverse itself, the Court has since held the opposite. *Alfons Lütticke*, supra; *Aktien–Zuckerfabrik Schöppenstedt v. Council* (1971) Eur.Comm.Rep. 975. Similarly, private parties need not challenge the validity of EC acts in national litigation prior to seeking damages relief before the Court. Here again the Court of Justice reversed its initial ruling to the contrary in the interest of the "proper administration of justice ... and procedural efficiency." *Merkur–Assenhandels GmbH v. Commission* (1973) Eur.Comm.Rep. 1055.

Nevertheless, the chances of obtaining individual damages relief for legislative acts of the Community are not great. The Court has limited this possibility to manifest and grave disregard by EC institutions of the limits of their powers in breach of superior rules of law protecting individuals. *Bayerische HNL Vermehrungsbetriebe GmbH & Co. KG v. Council and Commission* (1978) Eur.Comm.Rep. 1209; *Amylum NV v. Council and Commission* (1979) Eur.Comm.Rep. 3497. And when EEC directives are implemented at the national level in ways which cause damages, national remedies (if available and effective) must first be pursued. *Krohn & Co. Import–Export GmbH v. Commission* (1986) Eur.Comm.Rep. 753; *Asteris AE + Ors v. Hellenic Republic* (1990) Eur.Comm.Rep. ___ (Cases 106–120/87).

Judicial Practice and Procedure

The structure and procedures of the European Court of Justice (ECJ) and the Court of First Instance (CFI) are quite similar. Each has, for example, 13 judges who serve six-year renewable terms upon appointment by the member states acting in common accord. There is one judge from each member state, plus a thirteenth judge who rotates from the five largest EC states. The Court of First

Instance does not, however, have Advocates–General (infra) appointed to it, although members of the Court may serve in that role. Moreover, the CFI only sits in chambers of three to five judges. The Court of Justice is also divided into chambers, but sits en banc whenever cases are brought before it by member states or Community institutions, and in many Article 177 preliminary rulings. Some case reporters now identify the Court's opinions by chamber number. To an American, the Court's most distinguishing features are its emphasis on written (versus oral) procedures, the dominance of the Court (not the parties) over development of the evidence, and the absence of dissenting opinions.

The Protocol on the Statute of the Court of Justice annexed to the Treaty of Rome and the Court's Rules of Procedure (approved by the Council) establish a two-part proceeding. The written part commences with an application to the Court's registrar and designation of an agent or legal representative. This designation must occur. In other words, litigants may not represent themselves before the Court. Any lawyer entitled to practice before a national court in the EC may act before the Court of Justice or Court of First Instance. The application serves as a "complaint" for notice purposes and thereby limits (in most cases) the issues and evidence that can be raised in the proceeding. Its filing also triggers the assignment of a reporting judge and an Advocate–General to the case. The fact of the application and a summary of the issues presented is published in the Official Journal.

The application is also sent to the respondent who has one month to file a written "defense." Plaintiff may then reply, to which the defendant may submit a rejoinder. All of these written submissions to the court resemble full evidentiary and legal briefs more than pleadings. When the Article 177 preliminary ruling procedure is being used, the parties, member states, the Commission and (where appropriate) the Council may submit written briefs to the Court. The Parliament does not appear to have this right of submission. In general, the member states and the EC institutions (including Parliament) always have a right to intervene in cases before the Court. Individuals and enterprises with an interest in the litigation have the same right. Trade and professional associations, consumer groups and unions have been particularly active as intervenors.

At the discretion of the Court, a preliminary inquiry may be held. The Court (typically acting through the reporting judge) can pose questions to the litigants. The role of a court in posing questions is part of the civil law tradition which predominates on the Court. It is a procedure that most common law students familiar with a more adversarial system will find a bit unusual. The Court also has the power to examine witnesses, call experts and generally develop the evidence before it. Limited rights of cross-examination are allowed to counsel when this occurs.

The second part of the proceeding before the Court is oral. The Court first hears the views of the reporting judge in charge of the case and then counsel for both sides. At the end of the oral procedure, the Court of Justice hears the *Advocate–General,* a special lawyer employed by the Community to analyze and evaluate all cases before the Court and give public opinions on the proper result under EC law. Americans are typically unfamiliar with the role of an Advocate–General since there is no parallel in United States procedure. The closest parallel is the French Commissaire du Gouvernement at the Conseil d'Etat. The Advocate–General does not represent anyone and is a kind of permanent *amicus curiae* on behalf of justice in the Community.

There are six Advocates–General (AG) appointed for six-year terms to the Court of Justice by the member states acting in common accord. Four of the AG come from the largest EC member states, and the fifth and sixth "represent" the others. Their opinions are often much more informative than those of the Court in any given case. Whereas the Advocate–General is willing to spin out various hypotheticals and consider the broader ramifications of the legal principles at issue, the Court tends to write its opinions in a terse and summary fashion. It should be stressed that lawyers working with EC law commonly use the opinions of the Advocate–General in their practice to forecast future developments and to better understand the judgments issued by the Court. Some of the most controversial cases in EC law have involved instances where the Court has declined to agree with the opinions of the Advocate–General. See *Van Gend en Loos v. Nederlandse Administratie der Belastingen* (1963) Eur.Comm.Rep. 1; *Consten and Grundig v. Commission* (1966) Eur.Comm. Rep. 299; *Defrenne v. Sabena* (1976) Eur.Comm. Rep. 455; *Commission v. Council* (1971) Eur.Comm. Rep. 263 (*ERTA*).

The Court's judgment is drafted in French by the reporting judge. This draft is then discussed by the full court or chamber. The Court's decision is rendered *without dissent* in the language of the case (chosen by the plaintiff unless the defendant is from or is a member state). The absence of dissenting opinions shelters the judges from nationalistic pressures and critics. But it also makes analysis of opinions and projection of trends in the case law more difficult.

Costs are normally born by the losing party. Costs, for these purposes, generally include the Court's expenses, witnesses and experts, travel and subsistence of the parties to the Court's proceedings and reasonable legal fees. See Article 72 of the ECJ Rules of Procedure. The Court's assessment powers on costs are wide and substantial litigation over costs has ensued. However, most litigation results in a settlement agreement as between the parties on payment of costs. The loser must also pay the costs of intervenors who have supported the successful litigant. *Hoogovens v. High Authority* (1962) Eur.Comm.Rep. 253. The Court may make cash legal aid awards in appropriate cases and in the absence of national legal aid. *Lee v. Minister for Agriculture* (1980) Eur.Comm. Rep. 1495 (Article 177 reference in a civil case from Ireland).

Litigation brought before the Court of Justice does not automatically suspend the act being challenged. It continues to operate pending the Court's decision. Article 186. The Court (i.e. the President of the Court) may order suspension when it considers this necessary, along with any "interim measures." This is done only in exceptional circumstances of harm to the applicant. *NTN Toyo Bearing Co. Ltd. v. Council* (1977) Eur.Comm. Rep. 1721; *Commission v. Ireland* (1977) Eur. Comm.Rep. 1411. Pecuniary judgments of the Court against persons (not member states) are enforceable under the terms of Article 192. Once authenticated, the Court's judgment is enforced according to the ordinary judgment-creditor procedures of the member state where it is executed.

The Rules of Procedure for the Court of Justice permit revisions of Court judgments. Articles 98–100. No revision can occur more than ten years after judgment, and requests for revisions must be submitted within three months of the knowledge of new facts of decisive importance justifying revi-

sion. Such facts must have originally been unknown to both the Court and the litigant. *Acciaieria di Roma v. High Authority* (1960) Eur.Comm. Rep. 165. Moreover, if the information could have been easily obtained during litigation, no revision of judgment will be allowed. *Fonderie Acciarierie Giovanni Mandelli v. Commission* (1971) Eur. Comm.Rep. 1.

The Rules of Procedure also permit requests for interpretation of Court judgments when there are "difficulties" as to its meaning or scope. Article 102. Such requests can be made by the parties or any Community institution with an interest in the judgment. They are granted when the effect of the judgment on the parties is uncertain, not when its consequences for others is at issue. *High Authority and European Court v. Collotti* (1965) Eur. Comm.Rep. 275. Finally, third parties may seek reconsideration of Court judgments which will cause them damage. Requests for reconsideration must be made within two months of judgment, and the applicant must demonstrate no prior notice of the litigation. *Re Breedband* (1962) Eur.Comm. Rep. 145.

Enforcement of Civil and Commercial Judgments of National Courts

The EC has adopted two conventions of considerable importance to international traders litigating disputes within the Community. These are the Rome Convention on Law Applicable to Contractu-

al Obligations (Choice of Law) (1980) and the Brussels Convention on Jurisdiction and Enforcement of Judgments in Civil and Commercial Matters (1968). These Conventions are not automatically applicable in all EC nations. They are binding only in those nations that have ratified them. Article 220. The Choice of Law Convention affirms the right of parties to commercial contracts to designate the law which will govern those contracts. In the absence of such a designation, the law of the country most closely connected to the contract controls. The Choice of Law Convention became effective in 1991. France, Italy, Belgium, Luxembourg, Germany, Denmark and the United Kingdom have ratified it.

The Enforcement of Judgments Convention is an extremely detailed agreement generally facilitating enforcement of civil and commercial judgments of the courts of the member states in each others' courts. However, the Convention does not ordinarily apply to marital, inheritance, bankruptcy, tax or social security judgments. Nor does it apply to arbitration awards, but all EC states save Portugal are parties to the New York Convention on Recognition and Enforcement of Foreign Arbitral Awards (1958). The Judgments Convention is now effective in all twelve EC nations. Much of its substance is reproduced in the Lugano Convention on Jurisdiction and Enforcement of Judgments in Civil and Commercial Matters (1988). The Lugano Convention extends these principles to all ratifying EC and EFTA countries.

The Brussels Enforcement of Judgments Convention denies enforcement by EC domiciliaries against EC domiciliaries of certain judgments deemed to be based on "extraordinary jurisdiction" (e.g. French jurisdiction based solely on French citizenship of the plaintiff). But, in a discriminatory measure of importance, it permits EC domiciliaries to enforce judgments based upon extraordinary jurisdiction against non–EC domiciliaries. See Article 28(1). Thus, a North American trader with assets somewhere in the Community could find itself at the wrong end of such discrimination.

The Brussels Convention has been extensively construed by the European Court. The Court is granted jurisdiction to interpret the Convention in Article 3 of a 1971 Protocol. It does so through a preliminary ruling procedure analogous to Article 177 (supra). In the torts field, the Convention confers jurisdiction upon the courts of the states where the tortious acts occurred. This has been construed to mean either the place where the defendant acted (e.g. manufactured a product) or where the injury was suffered. *Handelswerkerij G.J. Bier B.V. v. Mines de Potasse d'Alsace SA* (1976) Eur.Comm.Rep. 1735 (environmental tort of dumping chloride into the Rhine actionable in Holland). Contracts disputes are generally governed by the courts where the obligation has been or is to be fulfilled. This "place of performance" test turns, according to the Court, upon substantive national contract law. *Industrie Tessili Italiana v. Dunlop A.G.* (1976) Eur.Comm.Rep. 1473. If there are several contractual obligations in question, the national court must distinguish between principal and secondary obligations. *Schenavai v. Kreischer* (1987) Eur.Comm.Rep. 239. In this case, a German architect sued a Dutch client for fees for plans for construction of buildings located in Germany. The principal obligation at issue was payment, not the plans or construction, which could be pursued in the courts of the Netherlands where the fees were to be paid. However, labor employment contracts may come under special analysis focused upon the place of work and not the place of the payment obligation when that would favor employees. See *Ivenel v. Schwab* (1982) Eur.Comm.Rep. 1891.

When the parties have selected a particular court in which to resolve their disputes, the Court of Justice has been careful to ensure that this was the product of informed written consent. *Estasis Salotti v. RÜWA* (1976) Eur.Comm.Rep. 1831 (placement of choice of court clause on reverse side of offer insufficient). Article 17 permits parties from outside the Community to join in the selection of a member state court without fear of an exercise of jurisdiction elsewhere (e.g. the place of performance) in the EC. Article 17 also provides that if any judicial forum selection was concluded for the benefit of only one party, *that* party may sue elsewhere. The idea of permitting the sole beneficiary of what some might see as an adhesion clause to escape from its forum selection obligations has not been found compelling. See *Anterist v. Crédit Lyonnais* (1986) Eur.Comm.Rep. 1951 (selection of bank's domicile court insufficient proof of intent to benefit bank exclusively).

CHAPTER 4

FREE MOVEMENT

Part II of the Treaty of Rome is entitled "Foundations of the Community." These articles concern the free movement of goods, trade in agriculture, transport and the free movement of persons, services and capital. The implementation since 1957 of free movement has been a slow and not entirely successful process. Indeed, as the 1992 campaign for a fully integrated market illustrates, considerable amendment and rejuvenation of the Treaty of Rome has been required. The Single European Act of 1987 amended the Treaty of Rome to establish the goal of creating a Europe genuinely "without internal frontiers," leaving customs and other controls solely to points of entry into the EC. The target for the completion of this task is the end of December, 1992. Hundreds of new legislative acts have already been adopted in its pursuit. See "1992 at a Glance" in the Appendix.

In 1990, the Benelux states, Germany, Italy and France agreed to remove their internal frontier controls on people under the "Schengen accord." This accord covers such sensitive issues as visas, asylum, immigration, gun controls, extradition and police rights of "hot pursuit." The main points of contention were cross-border traffic of immigrants and criminals, especially terrorists and drug dealers. These issues were resolved largely by promises of greater intergovernmental cooperation. In December of 1990, for example, the Council reached agreement on a directive that will make drug money laundering a crime in all member states. The Schengen accord serves as model for the 1992 campaign.

Free Movement of Goods

The free movement of goods within the European Community is based upon the creation of a customs union. Under this union, the member states have eliminated customs duties among themselves. Articles 12–16 of the Treaty of Rome. They have established a common customs tariff (CCT) for their trade with the rest of the world. See Chapter 6. Quantitative restrictions (quotas) on trade between member states are also prohibited, except in emergency and other limited situations. Articles 30–34. The right of free movement applies to goods that originate in the Common Market *and* to those that have lawfully entered it and are said to be in "free circulation." Articles 9 and 10.

The establishment of the EC customs union has been a major accomplishment, though not without difficulties. The member states not only committed themselves to the elimination of tariffs and quotas on internal trade, but also to the elimination of "measures of equivalent effect." See especially Articles 12, 16, 30 and 34 of Treaty of Rome. The elastic legal concept of measures of equivalent effect has been interpreted broadly by the European Court of Justice and the Commission to prohibit a wide range of trade restraints, such as administrative fees charged at borders which are the equivalent of tariffs. *Rewe Zentralfinanz v. Landwirtschaftskammer Westfalen–Lippe* (1973) Eur. Comm.Rep. 1039. Charges of equivalent effect to a tariff must be distinguished from internal taxes that are applicable to imported and domestic goods. The latter must be levied in a nondiscriminatory manner (Article 95), while the former are prohibited entirely (Articles 9, 12). There has been a considerable amount of litigation over this distinction. See e.g. *Industria Gomma, Articoli Vari v. Ente Nazionale ENCC* (1975) Eur.Comm.Rep. 699.

In a famous case, the Court of Justice ruled that Belgium could not block the importation via France of Scotch whiskey lacking a British certificate of origin as required by Belgian customs law. *Procureur du Roi v. Dassonville* (1974) Eur.Comm. Rep. 837. The Court of Justice held that any national rule directly or indirectly, actually or potentially capable of hindering internal trade is generally forbidden as a measure of equivalent effect to a quota. However, *if* European Community law has not developed appropriate rules in the area concerned (here designations of origin), the member states may enact "reasonable" and "proportional" (no broader than necessary) regulations to ensure that the public is not harmed. See the

"Cassis de Dijon" case, *Rewe Zentral AG v. Bundes-monopolverwaltung für Branntwein* (1979) Eur. Comm.Rep. 649 (German *minimum* alcoholic beverage rule not reasonable). Products meeting reasonable national criteria, the *Cassis* opinion continues, may be freely traded elsewhere in the Community. This is the origin of the innovative "mutual reciprocity" principle being used in significant parts of the 1992 legislative campaign.

The *Cassis* decision suggests use of a Rule of Reason analysis for national fiscal regulations, public health measures, laws governing the fairness of commercial transactions and consumer protection. Environmental protection and occupational safety laws of the member states have been similarly treated. Under this approach, for example, a Danish "bottle bill" requiring use of approved soft drink and beer containers was held disproportionately restrictive of Community trade. The use of only *approved* containers was therefore unreasonable. *Commission v. Denmark* (1988) Eur. Comm.Rep. 4607. However, the Danes' argument that a deposit and return system was environmentally necessary prevailed. This was (absent the approved container rules) a reasonable restraint on Community trade recognized by the Court under the *Cassis* precedent.

British, French and Belgian bans on Sunday retail trading have survived scrutiny under the *Cassis* formula. *Torfaen Borough Council v. B+Q PLC Ltd,* (1989) Eur.Comm.Rep. ___ (Case 145/88);

UDS v. Sidef Conforma & Ors (1991) Eur.Comm. Rep. ___ (Case C–312/89); *Re Marchandise & Ors* (1991) Eur.Comm.Rep. ___ (Case C–332/89). British prohibitions of sales of sex articles except by licensed sex shops are also EC compatible. *Quietlynn Ltd. v. Southend Borough Council* (1990) Eur. Comm.Rep. ___ (Case C–23/89). These cases vividly illustrate the extent to which litigants are invoking the Treaty of Rome in attempts at overcoming commercially restrictive national laws.

The Court has made it clear that all of the Rule of Reason justifications for national laws are temporary. Adoption of Common Market legislation in any of these areas would eliminate national authority to regulate trading conditions under *Dassonville* and *Cassis*. These judicial mandates, none of which are specified in the Treaty of Rome, acutely demonstrate the powers the Court of Justice to expansively interpret the Treaty and to rule on the validity under EC law of national legislation affecting internal trade in goods.

Article 36 and the Problem of Nontariff Trade Barriers

The provisions of Part II of the Treaty of Rome dealing with the establishment of the customs union do not adequately address the problem of nontariff trade barriers (NTBs). As in the world community, the major trade barrier within the European Community has become NTBs. To some extent, this is authorized. Article 36 of the Treaty of

Rome permits national restraints on imports and exports justified on the grounds of:

(1) public morality, public policy ("ordre public") or public security;

(2) the protection of health and life of humans, animals or plants;

(3) the protection of national treasures possessing artistic, historical or archeological value; and

(4) the protection of industrial or commercial property.

Article 36 amounts, within certain limits, to an authorization of nontariff trade barriers among the EC nations. This "public interest" authorization exists in addition to but somewhat overlaps with the Rule of Reason exception formulated under Article 30 in *Dassonville* and *Cassis* above. However, in a sentence much construed by the European Court of Justice, Article 36 continues with the following language: "Such prohibitions or restrictions shall not, however, constitute a means of arbitrary discrimination or a disguised restriction on trade between member states."

In a wide range of decisions, the Court of Justice has interpreted Article 36 in a manner which generally limits the ability of member states to impose NTB barriers to internal Community trade. Britain, for example, may use its criminal law under the public morality exception to seize pornographic goods made in Holland that it outlaws

(*Regina v. Henn and Darby* (1979) Eur.Comm.Ct. J.Rep. 3795), but not inflatable sex dolls from Germany which could be lawfully produced in the United Kingdom. *Conegate Ltd. v. H.M. Customs and Excise* (1986) Eur.Comm.Rep. 1007. Germany cannot stop the importation of beer (e.g. Heineken's from Holland) which fails to meet its "pure standards." *Commission v. Germany* (1987) Eur. Comm.Rep. 1227. This case makes wonderful reading as the Germans, seeking to invoke the public health exception of Article 36, argue all manner of ills that may befall their populace if free trade in beer is allowed. Equally fun are the unsuccessful Italian health protection arguments against free trade in pasta made from common (not durum) wheat. *Re Drei Glocken GmbH* and *Criminal Proceedings Against Zoni* (1988) Eur.Comm. Rep. 4233, 4285.

An unusual case under the public security exception contained in Article 36 involved Irish petroleum products' restraints. *Campus Oil Ltd. v. Minister for Industry and Energy* (1984) Eur.Comm.Rep. 2727. The Irish argued that oil is an exceptional product always triggering national security interests. Less expansively, the Court acknowledged that maintaining minimum oil supplies did fall within the ambit of Article 36. The public policy exception under Article 36 has been construed along French lines (ordre public). Only genuine threats to fundamental societal interests are covered. See *Regina v. Thompson* (1978) Eur.Comm. Rep. 2247 (coinage). Consumer protection (though a legitimate rationale for trade restraints under *Dassonville* and *Cassis,* supra) does not fall within the public policy exception of Article 36. *Kohl KG v. Ringelhan and Rennett SA* (1984) Eur.Comm. Rep. 3651.

Intellectual Property Rights as Trade Barriers

A truly remarkably body of case law has developed around the authority granted national governments in Article 36 to protect industrial or commercial property by restraining imports and exports. These cases run the full gamut from protection of trademarks and copyrights to protection of patents and know-how. There is a close link between this body of case law and that developed under Article 85 concerning restraints on competition. See Chapter 7. Trade restraints involving intellectual property arise out of the fact that such rights are nationally granted. Although considerable energy has been spent by the Commission on developing Common Market trademarks and patents that would provide an alternative to national intellectual property rights, these proposals have yet to be fully implemented. The Council has adopted Directive 89/104, which seeks to harmonize member state laws governing trademarks. Nevertheless, owners of intellectual property rights within the Community are free under most traditional law to block the unauthorized importation of goods into national markets. There is a strong tendency for national infringement lawsuits to serve as vehicles for the division for the Common Market.

The European Court of Justice has addressed these problems under Article 36 and generally resolved against the exercise of national intellectual property rights in ways which inhibit free trade inside the EC. In many of these decisions, the Court acknowledges the existence of the right to block trade in infringing goods, but holds that the *exercise* of that right is subordinate to the Treaty of Rome. The Court has also fashioned a doctrine which treats national intellectual property rights as having been *exhausted* once the goods to which they apply are freely sold on the market. One of the few exceptions to this doctrine is broadcast performing rights which the Court treats as incapable of exhaustion. See *Coditel v. Ciné Vog Films SA* (1980) Eur.Comm.Rep. 881; (1982) Eur.Comm. Rep. 3381. Records and cassettes embodying such rights are, however, subject to the exhaustion doctrine once released into the market. *Musik–Vertrieb membran GmbH v. GEMA* (1981) Eur.Comm. Rep. 147. Such goods often end up in the hands of third parties who then ship them into another member state.

The practical effect of many of the rulings of the Court of Justice is to remove the ability of the owners of the relevant intellectual property rights to successfully pursue infringement actions in national courts. When intellectual property rights share a common origin and have been placed on goods by consent, as when a licensor authorizes their use in other EC countries, then infringement actions to protect against trade in the goods to which the rights apply are usually denied. It is only when intellectual property rights do not share a common origin or the requisite consent is absent that they stand a chance of being upheld so as to stop trade in infringing products. See *CNL–Sucal v. Hag* (1990) Eur.Comm.Rep. ___ (Case C–10/89).

An excellent example of the application of the judicial doctrine developed by the Court of Justice in the intellectual property field under Article 36 can be found in the *Centrafarm* case. *Centrafarm BV and Adriann de Peipjper v. Sterling Drug Inc.* (1974) Eur.Comm.Rep. 1147. The American pharmaceutical company, Sterling Drug, owned the British and Dutch patents and trademarks relating to "Negram." Subsidiaries of Sterling Drug in Britain and Holland had been respectively assigned the British and Dutch trademark rights to Negram. Owing in part to price controls in the UK, a substantial difference in cost for Negram emerged as between the two countries. Centrafarm was an independent Dutch importer of Negram from the UK and Germany. Sterling Drug and its subsidiaries brought infringement actions in the Dutch courts under their national patent and trademark rights seeking an injunction against Centrafarm's importation of Negram into The Netherlands.

The Court of Justice held that the intellectual property rights of Sterling Drug and its subsidiaries could not be exercised in a way which blocked EC trade in "parallel goods." In the Court's view, the exception established in Article 36 for the protection of industrial and commercial property covers only those rights that were specifically intended to be conveyed by the grant of national patents and trademarks. Blocking trade in parallel goods after they have been put on the market with the consent of a common owner, thus exhausting the rights in question, was not intended to be part of the package of benefits conveyed. If Sterling Drug succeeded, an arbitrary discrimination or disguised restriction on Community trade would be achieved in breach of the language which qualifies Article 36. Thus the European Court of Justice ruled in favor of the free movement of goods within the Common Market even when that negates clearly existing national legal remedies. Only in the unusual situation where the intellectual property rights in question have been acquired by independent proprietors under different national laws may such rights inhibit internal Community trade. See *Terrapin (Overseas) Ltd. v. Terranova Industrie CA Kapferer & Co.* (1976) Eur.Comm.Rep. 1039; *CNL–Sucal v. HAG* (1990) Eur.Comm.Rep. ___ (Case C–10/89). While the goal of creation of the Common Market can override national intellectual property rights where internal trade is concerned, these rights apply fully to the importation of goods from outside the European Community. See *E.M.I. Records Ltd. v. CBS United Kingdom Ltd.* (1976) Eur.Comm.Rep. 811. North American exporters of goods subject to rights owned by Europeans may therefore find entry into the EC challenged by infringement actions in national courts.

NTBs and 1992

Nontariff trade barrier problems are the principal focus of the 1992 campaign for a fully integrated Common Market. Estimates are that the retention of customs frontiers, even in the absence of tariffs and quotas, costs the Community approximately 11 billion dollars a year. Many new legislative acts have been adopted or are in progress which target NTB trade problems inside the EC. *See* "1992 at a Glance" in the Appendix. There are basically two different methodologies being employed. When possible, a common European Community standard is adopted. For example, legislation on auto pollution requirements adopts this methodology. Products meeting these standards may be freely traded in the Common Market. Traditionally, this approach (called "harmonization") has required the formation of a consensus within the Community as to the appropriate level of protection.

Under Article 100A, added by the Single European Act of 1987, most 1992 legislation can be adopted by qualified majority voting in the Council of Ministers. Notable exceptions requiring a unanimous vote include new laws on taxation, employment and free movement of persons. However, when a 1992 measure is adopted by a qualified majority, the public interest exceptions to free internal trade specified in Article 36 (supra) apply. This may provide an escape clause for member states that are outvoted in the Council on 1992 legislation. Indeed, Article 100A extends the scope of Article 36 to include "major needs" relating to national protection of the working or natural environments. The Commission must be notified of any member state use of such an exception, which it or another member state can then challenge directly before the European Court as an "improper use." In doing so, the Commission need not adhere to the lengthy procedures (see Chapter 3) used with Article 169 prosecutions of member states.

Many efforts at the harmonization of European environmental, health and safety, standards and certification, and related law have been undertaken. Nearly all of these are supposed to be based upon "high levels of protection." Article 100A. In contrast, Article 118A on occupational health and safety legislation contains no such requirement. Many have criticized what they see as the "least common denominator" results of harmonization of national laws under the 1992 campaign. One example involves the safety of toys. Directive 88/378 permits toys to be sold throughout the Common Market if they satisfy "essential requirements." These requirements are broadly worded in terms of flammability, toxicity, etc. There are two ways to meet these requirements: (1) produce a toy in accordance with CEN standards (drawn up by experts); or (2) produce a toy that otherwise meets the essential safety requirements.

The lease common denominator criticism may be even more appropriate to the second legislative methodology utilized in the 1992 campaign. The second approach is based on the *Cassis* principle of mutual reciprocity (supra). Under this "new" approach, EC legislation requires member states to recognize the laws of other member states and deem them acceptable for purposes of the operation of the Common Market. For example, major Community legislation has been adopted in the area of professional services. See Council Directive No. 89/48. By mutual recognition of vocational diplomas based upon at least three years of courses, virtually all professionals have now obtained legal rights to move freely within the EC in pursuit of their careers. This is a remarkable achievement.

The mutual recognition methodology is the fallback position in the 1992 legislative campaign. Article 100B requires the Commission *during 1992* to draw up an inventory of national laws, regulations and administrative provisions which have not been harmonized under Article 100A. The Council, acting by the voting rules of Article 100A, may decide which of these rules must be recognized as mutually equivalent. The exceptions of Article 36 will apply to allow member states to escape from Article 100B mutual recognition.

General Rights of Residence

A general right of free movement for purposes of residence throughout the Community has been recognized since 1990 and will benefit students, retirees and the populace at large. This right should be distinguished from the free movement rights of workers (infra). The chief concern about a general right of residence is coverage for health and social welfare purposes, and a possible run towards those states with more generous programs. Council Directive 90/364 (effective in 1992) extends a general right of residence to all member state nationals and their families provided they do not become a burden on the public finances of the host country. Spouses and dependent children who are *not* EC nationals are nevertheless entitled to work in the country where the nonworking EC spouse has taken up residence. These principles also apply to employees and the self-employed who have ceased their occupational activity. Directive 90/365. EC students have a general right of residence throughout the Community provided they can show sufficient resources and enrollment in the host state. The student's family may accompany him or her and work in that state. Directive 90/366.

Students seeking vocational training in another member state cannot be subjected to discriminatory tuition fees not charged to nationals. *Gravier v. City of Liege* (1985) Eur.Comm.Rep. 593. In this decision, the Court of Justice took a broad view of "vocational training" under Article 128 of the

Treaty of Rome. Any form of education which prepares for qualification for a particular trade, profession or employment is included. This is the case regardless of age or the level of the training, and even if the study program involves some general education. A French national was therefore entitled to train in strip cartoon arts without paying special fees at a Belgian city academy. Students also benefit from a Community initiative known as ERASMUS. This program supports "vocational" student mobility and enrollment rights, even when research is primarily involved. See *Commission v. Council* (1989) Eur.Comm.Rep. 1425. University education is treated as vocational by the Court of Justice in this opinion.

Free Movement of Workers and the Self–Employed

The foundations of the Community created in Part II of the Treaty of Rome concern the free movement of persons, services and capital. These are often referred to in economic literature as the "factors of production." Their inclusion in the Treaty of Rome distinguishes the Treaty from others which merely create customs unions.

Freedom of movement for workers is secured in Article 48, and by an extensive range of legislative acts which have implemented this right. Whereas, for example, North Americans must obtain work permits in order to undertake employment within the European Community, this is not required of citizens of the member states. They may seek

employment on the same basis as nationals of the
EC state where the job is located. In other words,
workers from Community countries enjoy "national treatment." Council Regulation 1612/68; *Commission v. France* (1974) Eur.Comm.Rep. 359.
(French citizenship quota for crews on ships invalid). This right has caused renewed interest by
North Americans in becoming "dual nationals."
Irish and Italian "laws of return" generally permit
emigrants born in Europe *and* their children to
obtain Irish and Italian citizenship. Although the
U.S. government discourages dual citizenship status for Americans, the benefits of being an EC
national under the Treaty of Rome make this status quite attractive.

The right of expatriate European Community
workers to bring their families, obtain social services, housing, education and pensions in a nondiscriminatory manner is all provided in a wealth of
EC law. There is no Community social security
system. Rather, the Community assures equal
treatment of claims made against national systems. See, e.g., *Regina v. Warry* (1977) Eur.Comm.
Rep. 2085 (health care), *Frilli v. Belgium* (1972)
Eur.Comm.Rep. 457 (old age), *DiPaolo v. Office
National de l'Emploi* (1977) Eur.Comm.Rep. 315
(unemployment), *Reina v. Landeskreditbank Baden–Württemberg* (1982) Eur.Comm.Rep. 33 (family
benefits), *Pennartz v. Caisse Primaire d'Assurance
Maladie des Alpes–Maritimes* (1979) Eur.Comm.
Rep. 2411 (workers' compensation). The exercise
of the right of free movement by EC workers

cannot be subject to the issuance of restrictive residency or entrance permits. *State v. Royer* (1976) Eur.Comm.Rep. 497; *Regina v. Pieck* (1980) Eur.Comm.Rep. 2171. They can be required within a reasonable time to report their presence to the host member state. *Re Watson and Belman* (1976) Eur.Comm.Rep. 1185. A valid identity card from their home state is all that is required to prove a worker's right to reside elsewhere in the Community. *Giangoundis v. City of Reutlingen* (1991) Eur. Comm.Rep. ___ (Case C–376/89). Part-time and probationary workers (such as teachers seeking licensure) are included, as are the unemployed who actively seek work. *Lawrie Blum v. Land Baden– Württemberg* (1986) Eur.Comm.Rep. 2121; *Kempf v. Staatssecretaris van Justitie* (1986) Eur.Comm. Rep. 1741; *Regina v. Antonissen* (1991) Eur.Comm. Rep. ___ (Case C–292/89). In a notable decision, the European Court of Justice even struck down a longstanding Greek law restricting ownership of land to Greeks as contrary to the free movement rights of the Treaty of Rome. *Commission v. Greece* (1989) Eur.Comm.Rep. ___ (Case 305/87).

The only blanket exception to the regime of free movement of workers is established in Article 48(4) of the Treaty of Rome. Employment in the "public service" of member states is exempted. The public service, for these purposes, involves jobs with official authority, including the judiciary, the police, defense forces and tax inspectors. *Sotgiu v. Deutsche Bundespost* (1974) Eur.Comm.Rep. 153. Licensed attorneys fall outside the public service, even though they may be required in order to litigate in national courts. *Reyners v. Belgium* (1974) Eur.Comm.Rep. 631. Municipal positions are included when there is participation in the exercise of public power, which was the case in Brussels with the city architect but not city hospital nurses. *Commission v. Belgium* (1982) Eur. Comm.Rep. 1845.

Member states may restrict the free movement of workers from other Community nations on grounds of public policy (ordre public), public security or public health. Article 48(3); Council Directive 64/221. These provisions have been litigated extensively. In a long series of decisions, the European Court has evolved rules which limit the power of EC states to expel or deny admission to workers whose past conduct is objectionable. Only when that conduct is effectively combatted if engaged in by its own nationals may restraints on expatriate Community workers be applied. Compare *Van Duyn v. Home Office* (1974) Eur.Comm. Rep. 1337 (denial of right of Church of Scientology secretary from Holland to work in U.K. upheld) with *Adoui and Cornuaille v. Belgium* (1982) Eur. Comm.Rep. 1665 (denial of right of French waitresses suspected of prostitution to work in Belgium invalid). Public policy reasons for limiting the free movement rights of EC workers must be based on the existence of a genuine and serious threat affecting fundamental societal interests. *Regina v. Bouchereau* (1977) Eur.Comm.Rep. 1989. Past criminal convictions, alone, are insufficient.

The Common Market law prohibiting discrimination against workers from member states does not reach national laws that discriminate against a country's own citizens regarding free movement and employment. In other words, "reverse discrimination" can occur where EC law protects the rights of workers from other states but national law denies similar rights to workers of that nation. *Regina v. Saunders* (1979) Eur.Comm.Rep. 1129; *Moser v. Land Baden–Württemberg* (1984) Eur. Comm.Rep. 2539. Conversely, when a worker has exercised the right to employment elsewhere in the Community, he or she is entitled to rely on the Treaty of Rome upon returning home. *Knoors v. Secretary of State for Economic Affairs* (1979) Eur. Comm.Rep. 399.

In the early years of the Community, many Italian workers moved north into the factories of West Germany and to a lesser extent France as the rebuilding of the European economy took place. Membership in the EC was eagerly sought in later years by Greece, Portugal and Spain so as to acquire these rights for their expatriate workers. Prior to membership, Greek, Portuguese and Spanish workers in the EC were subject to much less liberal national laws on guest workers. These national laws continue for the most part to govern the rights of the large number of Turkish and Yugoslav employees in Germany, North Africans in France and Commonwealth citizens in Britain. Special employment rights (but not national treatment rights) have been given to Turkish workers

in the Community under the "Ankara Agreement", which acknowledges Turkey's associate status with the EC.

Right of Establishment—Professionals

The right to go into business as a self-employed
person in another member state is secured by
Article 52 of the Treaty of Rome. This is known as
the "right of establishment." Many Community
entrepreneurs, for example, have used this right to
open restaurants throughout the EC. Cuisine in
Britain is thought by some to have greatly benefited from this freedom. The right of self-establishment carries with it nearly the same bundle of
national treatment rights and exceptions associated with employed workers. See The Council's General Program for the Abolition of Restrictions on
Freedom of Establishment (1962).

Implementation of the right of establishment for
professionals is anticipated in Article 57 by the
issuance of Community legislation mutually recognizing diplomas and national licenses. Medical
doctors, dentists, veterinarians, architects and
many others have benefited from these provisions
and the substantial implementing law that now
accompanies them. For example, the Council in
1982 adopted directives about freedom to supply
services in the case of travel agents, tour operators,
air brokers, freight forwarders, ship brokers, air
cargo agents, shipping agents, and hairdressers. It
has been relatively easy to deal with those liberal

professions (e.g. medicine and allied professions) in which diplomas and other evidence of formal qualification relate to equivalent competence in the same skill. It did, however, take 17 years to negotiate the directive on free movement of veterinarians. And litigation over the implementation of these directives continues. In 1986 it took a Commission prosecution to remove the French requirement that doctors and dentists give up their home country professional registrations before being licensed in France. *Commission v. France* (1986) 1 Common Mkt.L.Rep. 57.

Typically, European Community law on the right of establishment creates minimum professional training standards which, if met, will result in mutual recognition. Substantial variations in training may trigger special admissions requirements, such as time in practice, an adaptation period or an aptitude test. A major 1992 campaign directive applies this approach to virtually all EC professionals receiving diplomas based upon a minimum of three years of study. Council Directive 89/48. Mutual recognition in this instance means that access is gained to host country professional bodies. This is different from the home country licensing method of mutual recognition used for banking, insurance and investment advisors (infra). Even in the absence of such legislation, professional disqualification on grounds of nationality is prohibited. *Patrick v. Ministre des Affaires Culturelles* (1977) Eur.Comm.Rep. 1199 (architects).

Considerable difficulty has been encountered in lifting restrictions within member states on the freedom to provide legal services. For example, within the legal profession there may be only a small amount of training or required knowledge held in common by a "lawyer" from a civil law jurisdiction (e.g. an avocat from France) and a "lawyer" from a common law jurisdiction (e.g. a solicitor from England). As a result, the directive relating to lawyers' services takes a delicate approach to the question of freedom to provide legal services and stops short of dealing with a right of establishment. See Council Directive 77/249. This directive allows a lawyer from one member state, under that lawyer's national title (e.g. abogado, rechtsanwalt, barrister), to provide services in other member states. This includes the right to appear in court without local co-counsel unless representation by counsel is mandatory under national laws. *Commission v. Germany* (1988) Eur. Comm.Rep. 1123. Directive 77/249 gave rise to lawyer identity cards issued under the auspices of *Commission Consultative des Barreaux Européans* (C.C.B.E.), which has been charged to propose a specific directive about a right of establishment for lawyers. However, the mutual recognition of diplomas accomplished in Council Directive 89/48 (supra) applies to lawyers.

Admission to the practice of law is still governed by the rules of the legal profession of each member state. Several European Court judgments have upheld the right of lawyer applicants to be free from discrimination on grounds of nationality, residence or retention of the right to practice in home jurisdictions. *Reyners v. Belgium* (1974) Eur. Comm.Rep. 631; *Thieffry v. Conseil de l'Ordre des Avocats de Paris* (1977) Eur.Comm.Rep. 765. By joining the bar in another EC country, lawyers acquire the right to establish themselves in more than one nation. The multinational law firm, pioneered by Baker and McKenzie in the United States, has only a few regional counterparts in the practice of European Community law. Slowly, however, attorneys from member states are establishing affiliations and sometimes partnerships which reflect and service the economic, political and social integration of Europe. These "European law firms" often compete with existing branches of American multinational firms for the lucrative practice of EC law.

In professional fields, the real barrier to movement of people across borders is language. In some instances, linguistic requirements for jobs are lawful despite their negative impact on free movement rights. See *Groener v. Minister for Education* (1989) Eur.Comm.Rep. ___ (Case 379/87) (Irish required for vocational teaching job). As much as the Community may succeed in its 1992 campaign at truly establishing an integrated market, the language barriers within the EC will remain. Although younger generations are increasingly multilingual, a professional who cannot speak to his or her clients or students is unlikely to succeed in another member state.

Freedom to Provide Services Across Borders

The freedom of nonresidents to provide services within other parts of the Community is another part of the foundations of the Treaty of Rome. Articles 59 and 60. The freedom to provide services implies a right to receive and pay for them by going to the country of their source. *Luisi and Carbone v. Ministero del Tesoro* (1984) Eur.Comm. Rep. 377. Industrial, commercial, craft and professional services are included within this right, which is usually not dependent upon establishment in the country where the service is rendered. *Commission v. Germany* (1986) Eur.Comm.Rep. 3755; *Ministère Public v. van Wasemael* (1979) Eur.Comm.Rep. 35 (employment agencies).

The Council has adopted a general program for the abolition of national restrictions on the freedom to provide services across EC borders. This freedom is subject to the same public policy, public security and public health exceptions applied to workers and the self-employed. Article 66. The Council's program has slowly been implemented by a series of legislative acts applicable to professional and nonprofessional services. As with the right of self-establishment, discrimination based upon the nationality or nonresidence of the service provider is generally prohibited even if no implementing EC law has been adopted. *Van Binsbergen v. Bestuur van de Bedrijfsvereniging voor de Metaalnijverheid* (1974) Eur.Comm.Rep. 1299 (legal representation); *Coenen v. Sociaal Economische Raad* (1975) Eur.

Comm.Rep. 1547 (insurance intermediary). However, in language that suggests a parallel with law it has developed in connection with the free movement of goods, the Court of Justice in *Van Binsbergen* indicated that EC governments may require providers of services from other states to adhere to professional public interest rules. These rules must be applied equally to all professionals operating in the nation, and only if necessary to ensure that the out-of-state professional does not escape them by reason of establishment elsewhere. In other words, if the professional rules (e.g. ethics) of the country in which the service provider is established are equivalent, then application of the rules of the country where the service is provided does not follow.

Bankers, investment advisors and insurance companies have long awaited the arrival of a truly common market. Their right of establishment in other member states has existed for some time. The right to provide services across borders without establishing local subsidiaries was forcefully reaffirmed by the Court of Justice in 1986. *Commission v. Germany* (1986) Eur.Comm.Rep. 3755. This decision largely rejected a German requirement that all insurers servicing the German market be located and established there.

New legislative initiatives undertaken in connection with the 1992 campaign promise to create genuinely competitive cross-border European markets for banking, investment and insurance services. It is envisioned, for example, that ordinary consumers will be able to hold multiple currency bank accounts and that the last vestiges of capital controls by national governments will be removed when these new laws are fully implemented. The cost of auto insurance, home loans and consumer credit is expected to fall significantly in many markets.

Licensing of insurance and investment service companies and banks meeting minimum capital, solvency ratio and other EC requirements (as implemented in member state laws) will be done on a "one-stop" home country basis. Banks, for example, cannot maintain individual equity positions in non-financial entities in excess of 15 percent of their capital funds and the total value of such holdings cannot exceed 60 percent of those funds. Council Directive 89/646. They can participate and service securities transactions and issues, financial leasing and trade for their own accounts. The proposed investment services directive requires home country supervision of the "good repute" and "suitability" of managers and controlling shareholders.

Other EC states must ordinarily recognize home country licenses and the principle of home country control. For example, Council Directive 89/646 ("the Second Banking Directive") employs the home country single license procedure to liberalize banking services throughout the Community. However, host states retain the right to regulate a bank's liquidity and supervise it through monetary policy and in the name of the "general good." Similarly, no additional insurance permits or requirements may be imposed by host countries when large industrial risks (sophisticated purchasers) are involved. However, when the public at large is concerned (general risk), host country rules still apply. Council Directive 88/357 ("the Second Non–Life Insurance Directive"). Major auto and life insurance directives employing one-stop licensing principles were adopted late in 1990. Council Directives 90/619 (life insurance) and 90/618 (auto insurance). The auto insurance directive reproduces the large versus general risk distinctions found in the Second Non–Life Insurance Directive. Host country controls over general risk auto insurance policies are retained until 1995. Host country permits are also required when life insurers from other member states actively solicit business.

There has been a rush by non-EC bankers, investment advisors and insurers to get established in the Community before January 1, 1993 in order to qualify for home country licenses. North Americans and others outside the Community have been particularly concerned about certain features of the new legislation mandating effective access in foreign markets for European companies before non-Community firms may benefit from the liberalization of services within the Common Market. Since state and federal laws governing banking, investment services and insurance are quite restrictive, and in no sense can it be said that one

license permits a company to operate throughout
the United States, it is possible that one result of
European integration will be reform of American
regulatory legislation. Unless there is "effective
market access" under American law for European
firms, U.S. companies entering the EC after 1992
may be unable to obtain the benefits of common
service markets throughout the Community. This
problem is generally referred to as the "reciprocity
requirement" of EC legislation. It is this kind of
requirement that gives the 1992 campaign the stig-
ma of increasing the degree of external trade barriers. Many outsiders, in rhetoric which sometimes
seems excessive, refer to the development of a
"Fortress Europe" mentality and threat to world
trading relations.

Capital Movements and the European Monetary System

The foundations of the Community established
in Part II of the Treaty of Rome end with provisions concerning the free movement of money and
transportation. "Current payments" associated
with import/export transactions in goods and services, as well as wage remittances, are routinely
made and protected by Articles 67 and 106. This
includes money taken abroad to make payment for
tourist, medical, educational or business travel services. *Luisi and Carbone v. Ministero del Tesoro*
(1984) Eur.Comm.Rep. 377. But it does not include
the unsubstantiated export of banknotes. *Re Casa-
ti* (1981) Eur.Comm.Rep. 2595.

The free movement of *capital* goals of the Treaty of Rome have been much delayed. In fairness, the Treaty only requires Member States to be "as liberal as possible" in granting exchange control authorizations for investment capital transfers. This provision acknowledges the sensitivity of the member states' concerns about disequilibriums in balance of payments and currency values. Articles 104–109. It was not until the implementation of the 1992 campaign that new legislative acts of the Community firmly entrenched the right of individuals and companies to move capital across borders without substantial limitation. Council Directive 88/361. Short-term monetary and exchange-rate national safeguards are preserved, but subject to Commission controls. Capital movements to and from the EC as a whole are expected to be similarly liberalized. This capital movements legislation, when combined with the various banking and investment services reforms in the EC, promises to bring forth a remarkable new financial sector in the Community. It also, some predict, makes inevitable a common Community currency replacing the national currencies. In moving toward monetary union, the member states have created the European Monetary System (EMS). When the EMS was established in 1979, member states deposited 20 percent of their gold and dollar assets with the European Monetary Cooperation Fund in exchange for an equivalent amount of European Currency Units (ECUs). This fund is used as a non-cash means of settlement between central banks undertaking exchange rate support (below).

Another part of the EMS is the European Exchange–Rate Mechanism (ERM). The ERM is similar in concept and form to the currency "snake" of the early 1970s, and allows limited fluctuation of national exchange rates from agreed central rate (ECU) parities. This intervention and planning stabilizes currency risks in EC transactions, thus generally promoting more trade within the Common Market. The Deutsche Mark and the French franc, for example, float within a band of exchange of 2.25 percent. Since 1990 the British pound sterling floats within a 6 percent band that acknowledges its relative weakness. The Spanish peseta also uses the 6 percent band. The Italian lire did likewise for many years prior to graduating to the 2.25 percent band. Only the Greek drachma and Portuguese escudo remain outside the ERM.

The member states have also established a joint credit facility for giving short and medium term financial support to ERM currencies under pressure. Basically, the central banks of ERM nations intervene in the currency markets, buying and selling as appropriate to keep the agreed parities. In cases of persistent strength or weakness, the central ECU rates can be realigned. This has not happened since 1987. Realignment results in the devaluation or revaluation of national currencies. It can only be done by common accord through the Committee of Central Bank Governors and Council of Finance Ministers. Many believe that the ERM is basically driven by the Deutsche Mark and the Bundesbank's strong distaste of inflation. Certainly its impact has been to draw currency values, monetary policies, and interest and inflation rates in the ERM Community close to those of Germany.

The European Currency Unit (ECU) has also been created. ECUs represent the weighted, average market value of the national currencies. The weighting is done according to the national shares of EC trade, which gives the Deutsche Mark about 30 percent of the ECU value. ECUs are called a "basket currency." ECUs, although not a tangible currency except as collectibles, are used as the basis of settlement between banks within the EMS, for budgetary purposes, to calculate agricultural subsidies and foreign aid, and levy fines and penalties. ECUs are increasingly used as reference values in private transactions and a large ECU bond and treasury bill market exists. Indeed, more ECU bonds are floated than all but U.S. dollar, Deutsche Mark, Swiss franc and Japanese yen issues. Visionaries foresee ECUs as the Common Market currency of the future.

Common Transport Policy

The Community's common transport policy is another objective that the Treaty of Rome outlines in Part II. Despite its critical role in the free movement of goods and people within the Common Market, transportation is an area in which the

Treaty's aspirations have long remained unful-
filled. Trade restraints in road, rail and air transportation within the European Community
abound. Indeed, the level of frustration with the
lack of integration in this field is reflected in a
lawsuit filed by the Parliament against the Council
before the European Court of Justice seeking to
force the Council to fully implement the Treaty's
goals for a more common and integrated transportation market. *European Parliament v. Council*
(1985) Eur.Comm.Rep. 1513. The Court found that
there had been a "failure to act" by the Council
which had to be remedied within a reasonable
time. Although there have been some reforms in
the transport field since then, transportation is
still one of the least successful areas of EC integration.

After much delay, progress has been made in
road transportation. Legislation has been issued
to abolish discriminations arising from different
(but still regulated) rates and from conditions applied to like goods in like circumstances. Community law also deals with common rules for international road carriage, restrictions upon drivers'
hours, and installation of tachygraphs that record
such hours. The latter requirement caused a furor
in Britain because it stopped drivers from "moon-
lighting" extra runs. *Commission v. United Kingdom* (1979) Eur.Comm.Rep. 419. Differences
among the Member States about road taxes, safety
requirements, noise levels, and truck weights and
dimensions have been mostly resolved. In 1988, a

Council directive vastly increased the number Community authorizations of interstate carriage of goods. By 1993, it is anticipated that such authorizations will be unlimited, though subject to qualitative licensing controls. Council Directive 1841/88. At least in this area, the Council has begun to fulfill its obligations under the 1985 Court of Justice judgment of inaction.

Council Regulations 4055-58/86 on maritime transport services move in the same direction (especially by removing so-called national flag reservations), but fail to deal with "cabotage" (maritime transport within one EC state). EC competition law rules apply, as do its antidumping rules. See Chapters 6 and 7. This represents the first application of dumping law in the services sector. Air transport has been a tougher nut to crack. Market-sharing, profit pooling and other restrictive cartel practices have long victimized Europe's flying public. Not surprisingly, many of the Community's airlines are governmentally owned. In the so-called "Nouvelles Frontieres" case, the Court of Justice struck a blow for greater competition and consumer benefit by legitimizing EC and national law enforcement actions against restrictive airline practices. *Ministère Public v. Asjes* (1986) Eur. Comm.Rep. 1425. See Council Directives 3975/87 and 3976/87. Price fixing by air carriers (including on flights to and from the Community) is unlawful unless specifically exempted by the Commission. *Ahmed Saeed Flugreisen v. Zentrale zur*

Bekämpfung unlauteren Wettbewerbs (1989) Eur. Comm.Rep. 838.

Since these decisions, Commission threats of prosecutions combined with new Community legislation of a mildly market-liberalizing character have made some headway at flying friendlier skies in Europe. For example, the old system that allowed any carrier on a route to veto low-fare proposals by other airlines has been replaced by the "double disapproval" rule. It now takes disapproval by two civil air authorities to negate low-fare proposals. Moreover, the right of governments to oppose the introduction of new fares has been limited. Council Directive 87/601. The Commission has also announced an intention to take over from the member states the responsibility for negotiating international air-traffic agreements. Traditionally, these agreements have been bilaterally undertaken at the national level.

CHAPTER 5

INTERNAL COMMUNITY POLICIES

Part III of the Treaty of Rome is entitled "Policy of the Community." It is in this part of the Treaty that some of the most dramatic surrenders of national sovereignty to EC institutions occur. If a common market is to result, many national economic policies must be coordinated or conformed to a common standard. Thus Part III of the Treaty of Rome seeks to minimize the trade distorting impact of national economic laws. Taxation is an excellent and perhaps the most difficult example.

Taxation

If each government were to legislate freely and differently on taxation, the operation of the Common Market would clearly be affected. Article 95 of the Treaty of Rome forbids discriminatory or protective taxation based on nationality or the origin of products. The goal of this article is to prohibit the use of tax laws as a trade barrier and ensure that goods which compete are equally taxed. The practical effect of Article 95 is to convey substantial powers of judicial review over national tax law and policy to the European Court.

Excise duties are an obvious example of the potential for trade distortion through taxation. Excise taxes on imported liquor, for example, must be levied at the same rate, on the same basis and by the same methods as domestic competitors. Low alcohol, cheap wines imported into Britain thus could not be taxed more than beer. *Commission v. United Kingdom* ("Wine and Beer") (1983) Eur.Comm.Rep. 2265. Nor could France discriminate in taxation of wine versus grain spirits. *Commission v. France* (1980) Eur.Comm.Rep. 347. But the prohibition against discriminatory internal taxation does not apply where there are no similar or competing national products. *Commission v. Denmark* (1991) Eur.Comm.Rep. ___ (Case C–47/88).

Sales taxes and what the Europeans refer to as "turnover taxes" can also have a trade distorting impact. Each member state now has a turnover tax generally referred to as the value-added tax (VAT). This was not always the case. Britain, for example, had to switch from a sales tax to a VAT upon joining the EC. The VAT is a cumulative multi-stage tax system encountered in virtually every transaction of goods *or services* throughout the Community. American attorneys might ponder what their clients' reactions would be if they added service taxes to their fees.

Although harmonization has been achieved as to the nature of the required tax system (the VAT), widely differing levels of VAT taxation within the

Community continue to distort trade relations. Britain, for example, has generally charged one uniform VAT rate of 15 to 17.5 percent but zero rates a number of "necessities." Italy, on the other hand, has had three levels of VAT with luxuries taxed at times as high as 38 percent. Furthermore, each country has established tax collection points at its borders in order to assure the collection of the proper amount of VAT for particular products in accordance with national law (the "destination principle"). These "tax frontiers" probably represent the most significant NTB in the Community today.

Many consider the ability of the Community to achieve a consensus as to the proper levels of VAT and excise taxation, or at least to reduce the degree of differences in such taxation among the member states, to be the litmus test of the 1992 campaign for a fully integrated market. In December of 1989, the Council agreed to the gradual alignment of VAT rates around a standard rate band of 14 to 20 percent. A reduced rate band of 5 to 9 percent is anticipated by 1993 for selected products. Existing zero rates are grandfathered. The tax frontiers will be eliminated by imposing VAT reporting and collection duties on importers and exporters using the destination principle on VAT rates. The excise tax frontier will be eliminated by moving to a system of interlinked bonded warehouses between which goods can move easily. As with the VAT, excise taxation will continue to follow the destination principle. The Commission hopes to move to taxation on the basis of origin principles later in the decade.

The Council has also been active in the corporate tax area, focusing particularly on double taxation issues. The Council adopted directives in 1990 on the taxation of mergers, the taxation of dividends paid by subsidiaries to parent companies, and the arbitration of tax disputes between member states. Additional directives on taxation of interest and royalties as between parent and subsidiary companies, and the allocation of losses as between them are expected to follow.

Competition Policy—Government Subsidies

The Community's competition policy is a natural consequence of its Common Market. The dismantling of internal tariffs, quotas and measures of equivalent effect opens up traditionally sheltered national markets to competition through trade in goods and services. Having created the playing field, so to speak, the Treaty of Rome seeks through its rules on competition to ensure that the field is level as possible for all who participate. These rules are of two basic types: business competition (i.e. antitrust) and government subsidies. The business competition rules of the EEC originate in Articles 85–90 of the Treaty of Rome. They are of such enormous importance to all who do business with the Community that Chapter 7 is devoted exclusively to them.

Subsidies by governments are one of the most intractable of world and Common Market trade problems. In the first place, there are subsidies everywhere. For example, most tax laws (including the Internal Revenue Code) are littered with subsidies. Secondly, identification and calculation of the amount of subsidy can be extremely difficult. The EC, like the GATT, has spent years just cataloging subsidies. In 1988, the Commission concluded that the member states spend approximately 100 billion ECUs annually on state subsidies. This amounts to about $2,000 per person engaged in manufacturing. Much of this aid goes to "crisis industries" that are declining, but a reasonable amount is targeted at growth sectors, technology development and general support. Moreover, subsidies are almost endemic where the member states own or are heavily invested in enterprises. Some enterprises have been acquired by governments out of bankruptcy in order to save jobs. Some have been established for strategic, prestige or capital requirements' reasons. Others have simply been nationalized as a matter of social policy. In recent years, there has been a trend (but not a stampede) towards privatization of enterprises owned by EC governments. Neither nationalization nor privatization is mandated or controlled by the Treaty of Rome. *Costa v. ENEL* (1964) Eur.Comm.Rep. 585 (Italian nationalization of electricity companies).

The Competition Policy Commissioner, Sir Leon Brittan, has recently taken the position that any action by a member state as an owner that is different from what a private investor would do can violate the subsidy or competition law (see Chapter 7) rules of the Treaty of Rome. Such actions may include cash payments, debt write-offs, acceptance of rates of return that are below market, implied or express guarantees of loans, cheap financing, new equity capital in circumstances a private investor would avoid and dividend waivers. In adopting this position, Sir Leon is relying heavily upon Article 92 of the Treaty of Rome.

Article 92(1) declares every national "aid" (subsidy) that distorts or threatens to distort competition by favoring certain businesses or goods incompatible with the Common Market. State aids intended to benefit workers but implemented through a reduction in public charges to textile corporations in Italy were caught within Article 92(1). The impact of the subsidy, not its purposes, determines its character. *Italy v. Commission* (1974) Eur.Comm. Rep. 709. French textile industry aids financed partly by import levies were similarly prohibited because of their discriminatory impact. *France v. Commission* (1970) Eur.Comm.Rep. 487. Though the money may be private in origin, a state aid exists when that money is distributed through a public body. *Commission v. France* (1985) Eur. Comm.Rep. 439. Provision of subsidies through state-owned enterprises are also caught by Article 92(1). *Italy v. Commission* (1991) Eur.Comm.Rep. ___ (Cases C–303/88, C–305/89). Investment subsidies that strengthen the position of a company in the Common Market fall within Article 92(1) as threats to the distortion of competition. *Philip Morris Holland BV v. Commission* (1980) Eur. Comm.Rep. 2671.

Article 92(2) declares the following subsidies *compatible* with the Treaty of Rome: (a) social aid granted to individuals without discrimination as to the origin of goods; (b) natural disaster aid; and (c) economic aid to East Germany (a reservation now mooted by German unification). Furthermore, Article 92(3) lists a number of aids which *may* be compatible with the Common Market if approved by the Commission. These include regional subsidies to promote development in areas of high unemployment or abnormally low standards of living, subsidies for important projects of common European interest, and subsidies to remedy serious disturbances in the economy of a member state. Also included are subsidies to facilitate the development of certain economic activities or areas (e.g. shipbuilding) provided they do not adversely affect trading conditions to an extent contrary to the common interest. Finally, any subsidy may be lawful if approved by the Council acting by qualified majority vote.

The Commission is charged in Article 93 with keeping all state aids under "constant review," which it does mostly by way of a reporting system. The duty of member state governments to report on the provision of subsidies to industry has been repeatedly upheld by the European Court. *France v. Commission* (1990) Eur.Comm.Rep. ___ (Case

301/87). If a subsidy is not compatible with the Common Market per Article 92 or is being misused, the Commission may render a decision to that effect against the member state unless the Council unanimously approves of the aid. Such Commission decisions terminate the ability to receive further state aid payments. *Capolongo v. Azienda Agricola Maya* (1973) Eur.Comm.Rep. 611. Absent compliance, the Commission can enforce its decision by bringing an action *directly* before the European Court of Justice. The Commission need not follow the more deliberate procedures established in Article 169 for ordinary prosecutions of member states not adhering to their EC obligations. See, e.g. *Commission v. United Kingdom* (1977) Eur.Comm.Rep. 921; *Commission v. Germany* (1973) Eur.Comm.Rep. 813.

Enterprises sometimes sue the Commission for failure to act against distortionary state subsidies. In one case, a French pasta maker sued the Commission for damages under Article 215 of the Treaty of Rome as a result of its failure to act against Italian subsidies to domestic pasta manufacturers. Holding that a causal link had not been established between the Commission's failure to act and the French company's damages, the Court of Justice agreed that the case was rightly dismissed. *Bertrand v. Commission* (1976) Eur.Comm.Rep. 1.

Certain patterns have emerged in the Community's law on state subsidies. Regional development aids are generally supported, especially since the

Single European Act of 1987 made elimination of regional economic disparities a priority. The whole of Greece, Portugal and Ireland, for example, are now treated as underdeveloped regions for subsidy law purposes. See Official Journal C 212/2. Indeed, the Community itself engages in the same subsidies under its Regional Policy, infra. Sectoral industrial aids to ease unemployment and modernize smokestack industries (coal, steel, textiles, shipbuilding) have generally been allowed. Production and marketing subsidies have generally been disallowed. Research and technological development subsidies, especially for energy saving projects, often pass muster. Since environmental protection subsidies violate the polluter must pay principle of the Community's Environmental Policy, these are not frequently approved.

The Commission's role relative to national subsidies has gradually changed over the years form prosecutorial watchdog against discriminatory and anticompetitive aids to coordinator of national subsidy policies and levels. In this capacity, the Commission can find itself negotiating specific subsidy amounts or refunds with national governments, e.g. French subsidies to state-owned Renault. The power of prosecution under Article 92 remains. No member state, for example, may match another EC nation's subsidy. *Steinike und Weinlig v. Germany* (1977) Eur.Comm.Rep. 595. The Court of Justice has affirmed the power of the Commission to order refunds of offending national subsidies. *Commission v. Germany* (1973) Eur.Comm.Rep. 813;

Commission v. Belgium (1988) 2 Common Mkt. L.Rep. 258 (failure of timely repayment is breach of Treaty obligations). Many have suggested authorizing the Commission to levy fines and penalties against member states that fail to adhere to Community law on subsidies.

Harmonizing National Laws—Procurement

Article 100 in Part III of the Treaty of Rome empowers the Council of Ministers, acting on Commission proposals, to issue directives for the "approximation" (better known as "harmonization" or "coordination") of national laws directly affecting the establishment or operation of the Common Market. Such directives must be adopted unanimously within the Council. Since a vast number of national laws affect the Common Market, the potential scope of Article 100 is very broad. This scope, over the years since 1957, was not fully exploited principally because of the unanimous Council voting requirement. Indeed, by 1986 and a Community of twelve nations, innovative legislation under Article 100 became quite difficult to obtain. That is why one major thrust of the Single European Act was the inclusion of Article 100A. It specifies qualified majority voting in the Council of Ministers for much of the 1992 legislative agenda. Qualified majority voting procedures also apply to directives used to harmonize national laws (e.g. subsidies) distorting the conditions of competition in the Common Market. Article 101.

Harmonization of national laws of concern to the Common Market is critical to advancing European Community integration. Harmonization can, for example, remove many of the barriers to free movement previously discussed in Chapter 4, e.g. those expressly permitted by Article 36 and the *Dassonville* line of cases. It can do the same for the public security exceptions to the free movement of workers and the self-employed, as well as to the freedom to provide services across borders. Harmonization is critical to removal of the tax and NTB frontiers within the Community which are a central focus of the 1992 campaign. In addition, harmonization can reach out to areas not specifically treated in the Treaty of Rome but which are of consequence to the functioning of the Common Market. A good example is government procurement law.

Every government, at whatever level, tends to favor local producers when spending the taxpayers' money. Various "Buy American" laws permeate much of the military and civil procurement of the federal, state and local governments in the United States. The governments of the European Community nations are no different. Nevertheless, through a long series of harmonizing directives issued by the Council and aggressive decisions of the European Court, the effects of Buy French, Buy Greek and Buy Greater London Council types of laws are slowly being overcome. For example, the Court's opinion in the *Buy Irish* case struck down a program of public advertisements urging consumers to voluntarily buy only goods marked with a "Guaranteed Irish" symbol. This program combined private and governmental funds and officials. It was declared a measure of equivalent effect to a quota hindering EC trade in breach of Article 30. *Commission v. Ireland* (1982) Eur. Comm.Rep. 4005.

The Council has issued a series of directives intended to open up government procurement to competitive bids from all Community enterprises. The first focus of this effort was on tendering procedures for public works projects. Discriminations on the basis of nationality which amount to the equivalent of trade quotas are prohibited under an early 1969 directive. Discriminatory procedural rules concerning the award of public works and construction contracts are standardized in a 1971 directive. These public works directives apply to contracts exceeding one million ECUs.

The second focus of the Community effort to combat discriminatory government procurement patterns is on supply contracts for goods and services to member governments, their regional and local subdivisions, public agencies and the like. A 1977 directive requires all public supply contracts in excess of 140,000 ECUs to be announced in advance in the Community's Official Journal. The announcement must also include the criteria for selection of bidders or suppliers, which may not be discriminatory. This directive does not apply to purchases of military supplies, but covers purchases of nonmilitary supplies used by military forces. Certain national governmental monopolies, e.g. water, gas and electricity, are excluded from its application. A 1980 directive amended these rules to bring them into conformity with the 1979 GATT Code on Government Procurement, to which the EC is a party. The GATT Code liberalizes government procurement rules on an international basis. The 1980 directive, nevertheless, maintains a margin of preference for EC enterprises seeking governmental supply contracts within the Community.

The early European Community procurement legislation did not live up to expectations. Purchasing entities and public authorities undertaking construction projects continued to give preference to domestic suppliers and contractors. A survey revealed the most common and serious breaches of the Community procurement rules: (1) failure to advertise contracts in the *Official Journal;* (2) abuse of the exceptions permitting single tendering; (3) discriminatory administrative, financial or technical requirements in tenders, especially the insistence on compliance with national standards even when EC law does not allow this; (4) illegal disqualification or elimination of bidders or applicants from other Member States, for example by discriminatory selection criteria; and (5) discrimination at the award stage. Public works contracts which contain standards that automatically exclude tenders from other member state companies using equivalent standards are unlawful impediments to the free movement of goods. *Commission v. Ireland* (1987) Eur.Comm.Rep. 1369.

It was reported in late 1986 that approximately 98 percent of all procurement contracts go to national suppliers in the EC. Single tendering (unpublicized, noncompetitive contract awards) and selective supplier arrangements (unpublicized, selectively competitive contract awards) continue to hurt Community efforts at overcoming buy-local preferences. Other problems exist with exemptions from EC procurement law for special needs such as "speed of delivery," "security" and "particular specifications." Procedural and substantive reforms of the existing directives were proposed by the Commission in 1986. These reforms would cover notice requirements, longer bid periods, publication of contract awards (who won), use of European specification standards (not national standards), and reduction of exemption industries (energy, transport, water and telecommunications).

Reform of procurement rules is part of the 1992 unified internal market campaign. Early in 1988, the Council adopted a directive tightening up the procedural aspects of the Community's procurement rules so as to reduce single tendering. Under another 1988 directive, public construction bidding was similarly reformed. In 1990, a directive was adopted which will (in 1993) open up public contracts to EC firms in the Community's telecommunications, energy, transport and water industries. This directive contains a controversial "Buy

EC" clause which allows public authorities to dismiss bids with less than 50 percent Community content, and gives Community suppliers a minimum margin of preference of 3 percent. The "Buy EC" clause may be dropped if satisfactory agreements are reached within the GATT on amendment of the Procurement Code.

Harmonizing National Laws—Product Standards and Liability

An important part of the 1992 campaign against nontariff trade barriers (NTBs) in the European Community involves product testing and standards. More than half of the legislation involved in the 1992 campaign concerns such issues. Since 1969, there has been a standstill agreement among the EC states to avoid the introduction of new technical barriers to trade. A 1983 directive requires member states to notify the Commission of proposed new technical regulations and product standards. The Commission can enjoin the introduction of such national rules for up to one year if it believes that a Community standard should be developed. Council Directive 83/169. The 1992 goal is to move from 12 sets of regulatory approvals to one unified Community system embodying essential requirements on health, safety, the environment and consumer protection. Goods that meet these essential requirements will bear an "EC mark" and can be freely traded. Manufacturers will self-certify their compliance with relevant EC standards.

Private regional standards bodies have been playing a critical role in the development of this system. These include the European Committee for Standardization (CEN), the European Committee for Electrotechnical Standardization (CENELEC) and the European Telecommunications Standards Institute (ETSI). Groups like these have been officially delegated the responsibility for creating thousands of technical product standards. They have been turning out some 150 common standards each year. For example, directives on the safety of toys, construction products and electromagnetic compatibility have been issued. See Council Directives 88/378, 89/106 and 89/336. These directives adopt the so-called "new approach" of setting broad standards at the Community level which if met guarantee access to every member state market. North American producers have frequently complained that their ability to be heard by European standards' bodies is limited. They have had little influence on EC product standards to which they must conform in order to sell freely in the Common Market.

Testing and certification of products is another part of the 1992 campaign. The main concern of North American companies is that recognition of U.S., Canadian and Mexican tests be granted by the EC. In the past, many North American exporters have had to have their goods retested for Community purposes. The Community is generally committed to a resolution of such issues under what it calls a "global approach" to product standards and testing. In negotiations undertaken as part of the Uruguay Round on revising the Standards Code of the GATT, the EC has indicated its commitment to giving recognition to "equivalent technical regulations" of other nations, and to avoidance of unnecessary obstacles to trade. Implementation of this commitment may come as a relief to U.S. exporters of beef and pork, both of which have encountered EC import bans in recent years because of the use of animal hormones and deficiencies (as a matter of Community law) in American meat processing plants.

Products liability law is one field where the Community acted before the 1992 campaign to harmonize national rules. Council Directive 85/374 established, for all twelve member states, a regime of strict (no-fault) defective products liability. Strict liability is tempered by certain defenses, notably the "state-of-the-art" defense which excludes liability where the manufacturer could not have discovered the defect when the product was made. Strict liability is also tempered in the award of damages by contributory negligence principles. The calculation and types of damages that may be recovered is largely left to national law. Thus the award of "pain and suffering" or punitive damages is under member state control, as is the imposition of total limits on recovery. A three-year statute of limitations ordinarily applies, and a ten-year absolute bar on liability is established in the Council directive on products liability.

For many EC nations, this directive mandated a fundamental switch away from liability systems grounded entirely in negligence principles. Americans who have studied the painstaking manner in which strict products liability doctrine was crafted in state courts are often surprised by the sweeping implementation of comparable law in the EC. The explanation lies in the goal of free movement and a desire to equalize the risks of liability (and the insurance costs) that most often accompany the distribution of goods to the public. There is, also, greater acceptance in Europe of the need to compensate accident victims regardless of fault. These factors facilitated the passage of the products liability directive and its implementation by the member states.

Consumer Protection

The Community has had a consumer protection and information policy since 1975. In addition to products liability, it focuses on health and safety product labelling and manufacture. Foodstuffs, cosmetics, detergents, vehicles, textiles, toys, dangerous substances, medicines, fertilizers, pesticides and animal feed are some of the areas now governed by Community consumer protection law. There is, for example, a directive which fixes the maximum level of pesticide residues on fruits and vegetables. Council Directive 76/895 (amended by Directive 90/642). A general "products safety" directive is anticipated as part of the 1992 campaign. It covers consumer and non-consumer goods and prohibits any "unacceptable risk" in their use. Permanent monitoring of all products put on the market must be maintained. Warning labels as to "significant risks" must be effective throughout the life of the product, including disposal. Consumer credit, false or misleading advertising, unfair contract terms, warranties and package holidays are also targeted for new or improved legislation under the 1992 campaign. Indeed, there is a sense in which the entire effort at creating a Europe without internal frontiers is proconsumer. The greater the reality of the Common Market, the wider the range of choices for consumers in search of goods and services.

Harmonizing National Laws—Securities, Business Organizations

The right of establishment and the freedom to provide services across borders (discussed in Chapter 4) apply to most business organizations operating in the Common Market. See Article 58 of the Treaty of Rome. They often exercise these rights by establishing subsidiaries or branches in other member states, or by acquiring businesses located there. Article 221 of the Treaty of Rome creates a right of national treatment as regards participation in the capital of profit-making companies. In other words, discrimination based upon nationality cannot be practiced when it comes to corporate capital. The cumulative effect which Community law has had upon persons doing business with or within member states is very substantial.

Several important EC directives have been adopted in the securities field. These concern admission of securities to stock exchange listings (1979 amended 1987), the issuance of a prospectus (1980 amended 1989), and regular information disclosures by publicly traded firms (1982 amended 1989). See, e.g., Council Directives 80/390, 89/298. Some commentators have suggested that the net result of these directives will be a "Common Market Prospectus." Once approved by a member state, a prospectus conforming to EC rules can be used throughout the Community subject to minimal additional disclosure requirements.

Council Directive 85/611 on mutual fund ("unit trust") management was implemented in 1985. It allows marketing in other member states based upon home country authorization. In 1988, the Council adopted an "anti-raider" directive requiring disclosure of the transfer of 10 percent or more of a publicly listed company. Council Directive 88/627. Until 1988, only three of the member states had laws regulating insider trading. Nevertheless, a directive on insider trading was finalized in 1989. Council Directive 89/592. This directive prohibits trading on the basis of inside information by primary and secondary insiders. Inside information is defined as non-public information which if made public would be "likely to have a significant effect on the price" of securities. Many perceive that the EC insider trading directive closely parallels U.S. securities' law principles. One concern with the directive is that it allows member states to choose which types of penalties apply to insider trading violations.

Article 220 of the Treaty of Rome obliges member states to enter into negotiations with each other about equal protection of citizens, abolition of double taxation, mutual recognition of firms and companies, the possibility of international mergers, and simplification of enforcement of judgments. Taken together with the right of establishment and the freedom to provide services, Article 220 was the backdrop against which member states signed in 1968 a Convention on Mutual Recognition of Companies and Other Bodies Corporate. This Convention seeks to ensure that Treaty benefits extend to such legal personae. Unfortunately, it is still awaiting full ratification by the member states.

In the interim, the Council has adopted a number of non-controversial coordination directives under Article 54 advancing Community company law. These in theory seek to avoid the race to the bottom problems associated with Delaware corporate law in the United States. The first directive sets out requirements for standardization of liability (including pre-incorporation liability) of companies. The second deals with the classification, subscription and maintenance of capital of public and large companies. The third concerns the internal merger of public companies. The sixth directive governs sales of assets of public companies, including certain shareholder, creditor and workers' rights. The fourth standardizes the treatment of annual accounts of public and large companies (e.g. in their presentation, content, valuation and publication). In this directive, there is a permissive provision relating to inflation or current cost accounting. Accounts are to show a "true and fair view" of the enterprise. There is some doubt about the degree of relation to similar requirements of the United Kingdom accounting bodies or "generally accepted accounting practices" in the United States. The fourth directive is followed by the seventh concerning requirements for accounts of groups of companies. The eighth provides certain minimum standards and qualifications for auditors of company accounts.

Several controversial proposals for company law directives are in varying stages of evolution. These include a fifth directive on company structure and administration which has been long delayed due to differing views about the functions of single and two-tier boards of directors and officers, and worker representation at these levels. Another controversial topic (the "Vredeling proposal") would require substantial information sharing between companies and their employees. Other less controversial directives are also planned. The ninth directive concerns liability on the part of parent companies for the debts of subsidiaries they effectively control. The tenth directive deals with cross-border company mergers. The eleventh (adopted in 1990) involves disclosure by branches operating in other EC states, and the twelfth affects private limited companies. Hostile takeovers, a sensitive area, are the subject of the thirteenth proposed company law directive. This directive would require equal treatment of shareholders and specify permissible defensive measures.

European Companies and Partnerships

Innovative company law proposals include those for a European Company Statute (SE) and a European Economic Interest Grouping (EEIG). The former is intended to create a Community corporate entity, overcoming the transnational problems associated with existing methods of incorporation within member states. The EEIG, adopted in 1985, is a vehicle with legal capacity formed in the manner of an international partnership of member state companies. The EEIG is prohibited from offering proprietary interests to the public and is a nonprofit enterprise. Limited liability is not obtained. The EEIG is intended for small or medium sized research and development or marketing ventures. Utilization of EEIG has been relatively low, in part because of perceptions of uncertainty about their tax status.

An amended proposal for a European Company was submitted by the Commission to the Council in August, 1989. Nineteen years had passed since the submission of the first proposal in 1970, and 14 years since the last amended proposal in 1975. In that period considerable harmonization had been accomplished by way of directives, and the new proposal is shorter, addresses fewer issues, and has a better chance of success. The European Company proposal is divided into two parts. The first proposes a European Company, to be called an SE (Latin "societas europaea"). The SE will not be mandatory. An SE could be formed by (1) public limited companies from at least two different EC states, (2) other companies from more than one EC member state establishing an SE as a joint subsidiary, or (3) an established SE creating another SE. It thus appears that an SE might only be formed by companies which are EC companies and which have their registered office and central administration in a member state. Non–EC companies wishing to establish an SE will have to establish a company in a member state.

If the European Company law does not cover a particular area, the general principles of the EC statute and the provisions of the national law of the country of registration control. Thus there will be some differences where national company law is applied. The SE proposes that either of two corporate forms may be used. The first is a single management board and the second is a two-tier structure with management and supervisory boards. If the two-tier form is adopted the members (and in some cases employees as well) appoint the supervisory board which in turn appoints the management board. The single management system may still require employee participation with the shareholders in the appointment of part of the board.

The second part of the European Company proposal is directed to the controversial worker participation concepts which have not been successfully adopted as a separate fifth directive. The second part brings employees into overall supervision and planning but not day-to-day management. It does not set down exact rules, acknowledging the different attitudes towards employee participation among the member states. Three models are recognized. First, employee representation on the supervisory or administrative board (differing from the employee participation in electing the board under the SE rules); second, a separate body of employees with some management role; and third, participation through some form of collective agreement. The last form would allow the United Kingdom to agree, since it has rejected any form but collective bargaining. An SE formed in Germany with a worker organization would not necessarily be able to demand such a board for its operation in another member state, since each member state can limit the model for all SEs registered in the state.

Environmental Policy

For many years, environmental law was a stepchild of the European Community. The Treaty of Rome of 1957 does not expressly authorize or anticipate such a policy. Clearly, however, differing national standards on the environment can have a substantial impact on the functioning of the Common Market. As environmental politics (remember the Green Party) and consciousness came of age in Western Europe, initial EC environmental efforts rested on Article 100 (harmonization) and Article 235, the Treaty's "necessary and proper" powers clause. The first Environmental Action Program commenced in 1973. The Community is now embarked on its fourth such program covering 1987–1992.

There are two basic thrusts to the Community's environmental policy. The first is the establishment of minimum quality standards (e.g. drinking water). The second involves specific emission controls (e.g. the discharge of pollutants into surface and ground water). On emission controls, the Community has proceeded slowly, industry by industry, after first identifying priority problems. The first water emissions directives involve mercury and cadmium discharges. Among the first air pollution directives, auto emissions and lead content in gasoline have had a high priority. Since 1989, Community law requires all member states to introduce lead-free gasoline into their markets and leaded gas is reduced to a minimum content. But there is no requirement, as yet, that all new cars use lead-free gasoline.

Waste control directives have targeted oil, PCB and PCT discharges as priorities. French law implementing the waste oil directive could not deny the right of oil companies to export wastes to an approved recycling center in another member state. *Syndicat National des Fabricants Raffineurs d'Huile de Graissage v. Groupement d'Intérêt Economique "Inter–Huiles"* (1983) Eur.Comm.Rep. 555. EC rules govern the biodegradability of detergents and the sulphur content of liquid fuels. *Commission v. Italy* (1980) Eur.Comm.Rep. 1099 and 1115. A strict liability directive for damages caused by commercial waste is proposed as part of the 1992 campaign. The producer (or transporter if negligent) would be strictly liable to individuals and public authorities for personal and property damages. If the producer of the waste cannot be found, holders or disposers will be strictly liable. When compared with the liability of companies under U.S. "superfund" legislation, however, the EC proposal may impose noticeably lower costs on industry. This is the result primarily of EC cost-benefit limitations on cleanup liability and the absence of any duty to pay governments for damages to natural resources. Commentators have noted that a competitive handicap may follow for American companies.

The Single European Act of 1987 added Articles 130R–130T to the Treaty of Rome. These articles firmly establish environmental policy as an important domain of the Community. Indeed, Article 130R(2) makes environmental protection requirements a mandatory component of *all* the Community's policies. One of the overriding legal principles of EC environmental policy is that the polluter shall pay. Article 130R(2). This may mean that national governments are limited in their ability to grant subsidies for environmental protection purposes. Another key principle is that member states may adopt more demanding environmental requirements, provided they are compatible with the Treaty of Rome. Article 130T.

The procedures for adoption of European Community environmental legislation and the conclusion of international environmental agreements are unusually detailed. Article 130R(3) requires the Community to consider available scientific and technical data, the environmental conditions in the regions of the EC, the potential benefits and costs of Community action or inaction, the economic and social development of the EC as a whole and balanced development of its regions when preparing environmental policy. The EC can legislate only when action at the Community level will better achieve the objectives at stake than action by individual member states. Article 130R(4) (the "subsidiarity principle").

Cooperation within international organizations on the environment is shared between the Community and its member states "within their respective spheres of competence." Article 130R(5). EC adoption of international environmental accords is subject to the same procedures regularly used for trade treaties. See Chapter 6. One important indicator of just how sensitive the environmental field is within the Community is provided by Article 130S. That article requires a unanimous Council vote before any legislative or international action on the environment is undertaken, specifically reserving to the Council the decision as to when qualified majority voting may be used. Most other authority added to the Treaty of Rome in 1987 by the Single European Act prescribes qualified majority voting. Compare Articles 100A, 118A.

Although Europe may have been relatively slow in joining the environmental movement when compared to North America, it is rapidly making up for lost time and forging ahead in some areas (e.g. fluorocarbons and the ozone layer). The European Parliament has been a strong supporter of this trend, backing up its commitment with new budgetary allocations and by promoting the creation of a European Environmental Agency. Its initial task will be to function as an information clearinghouse. The EC has also concluded a large number of international environmental agreements, including the Basel Convention on Transboundary Movements of Hazardous Wastes, the Bonn Agreement on the Prevention of Pollution of the North Sea, and the Washington Convention [against] International Trade in Endangered Species of Wild Flora and Fauna. One particularly innovative environmental agreement to which the EC is a party is the Barcelona Convention on the Mediterranean Sea. This Convention obligates the signatories to select from a menu of options on improvement and protection of the Med.

Regional Policy

The Treaty of Rome is premised upon the opening of national markets to competitive trade. The Treaty, especially as amended by the Single European Act in 1987, recognizes that some areas of the Community will not succeed under these conditions. These "less developed" parts of the EC benefit from the Community's Regional Policy. Since 1987, the basic provisions on Regional Policy are located in Articles 130A–130E of the Treaty of Rome under the title "economic and social cohesion."

The Community's Regional Policy operates in conjunction with other programs, notably agriculture, the Social Fund and coal and steel, to facilitate the growth and development of its poorer parts. The Mezzogiorno in Southern Italy was an early target for regional aid which now extends to most of Portugal, Greece and Ireland, as well as parts of the remaining member states. Some aid comes in the form of Community authorization for national subsidies. Other aid comes directly from the nonprofit European Investment Bank (EIB) established by Articles 129 and 130 of the Treaty of Rome. The EIB is funded by the Community and the capital market. It has financed a large number of regional development projects.

Article 130A commits the Community to the goal of reducing the disparities between its regions and the "backwardness" of its least-favored regions. A region is least-favored if its per capita GDP is less than 50 percent of the EC average. A major step towards this goal, accomplished by the Single European Act, was formal recognition of the European Regional Development Fund. This fund has operated since 1975 in addition to and coordinated with those that function under the Community's Common Agricultural Policy and its Social Policy. See Regulation 2052/88. The Regional Development Fund targets structural adjustment and conversion of declining industrial regions with aid grants. Its monies have gone a long way towards convincing the poorer regions of the Community that the 1992 campaign for a fully integrated market will bring some benefit to them. Regional development has often become the grease that insures a unanimous vote whenever needed to move the Common Market closer to a full reality.

Energy

Despite the specificity of the EURATOM and ECSC treaties, and the oil shocks of the 1970s, it is hard to say that the European Community has developed a viable all-encompassing energy policy. One reason is that Europe is energy poor. Those EC states with oil and gas (Britain and Holland especially) are not keen to be obliged to share these resources in a crisis with their fellow members. Neither would, one suspects, Norway. Common ground has been reached on minimum crude oil reserves, funding for alternative fuels and energy efficiency, and defense of the massive Siberian natural gas pipeline project from early Reagan administration ("evil empire") attacks. The exclusive French government trading monopoly over petroleum products was finally eliminated in accordance with Article 37 of the Treaty of Rome. *Cullet v. Centre Leclerc Toulouse* (1985) Eur.Comm. Rep. 305. And cheap energy subsidies through state enterprises to industry have frequently been condemned by the Commission and Court of Justice. See *Commission v. Netherlands* (1988) Eur. Comm.Rep. 281.

In 1980, the Council did adopt a Resolution on Community Energy Objectives for 1990, since revised to project to 1995. The primary objective is to limit oil dependency to about 40 percent of the Community's total energy needs (down from 60 percent in 1973), and 15 percent of its electricity requirements. In practice, this has mostly meant more subsidies for coal and nuclear power production.

Broadcasting, Telecommunications and Technology Directives

The Council has acted to promote "television without frontiers" in the Community. Council Directive 89/552. Each state must admit television broadcasts from the others. The regulation of the content of those broadcasts is generally left to home state control, subject to various Community rules on advertising. The directive provides that "when practicable," broadcasters (many of which are government-owned) should reserve a majority of their time for programs of European (not just Community) origin. This directive, when first proposed, contained an absolute requirement of more than 50 percent European broadcasting content. Intense lobbying by the United States, a major exporter of films and TV shows to Europe, introduced the "when practicable" limitation. Nevertheless, the long-term goal of broadcasting European television productions at least half the time is clearly stated. Will "Dallas" and "L.A. Law" survive the cut? Tune in after 1992.

All joking aside, the broadcasting directive was one of the few early 1992 campaign laws to attract headlines in America. The entertainment industry is America's second largest source of export earnings after military products and technology. The broadcasting and the banking directives caused the United States business community to wake up and become pro-active in the European Community. They have been supported by Congressional resolutions denouncing the EC broadcasting directive, and repeated statements by USTR Carla Hills that it is the "enemy of free trade." More balanced observers note that the broadcasting directive reflects the sense of cultural invasion that many Europeans resent and associate with more than just television, e.g. a McDonald's on every corner. Generally, however, the fear of losing cultural identity within Europe is diminishing as younger generations are educated, travel, inter-marry and take up work around the Community. The beginnings of a European "melting pot" are evident, but concern about the cultural influence of "outsiders" is growing. This affects not just American broadcasters, but also Japanese exporters, and the racial and ethnic minorities of the Community. North Africans, blacks and Asians resident in the Community often feel the brunt of these sentiments, which at their worst are openly racist.

Telecommunications by phone, fax, telex and computers go to the heart of modern service-oriented economies. The European Community has recognized this and taken steps under its 1992 campaign to integrate and improve the Community's telecommunications network. In 1990, the Council finalized the Community's "Open Network Provision" framework directive. This legislation harmonizes the conditions of access and use of public telecommunications networks. Commission Directive 88/301 (issued under Article 90) deregulates the sale and servicing of telecommunications equipment. France failed when it challenged the authority of the Commission to issue this directive before the European Court. *France v. Commission* (1991) Eur.Comm.Rep. ___ (Case C–202/88). Commission Directive 90/387 eliminates public monopolies over all but voice telephones and infrastructure ownership. Private sector companies may move freely into electronic mail, interactive communications, data transmission and the like. U.S. firms are particularly thought to have competitive advantages that will benefit them under the new EC telecommunications regime.

There is every reason to believe from the case law of the European Court that state monopolies in the telecommunications area will be required to abandon discriminatory national practices. This case law is partly based upon the freedom to provide services across borders, and partly upon EC competition law. See *Procureur du Roi v. Debauve* (1980) Eur.Comm.Rep. 833 (ban on television advertising); *Italy v. Commission ("British Telecom")* (1985) Eur.Comm.Rep. 873 (use of leased lines for customer service upheld); *Bond van Adverteerders v. The Netherlands* (1988) Eur.Comm.Rep. 2085 (discriminatory cross-border advertising restraints). Maximum advertising time limits (generally 15 percent) are established in the television without frontiers directive (supra). This directive also regulates cigarette and childrens' advertising.

A major directive on computer software has been adopted. Council Directive 91/250 extends copyright protection to most computer software. However, the directive permits "decompilation" (reproduction and translation of the program code) when necessary to the interoperability of independently created programs with other programs. Other notable directives concern the patentability of biotechnology and semiconductor topographies (No. 87/54). The latter gives protection for topographies that are original ("not commonplace"). A Council decision (89/337) establishes basic objectives for European production of high definition television.

Research and Development

One important thrust of the Single European Act of 1987 was promotion of more research and technological development. The European Community strongly perceived itself to be falling behind the United States and Japan in these areas. The result was eleven new articles in the Treaty of Rome, Articles 130F–130Q. The opening sentence of Article 130F establishes the goals of strengthening the scientific and technological bases of European industry and encouraging it to become more competitive at the international level. This is to be achieved not only through coordination of national activities and a program of generous Community grants, but also via the whole of the 1992 campaign for a fully integrated Common Market. When less than all the EC states participate in Community-sponsored research and development, the Council has the power to decide to what degree the resulting knowledge must be shared.

In 1987, the Council of Ministers adopted the Framework Program for Community Research and Development. This framework focuses on eight areas; the quality of life, information and communication, modernization of industry, exploitation and optimum use of geological resources, energy, development, marine resources and improved European science and technology cooperation. Some research is done at the Community's own Joint Research Center. Other research is sponsored through national institutes and universities. Many of the Community's research and development programs are known by acronyms such as ESPRIT (information technologies), RACE (advanced communications), DRIVE (road transport informatics and telecommunications), DELTA (learning technologies), and JET (nuclear fusion). Participation by United States companies in EC research programs has been limited.

Social Policy—Occupational Safety, the Social Fund and Social Charter

The Treaty of Rome is dominated by economic affairs. Nevertheless, the Community has always sought to provide for some of the concerns of the human beings who are impacted by the winds of economic change. Articles 117–128 of the Treaty of Rome establish the Social Policy of the European Community. These articles seek to improve working conditions and standards of living on a harmonized basis throughout the Community. The right of EC nationals to move freely to take up employment has previously been discussed in Chapter 4 in connection with the foundations of the Treaty. The Community's social policy builds upon this basic right. Article 121, for example, led to the enactment of social security legislation by the EC to insure coverage for those who exercise their right to move freely to work.

A major impetus came in 1987 with the addition of Article 118A by the Single European Act. This article focuses on health and safety in the working environment. Acting by a qualified majority vote, the Council in cooperation with the Parliament is empowered to issue directives establishing minimum requirements in this field. It has already done so, for example, on visual display units, heavy load handling and exposure to biological agents and carcinogens. More generally, Council directives now establish minimum safety and health requirements for most workplaces, equipment used by workers, and protective devices. *See* Council Directives 89/654, 655, 656. Article 118A specifically requires such directives to avoid imposing administrative, financial and legal constraints that would hold back the creation and development of small and medium-sized enterprises. Like the 1987 Treaty amendments creating the Community's Environmental Policy, Article 118A allows member states to maintain or introduce more stringent legal rules on working conditions, provided these are compatible with the Treaty of Rome.

Articles 123–128 create the European Social Fund. This fund comes out of the Community budget. It is used to pay up to 50 percent of the costs of the member states under their vocational retraining and worker resettlement programs. Article 125. EC rules have substantially harmonized these programs. Unemployment compensation is also funded when plants are converted to other production for workers who are temporarily suspended or suffer a reduction in working hours. They retain the same wage levels pending full re-employment. Commission Decision 83/516 extended the operation of the European Social Fund to promoting employment among those under age 25, women who wish to return to work, the handicapped, migrants and their families, and the long-term unemployed.

The 1992 campaign has a social dimension. Labor unions have been especially concerned about the prospect of "social dumping," the relocation of companies to EC states with weaker unions and lower wages. There is no EC legislation on minimum wages and none is expected in the near future. The Community's response to these concerns led to the Charter of Fundamental Social Rights For Workers, adopted in 1989 by 11 member states less Britain through the European Council. The Charter proclaims the following fundamental social rights for workers:

(1) freedom of movement and choice of occupations;

(2) fair remuneration (sufficient to have a decent standard of living);

(3) improved living and working conditions by the end of 1992 (e.g. paid leave);

(4) adequate social security benefits;

(5) free association in unions, including the right *not* to join, and the right to strike;

(6) nondiscriminatory access to vocational training;

(7) equal treatment for women and men;

(8) development of rights to access to information, and rights of consultation and participation;

(9) satisfactory health and safety conditions at work;

(10) for the young, a minimum employment age of 15, substantial limitations on night work for those under 18, and start-up vocational training rights;

(11) for retirees, the right to assistance "as needed" and a decent standard of living; and

(12) for the disabled, assistance to integrate socially and professionally.

The Charter is to be implemented immediately by the member states in "accordance with national practices." In addition, for each item listed above, Community legislation is anticipated by the end of 1992.

Equal Pay for Equal Work

Article 119 is probably the most prominent element in the Community's social policy. It is derived from International Labor Organization Convention No. 100 which three EC states, including France, had adopted by 1957. The French were rightfully proud of this tradition of nondiscrimination between the sexes on pay. They also appreciated that gender-based inequality in pay in other member states could harm the ability of their companies to compete. Article 119 thus enshrines the principle that men and women shall receive equal pay for equal work. For these purposes, "pay" is defined in Article 119 to mean wages or salary, and any other consideration in cash or kind, received directly or indirectly respecting employment. "Equal pay without discrimination based on sex" means that piece rate payment must be calculated on the same units of measurement and that time rates must be equal for the same job.

Article 119 has been the subject of voluminous EC legislation and litigation. It applies, quite appropriately, to the Community as an employer. *Sabbatini, née Bertoni v. European Parliament* (1972) Eur.Comm.Rep. 345; *Razzouk v. Commission* (1984) Eur.Comm.Rep. 1509 (working conditions). Early on, the Court of Justice decided that the Article 119 on equal pay for equal work is directly effective EC law. *Defrenne v. Sabena* (1976) Eur. Comm.Rep. 455. This decision allows individuals throughout the community to challenge pay discrimination in public and private sector jobs. The ruling in *Defrenne* was applied prospectively by the Court of Justice so as to avoid large numbers of lawsuits for back pay. There is no express authority for the Court to rule prospectively.

In *Defrenne,* a flight attendant for Sabena Airlines was able to allege illegal discrimination in pay and pension benefits (as a form deferred pay) to stewards and stewardesses on the basis of EC law before a Belgian work tribunal. Indeed, Community law in this area enshrines the principle of "comparable worth," a most controversial issue in American employment law. Women who are paid less than men performing work of less worth may claim relief under Article 119. *Murphy v. An Bord Telecom Eireann* (1988) Eur.Comm.Rep. 673. The harder question is how to determine what constitutes "equal work" requiring equal pay under Article 119. For example, does secretarial work equal custodial work? Does the work of an airline attendant equal that of an airline mechanic?

Council Directive 75/117 complements Article 119. It makes the principle of equal pay apply to work of *equal value* (to the employer). This mandates establishment of nondiscriminatory job classifications to measure the comparable worth of one job with another. The Commission successfully enforced Directive 75/117 in a prosecution before the European Court of Justice against the United Kingdom. The Sex Discrimination Act of 1975, adopted expressly to fulfill Article 119 obligations, did not meet EC standards because employers could block the introduction of job classification systems. *Commission v. United Kingdom* (1982) Eur.Comm.Rep. 2601. Danish law's failure to cover nonunionized workers also breached the EC equal pay directive. *Commission v. Denmark* (1986) 1 Common Mkt.L.Rep. 44. But its implementation under German law, notably by constitutional provisions, sufficed to meet Community stan-

dards. *Commission v. Germany* (1986) 2 Common
Mkt.L.Rep. 588.

When a woman succeeds a man in a particular
position within a company (here a warehouse man-
ager), she is entitled to equal pay absent a satisfactory explanation not based upon gender. *McCar-
thays Ltd. v. Smith* (1980) Eur.Comm.Rep. 1275.
The same is true of part-time (female) workers
doing the same job as full-time (male) workers.
Jenkins v. Kingsgate (Clothing Productions) Ltd.
(1981) Eur.Comm.Rep. 911. Free travel to railway
employees upon retirement cannot go only to men.
Garland v. British Rail Engineering, Ltd. (1982)
Eur.Comm.Rep. 359. And "pay" includes retirement benefits paid upon involuntary dismissal,
which cannot be discriminatory. *Barber v. The
Guardian Royal Exchange Assurance Group* (1990)
Eur.Comm.Rep. ___ (Case 262/88). It also includes
employer-paid pension benefits which cannot be for
men only. *Worringham and Humphreys v. Lloyds
Bank Ltd.* (1981) Eur.Comm.Rep. 767. In this decision the Court refused to remove the retroactive
effect of its judgment suggesting that *Defrenne* was
adequate notice of the direct effect of Article 119
upon employers.

The principle of equal pay for equal work has
been extended to equal treatment regarding access
to employment, vocational training and promotion,
and working conditions (e.g. retirement deadlines).
Council Directive 76/207 (issued under Article
235). This directive prohibits discrimination based

upon sex, family or marital status. Equal treatment must be extended to small and household businesses. *Commission v. United Kingdom* (1983) Eur.Comm.Rep. 3431. Dutch Law compulsorily retiring women at age 60 and men at age 65 violated the directive. *Beets–Proper v. Van Lanschot Bankiers NV* (1986) Eur.Comm.Rep. 773. See Council Directive 86/378 (equal treatment regarding pensions). Women cannot be refused employment because they are pregnant even if the employer will suffer financial losses during maternity leave. *Dekker v. Stichting Vormingscentrum voor Jong Volwassenen Plus* (1990) Eur.Comm.Rep. ___ (Case C–177/88). Maternity leave benefits for women, however, need not be extended to men. *Hoffman v. Barmer Ersatzkasse* (1984) Eur.Comm.Rep. 3047; *Commission v. Italy* (1983) Eur.Comm.Rep. 3273 (adoption leave benefits). The dismissal of a woman because of repeated absences owing to sickness is lawful provided the same absences would lead to the dismissal of men. *Hertz and Aldi Marked* (1990) Eur.Comm.Rep. ___ (Case C–179/88).

Equality also governs social security entitlements (Council Directive 79/7) such as disability or caring for the disabled pay. *Drake v. Chief Adjudication Officer* (1986) Eur.Comm.Rep. 1995. Social security benefits cannot be based upon marital status. Id. Women police officers cannot be denied arms when men are not, even in the interest of "public safety" and "national security." *Johnston v. Chief Constable* (1986) Eur.Comm.Rep. 1651. On national security exceptions to the Treaty of

Rome, see generally Articles 223–225. Equal treatment requires the elimination of preferences based upon gender in laws governing collectively bargained employment agreements. *Commission v. France* (1990) Eur.Comm.Rep. ___ (Case 312/86) (preferences for women must be removed).

Although Article 119 on equal pay is directly effective EC law binding upon public and private employers throughout the Community (*Defrenne*), it is not yet clear to what degree the equal treatment directive cited above has that effect. Clearly this directive is binding on the member states and public corporations as employers. See especially *Marshall v. Southampton and South–West Hampshire Area Health Authority (Teaching)* (1986) Eur. Comm.Rep. 723 (discriminatory retirement ages unlawful); *Foster v. British Gas* (1990) Eur.Comm. Rep. ___ (Case 188/89). The private sector must comply after national implementing legislation is adopted, but if that legislation is deficient the only remedy is a prosecution of the member state by the Commission. See *Duke v. GEC Reliance Ltd.* (1988) All Eng.Rep. 626 (discriminatory retirement ages lawful). There is a trend within the jurisprudence of the Court of Justice towards recognition of a broad human right of equality before the law. This is evidenced in a number of Article 119 cases, which suggests that the private sector will eventually be bound by all Community legislation on equal pay and equal treatment even in the absence of or in spite of national implementing law.

European Investment Bank

Articles 129 and 130 of the Treaty of Rome established the nonprofit European Investment Bank (EIB). A Protocol on the EIB was annexed to the Treaty. The bank has played a major role in funding regional development projects within the Community and external development projects under the Lomé Convention and other EC trade agreements (see Chapter 6.)

The Board of Governors of the EIB consists of the Ministers of Finance of the member states. This board oversees the bank's capital resources and loan activities. In general, EIB loans are only made to private EC entities when other sources of financing are also available and the member state where the investment is located guarantees the loan. The European Investment Bank has raised substantial sums in the international money markets.

Common Agricultural Policy

The Treaty of Rome establishes the basic principles governing what is perhaps the most controversial of all Community policies, the Common Agricultural Program (CAP). The inclusion of agricultural trade in the Treaty of Rome was a critical element to the politics of the Community and remains largely without precedent in other regional economic treaties throughout the world. For many reasons, including the desire for self-sufficiency in food and the protection of farmers, free trade in agricultural products is an extremely sensitive issue. When the Common Market was established in 1957, France and Italy had substantial farming communities, many of which were family based and politically powerful. Both countries envisioned that free trade in agricultural products could threaten the livelihoods of these people. The solution, as outlined in Articles 38 through 42 of the Treaty of Rome, was to set up a "common organization of agricultural markets."

The objectives of the CAP stated in the Treaty of Rome include the increase of productivity, the maintenance of a fair standard of living for the agricultural community, the stabilization of markets and the provision of consumer goods at reasonable prices. It has not proved possible to accommodate all of these objectives. Consumer interests have generally lost out to farmers' incomes and trading company profits. Target prices for some commodities (e.g. sugar, dairy products and grain) are established and supported through Community market purchases at "intervention levels". "Variable import levies" (tariffs) are periodically changed to ensure that cheaper imports do not disrupt CAP prices. External protection of this type is also extended to meat and eggs. Fruit, vegetables and wine are subject to quality controls which limit their flow into the market.

The European Agricultural Guidance and Guarantee Fund (better known by its French initials as

FEOGA) channels the Community agricultural budget into export refunds, intervention purchases, storage, and structural adjustment. Agricultural policy regulations cannot discriminate against like or substitute products. Article 40(3). But the bias towards producers, not consumers, in the CAP has been consistently upheld by the Court of Justice. *Germany v. Commission* (1963) Eur.Comm.Rep. 131; *Balkan–Import–Export GmbH v. Hauptzollamt Berlin–Packhof* (1973) Eur.Comm.Rep. 1091 (CAP measures valid unless "obviously unreasonable" consumer prices produced).

Agricultural goods, like industrial products, can trigger free movement litigation. These issues are often raised under Articles 30–36, covered in Chapter 4. In one case, for example, the Court of Justice suggested that UK animal health regulations were a disguised restraint on Community trade in poultry and eggs. *Commission v. United Kingdom* (1982) Eur.Comm.Rep. 2793 (Newcastle disease). As with industrial goods, if the real aim is to block imports, such regulations are unlawful measures of equivalent effect to a quota. On the other hand, the United Kingdom could establish a Pear and Apple Development Council for purposes of technical advice, promotional campaigns (not intended to discourage competitive imports), and common quality standards for its members. But it could not impose a mandatory fee to finance such activities. *The Apple and Pear Development Council v. K.J. Lewis, Ltd.* (1983) Eur.Comm.Rep. 4083.

Apart from variable tariff protection, CAP quality control regulations can serve to keep foreign agricultural products from entering the EC market. For example, the ban on beef hormones adopted by qualified majority vote in the late 1980s stirred opposition internally. *United Kingdom v. Council* (1988) Eur.Comm.Rep. 855. In the United States, the beef hormones legislation was vehemently opposed by the White House, but accepted by the renegade Texas Department of Agriculture which offered as much hormone-free beef to the Community as it would buy. The Texas offer delighted the EC Commissioner on Agriculture who rarely has a U.S. ally and is said to have wired: "I accept."

European Community agricultural trade restraints are of enormous consequence to North American exporters. Equally significant are EC "export refunds" on agricultural commodities, refunds that affect the opportunities of North American exporters in other parts of the world. The United States has consistently argued (at times successfully) that these refunds violate the GATT rules on subsidies while at the same time increasing its own export subsidies on agricultural goods. The result has been an agricultural "trade war" between the U.S. and the EC. Each side has sought to outspend the other on agricultural export subsidies in a market that has been wonderful to buyers. Major attempts at a resolution or at least diminishment of the agricultural trade war were undertaken in the Uruguay Round of GATT negotiations during the late 1980s and early 1990s. These efforts have not proved successful to date.

A veritable maze of Community legislation and case law governs the CAP. For many years, special agricultural "monetary compensation amounts" (MCAs) have been collected at national borders, greatly contributing to the failure to achieve a Europe without internal trade frontiers. It was not until 1987 that firm arrangements were realized to dismantle the MCA system. In most years, the net effect of the CAP is to raise food prices in the EC substantially above world price levels. The CAP has meant that agriculture is heavily subsidized. Indeed, it continues to consume the lion's share of the EC budget and at times seems like a spending policy that is out of control.

The Common Agricultural Policy does include a variety of "structural" programs intended to reduce the size of the Community's farm population, increase the efficiency of its production and hold down prices. These programs have involved retirement incentives, land reallocations, and training for other occupations. There has been a gradual reduction in the number of Community's farmers over the years. In 1988, the Council adopted rules designed ultimately to reduce agricultural expenditures by linking total expenditures to the Community's rate of economic growth, establishing automatic price cuts when production ceilings are reached, and creating land set-aside and early retirement programs for farmers. In the main, however, like the United States, the European Community seems unable to stabilize the level of its agricultural subsidies. This results in overproduction ("butter mountains," "wine lakes") and frequent commodity trade wars. A significant amount of fraud to obtain CAP subsidy payments has occurred. In 1989, the House of Lords Select Committee on the European Community released a scathing report on subsidy abuses entitled "Fraud Against the Community." Others legitimately farm marginal land with lots of fertilizer. The excess produce is stored, used in social welfare programs and frequently "dumped" in cheap sales to the Soviets, Eastern European nations, and elsewhere.

France and Italy, in the early years of the EC, became major beneficiaries of CAP subsidies. West Germany, with a minimal agricultural sector, was the primary payor under the program. It, in turn, principally benefitted from the custom union provisions establishing free trade in industrial goods. Hence a basic tradeoff was established in 1957 by the Treaty of Rome. France and Italy would receive substantial agricultural subsidies out of the Community's budget while West Germany gained access for its industrial goods to their markets. Britain, like Germany, sees itself as a net payor under the CAP. It has repeatedly been able to negotiate special compensatory adjustments as a consequence. Greece, Spain, Portugal and Ireland, on the other hand, looked forward eagerly to EC membership as a means to CAP subsidies. These countries, along with unified Germany, are often the least efficient producers of agricultural products. As such, they stand to lose the most if the CAP is substantially replaced by market forces.

Despite its incredible cost, the CAP remains one of the political and economic cornerstones of the Community. External protests from North America notwithstanding, the CAP is unlikely to disappear. The provocative question much debated in the Uruguay Round of GATT negotiations is whether a mutually satisfiable reduction in the level of North American and European Community subsidies to agriculture can be achieved.

Common Fisheries Policy

Unlike agriculture, the Community is a net importer of fish and fish products. Nevertheless, a "common organization" for the fisheries' market in the EC has also been created. Council Regulation 2796/81. Following the lead of other nations, the Community extended its exclusive economic zone to 200 miles offshore in 1977. The most controversial feature of the Common Fisheries Policy (CFP) is the requirement that member states open their waters beyond six (sometimes twelve) miles to each other's fishing fleets to the limit of a "total allowable catch (TAC)" fixed by the Council. The TACs and related technical measures (e.g. minimum fish net sizes) are basically conservation measures.   TACs have even been zero for the evanescent herring in extreme years.

Each TAC is divided into member state fishing quotas by the nations where the fish are found. Those states are authorized to close a fishery when a quota is exhausted.   Fishery quotas are exchangeable as between the member states.   Each state is required to record all landings or transfers at sea which are deducted from the country quotas. Commission review and inspection of these records and decisions is undertaken to ensure compliance with Fisheries Policy rules.

Numerous cases have come before the European Court of Justice enforcing rights of entry and challenging discriminatory quotas.   *Commission v. Ireland* (1978) Eur.Comm.Rep. 417;   *Regina v. Kirk* (1984) Eur.Comm.Rep. 2689.   Even the practice of "quota hopping" by registering boats under the national laws of other member states must be tolerated.   *Regina v. Secretary of State for Transport* (1990) Eur.Comm.Rep. ___ (Case C–213/89).

The Fisheries Policy was initiated by the original six EC states in 1970 in anticipation of the enlargement of the Community to include fishery-rich nations (for whom it has become part of the price of membership).   This helps explain why many people in nations like Norway and Iceland shudder at the prospect of joining the Community.   The Common Fisheries Policy also governs the marketing and price of fish in the Community.   The Commission sets "official withdrawal prices" for various types of fish. These prices act as a floor to the market. When they are reached, fish producers can withdraw up to twenty percent of their catch and receive Community subsidies. Fish withdrawn in this manner cannot be used for human consumption. As in the agricultural area, the Community can grant export refunds to aid the sale of fish abroad, and it can protect the withdrawal price levels by limiting imports. Structural relief measures have emphasized reductions in the Community's fishing fleet and subsidies for fish farming. The European Community has numerous international fishery agreements, including one with the United States which primarily accesses U.S. waters and "surplus fish" to EC boats and opens the Common Market to American exports.

CHAPTER 6

EXTERNAL TRADE RELATIONS AND OPPORTUNITIES

Articles 110–116 of the Treaty of Rome vest in the European Community control over external commercial relations. This is referred to as the Community's "common commercial policy," and it covers both imports and exports. Article 113 provides some illustrative examples of the wide scope of this policy, including tariffs, quotas, trade agreements, export controls, dumping and subsidies. The Common Commercial Policy can involve the application of international boycott sanctions. The EC adhered to such sanctions against Rhodesia in 1976, Iran in 1980, and Argentina and the Soviet Union in 1982, and Iraq in 1990. The Community also participates in the United Nations Conference on Trade and Development (UNCTAD). It implements UNCTAD's integrated commodity program as well as the Cocoa, Tin, Jute, Natural Rubber and Coffee Agreements. The EC supports the International Tropical Timber Organization, the U.N. Conference on Copper and the International Cotton Advisory Committee.

The European Court of Justice has ruled that the member states cannot enact external commercial policy laws without "specific authorization" from the Community. *Criel and Schou v. Procureur de la République* (1976) Eur.Comm.Rep.1921. In this field, the Community should be supreme. Operationally speaking, however, this is not always the case. The following discussion of national import quotas, voluntary export restraints and "mixed" EC trade agreements illustrates this. Surrendering national sovereignty over external commercial relations is a most sensitive area.

Common Customs Law

The Common Customs Tariff (CCT) (also known as "TARIC") has been steadily reduced over the years as a result of the GATT tariff Rounds. After the Tokyo Round (1978), EC tariffs on manufactured goods dropped on average to about 8 percent. See Council Regulation 2658/87 (Schedule of Customs Duties). Member states may not alter the Common Customs Tariff by unilaterally imposing additional duties. *Sociaal Fonds voor de Diamant Arbeiders v. NG Indiamex* (1973) Eur.Comm.Rep. 1609.

The Community follows the Customs Cooperation Council harmonized nomenclature in its customs classification system. Council Regulations 1445/72, 2658/87. This generally corresponds to the classifications found in the Harmonized Tariff System (HTS) adopted by the United States in 1988. The valuation of goods for purposes of assessing the CCT is done according to the General Agreement on Tariffs and Trade (GATT) Customs

Valuation Code. Council Regulation 1224/80. This means that in most instances the transaction value is the basis for CCT assessments. See *Hauptzollamt Hamburg–Ericus v. Van Houten International GmbH* (1986) Eur.Comm.Rep. 447 (Costs of weighing imports on arrival excluded from transaction value); *Hauptzollamt Scheinfurt v. Mainfrucht Obstverwertung* (1985) Eur.Comm.Rep. 3909 (Costs of internal EC transport that are separately invoiced excluded).

New members are always phased into the EC customs union rules and tariffs over a transitional period. Portugal and Spain, for example, will not be fully aligned until the end of 1992. Thereafter, United States exporters to any one of the twelve EC nations will pay the same customs duties, regardless of the port of entry. Once U.S. goods enter an EC nation, in principle they may be freely traded inside the Community. Articles 9 and 10 of Treaty of Rome. In contrast, when U.S. goods enter an EFTA nation the absence of a common external tariff means that they cannot be freely traded within that group.

Differing import quotas on external trade continue to be applied by national governments, as in the case of automobiles from Japan. These quotas, in turn, cause "deflection of trade" restraints to be applied *internally* so that the external quotas cannot be avoided by shipping goods into quota-free EC nations. Such restraints, at least in theory, should only exist if authorized by the Commission and not be more onerous than necessary. See Articles 113–115 and *Criel and Schou v. Procureur de la Républic* (1976) Eur.Comm.Rep. 1921. One goal of the 1992 campaign is to harmonize all European Community import quotas. This should eliminate the need for internal licensing controls. Another is the adoption of a Common Customs Code. The Code, for example, will determine where goods originate.

As a general matter, the Community determines the origin of goods based upon where the "last substantial process or operation" that was economically justified was performed. Council Regulation 802/68. A process or operation is "substantial," for these purposes, only if the resulting product has its own properties and composition. *Ubersee-handel v. Handelskammer Hamburg* (1977) Eur. Comm.Rep. 41. Cleaning, grinding, grading and packaging a raw material do not meet this standard. Id. "Rules of origin" are critical to duty free entry of goods from Lomé Convention, Mediterranean Basin or GSP developing nations (infra). Many goods originate for tariff preference purposes in a beneficiary country only if 40–45 percent of their value was added locally. Special rules of origin and EC content requirements apply to high-technology products like printed circuit boards, integrated circuits and the like. These rules often have the effect of transferring technology and production to the EC. Processed EFTA exports originate therein and may be freely traded to the EC under rules that emphasize a change in tariff category.   The many variations on the origin of goods contained in Community law and EC trade agreements make these rules particularly complex.

The common customs law of the European Community also includes Council Regulation 3842/86 targeting counterfeit goods.   Such goods may not be imported into the Community, nor freely circulated within it.   They are subject to seizure by national customs authorities.   The definition of counterfeit goods contained in this regulation refers to goods bearing marks without authorization. Thus the regulation does not apply to trade in "gray market goods" (those produced abroad under license).

Generalized Tariff Preferences (GSP)

The Community participates in the generalized system of tariff preferences (GSP) initiated within the GATT to give duty free access to industrial markets for selected goods coming from the developing world.   This policy is implemented in the Community's Common Customs Tariff (CCT) regulations.   Poland and Hungary were added to the Community's GSP program in 1990 in recognition of restructuring and developmental problems in their economies.   Most of Eastern Europe seems likely to be similarly treated.

Approximately 150 non-European developing nations now benefit from the GSP trade preferences of the EC, including China.   Goods from most of the Four Dragons of East Asia (South Korea, Taiwan, Hong Kong and Singapore) still qualify. However, South Korean goods have been disqualified since 1987 because of inadequate intellectual property protection in that nation. In contrast, all of these countries were "graduated" (i.e. no longer treated as developing nations) out of the United States' GSP program in 1989.

The EC system of generalized tariff preferences is selectively applied when about 130 "sensitive products" are involved. In other words, there are limitations (quotas and tariff ceilings) on duty free access to the Common Market if the goods compete with Community manufacturers. However, these GSP limitations do not apply to products already receiving duty free access under the Lomé Convention or the Community's Mediterranean Policy (infra). Thus, nations that are covered by the latter trade rules still obtain some margin of preference over other third world GSP beneficiaries.

Escape Clause Proceedings and Voluntary Trade Restraints

Community commercial policy regulations establish common rules for imports and exports. Council Regulation 288/82. These rules authorize "escape clause" measures to curb exports in the face of shortages, or to curb surging imports that threaten serious injury to similar EC products. Special rules apply to escape clause proceedings when the imports are from state-trading countries.

Council Regulations 1765/82, 1766/82. European Community escape clause law on imports is derived from Article XIX of the GATT. Its counterparts in U.S. law are found in Sections 201 and 406 of the Trade Act of 1974 (19 U.S.C. §§ 2251, 2436).

The protective measures authorized by the EC escape clause regulations may include tariffs, quotas and, more controversially, agreements with exporting nations to voluntarily control the flow of certain goods into the Community *or* particular EC nations. Such "voluntary export restraints" (VERs) have been used by the Community on consumer electronics, machine tools, food products and steel imports. The Community itself "voluntarily" restrains the export of steel to the United States. Another variation on the VER theme has been the negotiation of private industry-to-industry export restraint agreements. These agreements have been undertaken at the national level so as to avoid Common Commercial Policy rules and Community authority. Though legally suspect (see *ERTA,* infra), they continue to function for footwear, automobiles and electrical equipment.

One goal of the 1992 campaign is to replace national quotas and VERs with common EC import controls. This is already done at the Community level in the case of textiles under the MultiFibre Arrangement. The Community's overall quota is divided into subquotas managed by each member state. The subquotas are not always uniform, as with textiles where they are divided on grounds which reflect the degree of sensitivity to such imports of each country. In such instances, national import licenses (used to ensure that no end runs are achieved around the national allocations) have been up upheld. *Tezi Textiel BV v. Minister for Economic Affairs* (1986) Eur.Comm.Rep. 887 and 993. Such EC trade restraints are inconsistent with the 1992 goal of a Europe without internal frontiers.

Illicit Commercial Practices

Another emerging area of the Common Commercial Policy was commenced in 1984 in response to efforts (ultimately withdrawn) by the Reagan Administration at limiting participation of European licensees of American technology in the Siberian natural gas pipeline project. This is sometimes called the "new commercial policy" and is embodied in Council Regulation 2641/84. This regulation covers situations not subject to escape clause, dumping or subsidy proceedings (infra). It concerns "illicit commercial practices" by foreign *countries* and roughly approximates Section 301 of the U.S. Trade Act of 1974 (19 U.S.C. § 2411).

When countries engage in practices that are incompatible with international law (e.g. the GATT) or incompatible with "generally accepted rules," and threaten injury to a Community industry, the EC may undertake international dispute settlement procedures (if appropriate) or unilateral retaliatory measures. The latter can include raising tariffs, suspending trade concessions or imposing quotas. Private parties can file complaints under the "A" procedures with the Commission to initiate examination of allegedly illicit and injurious commercial practices. Negative decisions by the Commission upon "A" complaints may be appealed to the Court of Justice. *FEDIOL v. Commission* (1989) Eur.Com.Rep. ___ (Case 70/87). Under the so-called "B" procedures found in Regulation 2641/84, the EC may assert its rights under international law or generally accepted rules if it wishes to challenge the commercial practices of other nations. In these proceedings, full exercise of the Community's rights are at issue, not injury to an EC industry nor the legality of the foreign country practices. The same remedies apply to both "A" and "B" illicit commercial practice proceedings.

Antidumping Duties

Another part of the Common Commercial Policy concerns unfair trading practices applied to goods exported to the Community. The two most important areas of law here concern dumping and subsidies. Regulation 2423/88. Similar rules apply to unfair shipping services used to bring goods to the Community. Council Regulation 4057/86. In recent years, EC use of antidumping proceedings to protect its market has risen substantially. Nearly half of these proceedings involve goods from non-market economy states (NMEs). Apart from

NMEs, Japanese and United States exports have most frequently been involved in Community antidumping proceedings. Many of these proceedings are settled by promises of the exporters to raise prices and refrain from "dumping." The standing of most exporters and complainants to challenge EC dumping decisions has been affirmed by the European Court. See Chapter 3. Such persons would otherwise lack any possible judicial remedy. Importers, on the other hand, have remedies in the national courts of the member states and are therefore generally unable to challenge EC dumping decisions directly before the European Court. *Alusuisse Italia v. Council and Commission* (1982) Eur.Comm.Rep. 3463.

Dumping involves selling abroad at a price that is less than the price used to sell the same goods at home (the "normal" or "fair" value). To be unlawful, dumping must threaten or cause material injury to an industry in the export market, the market where prices are lower. Dumping is recognized by most of the trading world as an unfair practice (akin to price discrimination as an antitrust offense). Dumping is the subject of a special GATT code which establishes the basic parameters for determining when dumping exists, what constitutes material injury and the remedy of antidumping tariffs. See the Agreement on Implementation of Article VI of the GATT (1979) ("Antidumping Code"). Such tariffs amount to the margin of the dump, i.e. the difference in the price charged at home and (say) the European Community.

Although much of the EC law on antidumping duties is consistent with the GATT code, and therefore generally conforms to American law on the subject (19 U.S.C. § 1673), some interesting twists have been applied. One of the most controversial is the so-called "screwdriver plant regulation" aimed mostly at Japanese exporters. Council Regulation 1761/87. These exporters, when faced with antidumping duties on top of the Common Customs Tariff, began to assemble consumer electronics and other products inside the Community using Japanese made components plus a screwdriver. The net effect of the Community's regulatory response is to reimpose dumping duties on these products unless at least 40 percent of the components originate outside the source country (Japan). The Japanese have challenged this regulation within the GATT.

Similar results have been achieved in certain cases when the Japanese export goods assembled in America to the EC. See Council Regulation 3205/88 (photocopiers) (assembly does not involve a substantial operation or process so as to alter origin of goods). Accord, *Brother International GmbH v. Hauptzollamt Gieben* (1989) Eur.Comm.Rep. ___ (Case 26/88) (suggesting typewriters assembled in Taiwan originate from Japan unless assembly causes the use to which components are put to become definite and the goods to be given their specific qualities). In the photocopiers case, the goods had actually qualified as American for purposes of U.S. procurement rules. This origin was rejected by the EC.

Some have asserted that the EC employs a double standard when calculating export prices and normal values for dumping law purposes. They claim that the EC has cloaked itself in the technical obscurity of the law so as to systematically inflate normal values and deflate export prices, thereby causing more dumping to be found. Use of asymmetrical methods to reach these determinations has been upheld by the European Court. *Miniature Bearings, Nippon Seiko v. Council* (1987) Eur.Comm.Rep. 1923. Additional criticism has been levied against the Commission's refusal to disclose the information upon which it relies in making critical dumping law decisions. Much of this information is admittedly confidential, but could be released under a protective order.

Countervailing Duties

The internal trade problems associated with member state "aids" (subsidies) to enterprises located inside the EC have already been discussed in connection with the Community's competition policy. See Chapter 5. Many of the same problems re-emerge in the context of the Common Commercial Policy. This time, however, the source of the subsidies are governments located *outside* the Common Market. Many subsidies, especially export subsidies, are treated as an unfair trading practice under the GATT. As with dumping, there is a separate GATT code which creates the ground rules in this area. See the Agreement on Interpretation and Application of Articles VI, XVI and XXIII of the GATT (1979) ("Subsidies Code"). This Code is implemented as a matter of Common Commercial Policy by the EC and therefore parallels similar law in the United States. 19 U.S.C. § 1671.

The types of "subsidies" subject to "countervailing duties" are in great dispute internationally. European Community regulations simply illustrate, without limitation, what constitutes a countervailable subsidy in a long listing of export subsidies. Council Regulation 2423/88. Certain domestic manufacturing, production, and transportation subsidies can also be countervailed if they (like export subsidies) threaten material injury to an EC industry. The European Court of Justice has said that the concept of a countervailable subsidy presupposes "the grant of an economic advantage through a charge on the public account." *FEDIOL v. Commission* (1988) Eur.Comm.Rep. 4193. For a domestic subsidy to be countervailable, it must have "sectoral specificity" (seek to grant an advantage only to certain firms). For an export subsidy to be countervailable, it must specifically benefit the imported product. Id. As with dumping proceedings, the Commission makes these judgments provisionally and the Council renders final judgment (issued as a CCT regulation). The amount of the extra EC duty corresponds to the amount of the subsidy.

Trade Relations

Article 116 of the Treaty of Rome contains a commitment to proceed within international economic organizations on matters of particular interest to the EC only by common action through Commission proposals adopted by a qualified majority vote in the Council of Ministers. Other provisions of the Treaty reinforce the general transfer of sovereignty over external trade policy achieved in Part III of the Treaty. Part IV, for example, details the Community's trade relations with many former colonies of the EC nations. Article 238 in Part VI anticipates the conclusion of "association agreements" linking favored nations to the EC. Most importantly, Article 229 gives the Commission the power to represent the Community within the General Agreement on Tariffs and Trade (GATT). This representation affords EC nations much more bargaining power over tariffs and other trade issues with Canada, the United States and Japan than they ever had individually. Throughout the GATT negotiating "rounds," most recently the Uruguay Round, the EC has become a force to be reckoned with. Many attribute the failure of the Uruguay Round to reach closure in December of 1990 to EC recalcitrance over agricultural trade barriers necessary to the preservation of its Common Agricultural Policy (see Chapter 5).

Trade between the United States and the European Community is voluminous, roughly in balance and increasingly fractious. While the focal point in recent years has been agricultural trade, especially the problem of export subsidies, there are many contentious issues. For example, Airbus subsidies are said to threaten Boeing, and the 1992 legislative campaign may erect a "Fortress Europe" in banking, insurance, broadcasting and other areas. There is a general concern in North America that Europe is turning inward and protective.

The Community, for its part, has begun imitating the United States' practice of issuing annual reports voicing *its* objections to U.S. trade barriers and unfair practices. The 1991 report targets Section 301 of the Trade Act of 1974 (19 U.S.C. § 2411 as amended). In recent years, the U.S. has invoked Section 301 in trade disputes with the EC over the use of animal hormones and EC regulation of oil seeds. The Community perceives Section 301 to be a unilateral retaliatory mechanism that runs counter to multilateral resolution of trade disputes through the GATT. This perception has not stopped the Community from partially duplicating this mechanism in EC law protections against "illicit commercial practices" (supra).

The 1991 report also highlights the problem (from the EC perspective) of the diversity of state and local regulation of procurement, product standards, the environment, financial services and taxation. U.S. critics of Europe's legislative diversity could not have said it better. Perhaps both sides are headed for stronger central government regulation of trade-impacting measures. See especially the discussion of EC product standards and liability law in Chapter 5. Each has a lot at stake in trade with the other. The tough question is whether the GATT or other dispute resolution procedures can be made to work so as to preserve mutually beneficial trade relations between the Community and North America.

The European Community's trade relations with Japan are less voluminous, less in balance and (at least superficially) less fractious than with the United States. Japan runs a growing surplus in its trade with the EC, but the amount is smaller than the huge surplus it accumulates in trading with the States. Many Europeans speak quietly and with determination about their intent to avoid the "United States example" in their trade relations with Japan. Less quietly, some national governments have imposed rigorous quotas on the importation of Japanese autos and instituted demanding local content requirements for Japanese cars assembled in Europe. The Community, for its part, has frequently invoked antidumping proceedings against Japanese goods and demonstrated a willingness to create arcane rules of origin that promote its interests at the expense of the Japanese. At the GATT level, however, Japan and the EC share common concerns about retaining their agricultural support systems. These concerns place them in opposition to the U.S. and others who seek to liberalize world trade in agricultural products.

Trade Agreements

Articles 113, 114, 228 and 238 of the Treaty of Rome establish the procedures used in the negotiation of most trade agreements with the EC. Basically, the Commission proposes and then receives authorization from the Council to open negotiations with third countries or within an international organization. When the Commission reaches tentative agreement, conclusion or ratification must take place in the Council after consulting the Parliament. The Council votes by qualified majority on Common Commercial Policy agreements (Article 114). These include most GATT agreements. The Council votes unanimously on association agreements (Article 238 infra) and on international agreements undertaken via Article 235 (e.g. environmental conventions prior to 1987).

An opinion of the European Court as to the compatibility with the Treaty of Rome of the proposed agreement and the procedures used to reach it may be obtained in advance at the request of the Commission, Council or a member state. There are no public proceedings when such opinions are sought. Use of this advance ruling procedure may forestall judicial review at a later date of the compatibility of Community agreements with the Treaty of Rome. See ECJ Opinion 1/75 (1975) Eur.Comm.Rep. 1355 (Local Cost Standards).

Article 210 of the Treaty of Rome conveys "legal personality" to the Community. This gives it the power to enter into international commitments. This is the case by implication even when there is no express Treaty authorization to enter into international agreements necessary to achieve internal Common Market objectives. ECJ Opinion 1/76 (1977) Eur.Comm.Rep. 741 (Inland Waterways). A well known decision of the European Court holds the scope of the Community's trade agreements power to be coextensive with all *effective* surrenders of national sovereignty accomplished under the Treaty of Rome. *Commission v. Council* (1971) Eur.Comm.Rep. 263 (the "*ERTA*" decision). Thus, if an internal economic policy matter is governed by existing EC law, the external aspects of that policy are (either expressly or *by implication*) exclusively within the Community's competence.

As a rule, member states may not negotiate trade treaties in EC-occupied fields. They may do so on a transitional basis in areas where the Community lacks authority or (less clearly) has not effectively implemented its authority. For example, in the early 1970s the EC had not developed an effective overall energy policy, although it clearly had competence in the coal and nuclear fields. Thus, the International Energy Agreement achieved through the Organization for Economic Cooperation and Development (OECD) in 1975 after the first oil shocks is not an EC agreement. In contrast, the Community clearly had competence in the field of export credits. OECD arrangements in this area are exclusively the province of the Community with no residual or parallel authority in the member states. ECJ Opinion 1/75 (1975) Eur.Comm.Rep. 1355 (Local Cost Standards).

The *ERTA* decision of the European Court, combined with the ever expanding internal competence of the Community, leaves relatively little room for national governments to enter into trade agreements. Several decisions suggest that the Community's external authority parallels its internal powers even if it has not effectively implemented those powers. *Kramer et al.* (1976) Eur.Comm.Rep. 1279 (North Atlantic Fisheries); ECJ Opinion 1/76 (1977) Eur.Comm.Rep. 741 (Inland Waterways). However, recognizing the sensitivities involved, "mixed agreements" negotiated by the Commission (acting on a Council mandate) and representatives of the member states are frequently used. Both the Community and the member states are signatories to such accords. This has been done with the "association agreements" authorized by Article 238 and certain of the Tokyo Round GATT Codes. The Court of Justice has upheld the validity of mixed international agreements and procedures, but suggested that absent special circumstances their use should not occur when the Community's exclusive jurisdiction over external affairs is fully involved. ECJ Opinion 1/78 (1979) Eur.Comm.Rep. 2871 (Natural Rubber Agreement). In other words, mixed procedures should be followed only when the competence to enter into and implement international agreements is in fact shared between the Community and its member states.

Article 234 of Treaty of Rome indicates that most treaties the member states reached prior to joining the EC continue to be valid even if they impact on areas now governed by Community law. Many bilateral treaties of Friendship, Commerce and Navigation fall within this category despite their impact on immigration, employment and investment opportunities. Member states are, however, required to take all appropriate steps (e.g. upon renewal) to eliminate any incompatibilities between national trade agreements and the Treaty of Rome. See generally *Kramer et al.* (1976) Eur. Comm.Rep. 1279 (North Atlantic Fisheries); Council Decision 91/167. Moreover, prior treaties cannot be invoked so as to negate or fail to fulfill Treaty of Rome obligations. *Re Van Wesemael* (1979) Eur.Comm.Rep. 35 (International Labor Organization Convention no ground for member state failure to apply Community law).

Lastly, because the Soviet Union and its Eastern European satellites refused for many years to even recognize the European Community, some bilateral trade and cooperation agreements between those nations and the member states continue in place. It was not until 1988 that official relations between the Community and COMECON were initiated. As more democracy has taken hold, first generation trade and aid agreements have been concluded by the EC with Hungary (1988), Poland (1989),

Czechoslovakia (1989), Bulgaria (1990) and nearly every other Eastern European nation. The Community is actively considering second generation "association agreements" (infra) with several of these countries.

Trade agreements and other international treaties of the European Community are subject to judicial review by the Court of Justice as "acts" of its institutions. See Articles 173, 175 and 177 and Chapter 3. Moreover, such agreements are binding on the member states which must ensure their full implementation. Article 228(2). When the European Court holds international agreements of the Community "directly effective" EC law, individuals may rely upon them in national litigation. See Chapter 3. The direct effects doctrine has led to cases where citizens end up enforcing the trade agreements of the EC despite contrary law of their own or other member state governments. *Bresciani v. Amministrazione Italiana della Finanze* (1976) Eur.Comm.Rep. 129 (Yaoundé Conventions); *Hauptzollamt Mainz v. Kupferberg* (1982) Eur. Comm.Rep. 3641 (EC–Portugal Free Trade Agreement).

Association Agreements—Mediterranean Policy

Article 238 of the Treaty of Rome authorizes the Community to conclude association agreements with other nations, regional groups and international organizations. The Council must act unanimously in adopting association agreements. Since the Single European Act of 1987, association agreements also require Parliamentary assent (which it has threatened to withhold from renewal of the Israeli–EC association agreement unless better treatment of Palestinian exports to the Community is achieved). The network of Community trade relations established by Article 238 association agreements covers much of the globe. Those who are "associated" with the EC usually receive trade and aid preferences which, as a practical matter, discriminate against nonassociates. Arguments about the illegality of such discrimination within the GATT and elsewhere have typically not prevailed.

Article 238 indicates that association agreements involve "*reciprocal* rights and obligations, common action and special procedures" (emphasis added). The reciprocity requirement found in Article 238 mirrors GATT law on nonpreferential trading and free trade area agreements. See Chapter 1. European Community association agreements usually establish wide-ranging but hardly reciprocal trade and economic links. Greece for many years prior to membership was an EC associate. Turkey still is and has been since 1963. These two agreements illustrate the use of association agreements to convey high levels of financial, technical and commercial aid as a preliminary to membership. Another type of association agreement links the remaining EFTA nations with the European Community. These agreements provide for industrial free trade and symbolize an historic reconciliation of the EC and EFTA trading blocks in 1973 when Britain and Denmark switched sides. See Chapter 1.

Still another type of association agreement involves pursuit of what the EC refers to as its "Mediterranean Policy." This policy acknowledges the geographic proximity and importance of Mediterranean basin nations to the Community. The Med is viewed as a European sphere of influence. Most of these association agreements grant trade preferences (including substantial duty free EC entry) and economic aid to Mediterranean nations *without* requiring reciprocal, preferential access for EC goods. Agreements of this type have been concluded with Algeria, Morocco, Tunisia, Egypt, Jordan, Lebanon, Syria, Israel, Yugoslavia, Malta and Cyprus. See Community Agreements with Mediterranean and ACP Countries in the Appendix.

In addition, the European Community has a host of other association agreements based upon most-favored-nation trading, not preferential access. These include agreements with Sri Lanka, Pakistan, Bangladesh, India, the ASEAN group (Thailand, Singapore, Malaysia, The Philippines, Brunei, and Indonesia), the Andean Pact (Bolivia, Colombia, Ecuador, Venezuela, Peru), Argentina, Uruguay, Brazil and Mexico. In 1990, a Cooperation Agreement was signed with the Gulf Council of Arab nations.

The Lomé Conventions

Part IV of the Treaty of Rome, entitled the "association of overseas territories and countries," was intended to preserve the special trading and development preferences that came with "colonial" status. In 1957, France, Belgium, Italy and The Netherlands still had a substantial number of these relationships. Article 133 completely abolished (after a transitional period) Community tariffs on goods coming from associated overseas territories and countries. There is no duty on the part of these regions to reciprocate with duty free access to their markets for EC goods. Although some territories continue to exist (e.g. French territories like Polynesia, New Caledonia, Guadaloupe, Martinique, etc.), most of the once associated overseas colonies are now independent nations. This is true as well for the former colonies of Britain, Denmark, Portugal and Spain (whose remaining territories are also covered by Part IV).

As independence arrived throughout Asia, Africa and elsewhere, new conventions of association were employed by the EC as a form of developmental assistance. The first of these were the Yaoundé Conventions (1964 and 1971) with newly independent French-speaking African states. These conventions were in theory free trade agreements, but the African states could block almost any EC export and the Community in turn could protect itself from agricultural imports that threatened its Common Agricultural Policy. A healthy dollop of financial and technical aid from the Community was thrown into the bargain.

When Britain joined the European Community in 1973, it naturally wished to preserve as many of the Commonwealth trade preferences as it could. The Yaoundé Conventions were already in place favoring former French colonies south of the Sahara. The compromise was the creation of a new convention, the first Lomé Convention (1975), to expand the Yaoundé principles to developing Caribbean and Pacific as well as English-speaking African nations. The fourth Lomé Convention (1990) is now operating and it governs trade and aid between the EC and a large number of African, Caribbean and Pacific (ACP) states. The Lomé nations presently include: Angola, Antigua & Barbuda, Bahamas, Barbados, Belize, Benin, Botswana, Burkina Faso, Burundi, Cameroon, Cape Verde, Central African Republic, Chad, Comoros, Congo, Djibouti, Dominica, Dominican Republic, Equatorial Guinea, Ethiopa, Fiji, Gabon, Gambia, Ghana, Grenada, Guinea, Guinea Bissau, Guyana, Haiti, Ivory Coast, Jamaica, Kenya, Kiribati, Lesotho, Liberia, Madagascar, Malawi, Mali, Mauritania, Mauritius, Mozambique, Namibia, Niger, Nigeria, Papua New Guinea, Rwanda, St. Christopher & Nevis, St. Lucia, St. Vincent & The Grenadines, Sao Tomé & Principe, Senegal, Seychelles, Sierra Leone, Solomon Islands, Somalia, Sudan, Surinam, Swaziland, Tanzania, Togo, Tonga, Trinidad & Tobago, Tuvalu, Uganda, Western Samoa, Vanuatu, Zaire, Zambia and Zimbabwe.

Perhaps the most important feature of this lengthy listing is the developing nations that are *not* Lomé Convention participants. Unless they fall within the Community's Mediterranean Policy (supra), they are apt to perceive the Lomé Conventions as highly discriminatory against their exports and economic interests.

Unlike the Yaoundé Conventions, the Lomé Conventions do not create (even in theory) reciprocal free trading relationships. While the Lomé states retain substantial duty free access to the Common Market, the Community obtains no comparable benefit. The Lomé nations do promise not to discriminate in trading among EC countries and to grant each most-favored-nation benefits. This has meant, in practice, that they are free to block imports from the EC whenever desired. A variety of "development" preferences are also granted by the Community in the Lomé Conventions. These include expensive purchasing obligations on sugar, for example. There is no free movement of persons as between the ACP states and the Community. However, whenever such persons are lawfully resident and working in the other's territories, they must be given national treatment rights.

Most significantly, the Lomé nations now participate in two innovative EC mechanisms designed to stabilize their agricultural and mineral commodity export earnings. These programs are known as STABEX and MINEX (also known as SYSMIN). STABEX covers (*inter alia*) ground nuts, cocoa, coffee, cotton, coconut, palm, rawhides, leather and wood products, and tea. MINEX deals with copper, phosphates, bauxite, alumina, manganese, iron ore, and tin. These programs are an acknowledgement of the economic dependence of many Lomé nations on commodity exports for very large portions of their hard currency earnings.

Some have argued vigorously that STABEX and MINEX perpetuate rather than relieve this dependence. Both programs provide loans and grants in aid to Lomé nations who have experienced significant declines in export earnings because of falling commodity prices, crop failures and the like. The greater the dependency and decline, the larger the EC financial transfers. In 1989, these amounted to 315 million ECU. These sums are not, for the most part, tied to reinvestment in the commodity sectors causing their payment nor to the purchase of Community products or technology. In a world where most development aid is tied (i.e. must usually be spent on the donor's products or projects), STABEX and MINEX represent a different approach. Many Latin American nations have lobbied the United States to create similar mechanisms for their commodities.

The Lomé IV Convention (1990) added several new features. The European Community now financially supports structural adjustments in ACP states, including remedies for balance of payment difficulties, debt burdens, budget deficits and public enterprises. Cultural and social cooperation, trade in services and environmental issues are also addressed. For example, an agreement not to ship toxic and radioactive waste was reached. The Lomé IV Convention builds upon earlier provisions by specifying protected human rights such as equal treatment, civil and political liberty, and economic, social and cultural rights. Financial support from the EC is given to ACP nations that promote human rights.

Duty Free Access to the Common Market

The end-game so far as exporters to the European Community are concerned is unlimited duty free access. Except for raw materials, few North American exports will qualify for such treatment. However, subsidiaries based in developing or EFTA nations may achieve this goal. This is possible because of the Community's adherence to the GSP program, its Mediterranean basin trade agreements, the Lomé Conventions and the industrial free trade treaties with EFTA. It may also be possible to ship goods produced in Eastern European nations duty free into the EC under the "second generation" trade agreements presently being negotiated. All of these topics have been previously discussed. There are, of course, exceptions and controls (quotas, NTBs) that may apply under these programs. Nevertheless, the Common Market is so lucrative that careful study of its external trade rules is warranted.

Such studies can realize unusually advantageous trade situations. For example, many developing nations are Lomé Convention participants or GSP beneficiaries. The goods of some of these nations are also entitled to duty free access to the United States market under the U.S. version of the GSP program (19 U.S.C. § 2461) or the Caribbean Basin Economic Recovery Act (1983) (19 U.S.C. § 2701). A producer strategically located in such a nation (e.g. Jamaica) can have the best of both worlds, duty free access to the European Community and the United States.

Commercial Agents

Council Directive 86/653 coordinates member state laws regarding self-employed commercial agents. This directive was inspired by existing French and German law. In Denmark and Britain new legislation was required for its implementation. From a United States perspective, the directive is remarkably protective of the agent. It is particularly significant because many North American firms do business in Europe through commercial agents.

Directive 86/653 establishes various rights and obligations for commercial agents and principals, e.g. the agent's duty to comply with reasonable instructions and the principal's duty to act in good faith. In the absence of an agreed compensation, customary local practices prevail (and if none, reasonable remuneration). Compensation rights before and after the effective period of the agency contract are specified. Directive 85/653 also establishes when the agent's commission becomes due and payable, as well as the conditions under which it is extinguishable. Agency agreements for fixed periods of time that continue to be performed by both parties upon expiration become contracts for an indefinite period.

An important element concerns the notice and termination rights of the agent. Minimum notice requirements of one month per year of service up to three years, and optional notice requirements up to six months for six years are created. The member states must provide for either a right of indemnification or for damages compensation. The agency agreement cannot waive or otherwise "derogate" these rights. The indemnity cannot exceed one year's remuneration but does not foreclose damages. The indemnity is payable if the agent has brought in new customers or increased volumes with existing customers to the substantial continuing benefit of the principal and is equitable in light of all circumstances.

The right to damages as a result of termination occurs when the agent is deprived of commissions which would have been earned upon proper performance to the substantial benefit of the principal. The agent may also seek damages relief when termination blocks amortization of the costs and expenses incurred on advice of the principal while performing under the agency contract. The death of the agent triggers these indemnity or compensation rights. They are also payable if the agent must terminate the contract because of age, infirmity or illness causing an inability to reasonably continue service. No indemnity or damages may be had under specified circumstances, including when the agent is in default justifying immediate termination under national law. "Restraint of trade" clauses (covenants not to compete) are permissible upon termination to the extent that they are limited to two years, the goods in question and the geographic area and/or customers of the agent. Such clauses can be made a pre-condition to the payment of an indemnity.

CHAPTER 7

BUSINESS COMPETITION LAW

The primary purpose of competition policy in the European Community is preservation of the trade and other benefits of economic integration. The removal of governmental trade barriers unaccompanied by measures to ensure that businesses do not recreate those barriers would be an incomplete effort. Competing enterprises might agree to geographically allocate markets to each other, making the elimination of national tariffs and quotas by the Treaty of Rome irrelevant. Similarly, a dominant enterprise in one state might tie up all important distributors or purchasers of its goods through long-term exclusive dealing contracts. The result could make entry into that market by another business exceedingly difficult. By assisting in the formation and maintenance of an economic community, business competition law is an important component in EC competition policy. It prevents enterprise behavior from becoming a substantial nontariff trade barrier to economic integration.

The secondary purpose of European Community competition policy is not unique to regional integration. This purpose is the attainment of the economic benefits generally thought to accrue in any economy organized on a competitive basis.

These benefits are many. Perhaps most important of all, an economy characterized by competitive enterprise answers the questions of economic organization by maximizing the market desires of its human constituents. A genuinely competitive market is responsive to individual choice and libertarian in a way that acknowledges and promotes diversity. Competition among businesses protects the public interest in having its cumulative demand for goods and services provided at the lowest possible prices and with the greatest possible degree of responsivity to public tastes. It is in this sense that a competitive economy is said to be guided by the principle of "consumer welfare or consumer sovereignty." When, for example, EC law prevents competing enterprises from fixing prices for their goods or prevents a dominant enterprise from charging monopoly prices at the consumers' expense, such law helps to realize the economic benefits of competition within the Euro-economy.

Coal and Steel Business Competition Rules

The first body of business competition law was created in the Treaty of Paris establishing the European Coal and Steel Community in 1951. ECSC business competition rules are found largely in Articles 65 and 66 of the Treaty of Paris. Article 80, which defines "enterprise" for Article 65 and 66 purposes, subjects both public and private coal and steel firms to the rules of ECSC competition law. This is important because many coal and steel businesses in the Community are state-owned. Article 65(1) prohibits and voids business agreements and concerted practices "tending directly or indirectly" to prevent, restrict or distort "normal" competition within the ECSC. Such agreements may not be relied upon before any court or tribunal in the member states. However, certain joint-buying, joint-selling and specialization agreements must, notwithstanding Article 65(1), be authorized by the Commission when the conditions of Article 65(2) are met. Authorizations follow when the Commission determines that these agreements:

(1) make a substantial improvement in the production or distribution of coal or steel;

(2) are no more restrictive than necessary to achieve those results;

(3) do not convey power over price, production or marketing of a substantial portion of the products concerned; and

(4) do not shield firms against effective competition in the common coal and steel markets.

Article 65(2) authorizations are valid for limited time periods, subject to conditions and can be revoked.

As a general matter, the coal and steel business competition rules have not been vigorously pursued. However, in 1961 the Commission refused to authorize a joint-selling organization for thirty-five colliery companies operating the great majority of the mines in the Ruhr valley. The organization would have supplied 73 percent of the coal consumed in West Germany and 59 percent of the Community's entire coal sales. These firms had already obtained provisional authorization for three separate joint-selling coal agencies. The Commission, backed by the Court of Justice, found that authorization of a single agency would have conveyed the "power to determine prices" in violation of Article 65(2). The Commission noted that neither cheaper coal nor cheaper fuel oil imports in the past had caused the companies to lower their prices to competitive levels. Included in the Court's opinion is a rare and learned discussion of "pure competition" theory and the "normal" and "imperfect" competitive conditions of oligopoly in the Community's coal sector. *Geitling v. High Authority* (1962) Eur.Comm.Rep. 83.

Article 66 of the Treaty of Paris establishes extensive Commission controls over coal and steel mergers causing a "concentration." Merger authorizations are granted when the concentration does not convey the power

"to determine prices, to control or restrict production or distribution, or to hinder effective competition in a substantial part of the market for [the] products; or to evade the rules of competition instituted under this Treaty."

No merger guidelines or regulations have been issued by the Commission under its Article 66 powers. Compare the Commission Regulation on

Concentrations under the Treaty of Rome, infra.
Coal and steel mergers law has developed on a
case-by-case basis with authorizations frequently
granted. Steadily increasing industrial concentration in the coal and steel sectors has been given
Commission approval. The Commission has thus
consistently fostered market structures for coal
and steel that may be inimical to effective Common Market competition. The basis for this policy
is the belief that larger and, ideally, more efficient
Community enterprises are required in order to
compete internationally with East Asian and
North American firms.

Under Article 66(7) the Commission may take
action when it finds:

"public or private undertakings which, in law or
in fact, hold or acquire in the market for [coal or
steel] a dominant position shielding them against
effective competition in a substantial part of the
common market."

The Commission is ultimately empowered to determine the prices, conditions of sale, production, or
delivery schedules of a dominant firm. A dominant coal or steel enterprise need not *abuse* its
market position to become subject to Commission
controls. Compare Article 86 of the Treaty of
Rome (infra). The existence of the dominant position is enough, although abuse may be a reason for
action by the Commission.

Relatively little use has been made of Article
66(7) against dominant coal and steel businesses in

the Community. In 1975, however, the Commission decreed interim measures against the publicly owned National Coal Board of Britain requiring it to sell coal at a lower, nondiscriminatory price to a private producer of hard coke. The National Coal Board held 88 percent of the market for the production of domestic hard coke. The price margin between NCB's coal and hard coke sales was alleged to be insufficient to allow the private firm to operate economically and thus shielded NCB from effective competition. *In Re National Carbonising Co. Ltd.* (1975) Common Mkt.L.Rep. D82.

The Commission exercises exclusive jurisdiction over Articles 65 and 66, subject to an appeal to the European Court of Justice. Since 1989, most of these appeals are lodged with the Court of First Instance. This exclusive jurisdiction prohibits private parties from raising ECSC business competition law issues in national courts. In other words, Articles 65 and 66 are not "directly effective" Community law. See Chapter 3. This contrasts sharply with the concurrent jurisdiction of national courts and authorities in many EEC competition law matters. Thus, despite its earlier birth, the facilitating "tending to" language of Article 65, and the broad coverage of Article 66, there has been limited case and regulatory development of coal and steel competition law. This is the complete opposite of what has occurred under the Treaty of Rome establishing the EEC. The utilization by the Commission of some market managing techniques (e.g. occasional price and production controls), the exclusivity of its jurisdiction and (one suspects) the presence of so many publicly owned coal and steel enterprises account for this underdevelopment.

Early in 1991, Competition Commissioner Sir Leon Brittan announced that every effort would be made to align so far as possible the Commission's law enforcement practices under the Coal and Steel Treaty with those under the Treaty of Rome. Sir Leon noted that he would have preferred ending the Coal and Steel Treaty early, prior to its "natural expiration" in 2002.

Nondistorted Competition Policy

One of the basic tasks of the European Economic Community, as set out in Article 3(f) of the Treaty of Rome, is the institution of a "system ensuring that competition in the common market is not distorted." In this regard, the Treaty of Rome appears to reflect a more German perspective on economic organization, whereas the Treaty of Paris was more heavily influenced by French views. Distorted competition is a broad English translation for the French concurrence faussée. Nondistorted competition is close to the German concept of funktionsfähiger Wettbewerb, but it is not clear to what extent this concept is a correlative of what Americans call workable or effective competition. There is some suggestion that workable competition is the minimum level required in business competition law analyses. See *Metro SB–Gross-*

märkte GmbH & Co. KG v. Commission (1977)
Eur.Comm.Rep. 1875. Nondistorted competition is
thus a complex, evolving and distinctly European
perspective on economic organization. It includes,
for example, the heavy hand of agricultural price
regulation and subsidies embodied in the Common
Agricultural Policy. See Chapter 5.

Public and private business competition law is
only one facet of nondistorted competition policy.
Equally, if not at times more important, are a wide
range of other Community concerns and decisions.
Foremost of these concerns has been the implementation and maintenance of the EC customs
union and rights of free movement, which by their
very nature promote competition across borders.
See Chapter 4. Indeed, the whole of the 1992
campaign could be said to underwrite more economic competition within the Community.

Trade treaties and the Common Commercial Policy are another important element in the Community's competition regime since they heavily influence external competitive pressures. See Chapter
6. Two areas of Community law with specific
implications for competition policy are government
subsidies and procurement. See Chapter 5. In
none of these fields of Community law, however, is
there the depth and expansiveness that can be
found in EEC competition law. It is very nearly
impossible to avoid contact with this law in doing
business with the European Community. Hence,
business competition rules are often the first en-

counter that the North Americans have with EC law.

The coverage of EEC competition law that follows is highly selective. No attempt at a comprehensive survey of this vast field has been made or is possible in a Nutshell. The general principles and examples chosen are merely illustrative of the types of legal problems that can be encountered.

Article 85

Article 85(1) of the Treaty of Rome deals with concerted business practices, business agreements and trade association decisions. When they have the potential to affect trade between member states *and* have the object or effect of preventing, restricting or distorting competition *within* the Community, such business activities are deemed incompatible with the Common Market and prohibited. The focus of Article 85(1) is thus on cartels. By way of example, Article 85(1) lists certain prohibited activities:

(1) the fixing of prices or trading conditions;

(2) the limitation of production, markets, technical development or investment;

(3) the sharing of markets or sources of supply;

(4) the application of unequal terms to equivalent transactions, creating competitive disadvantages; and

(5) the conditioning of a contract on the acceptance of commercially unrelated additional supplies.

Article 85(2) voids agreements and decisions prohibited by Article 85(1). Thus the prohibitions of Article 85(1) against anticompetitive activity are absolute and immediately effective under 85(2) without prior judicial or administrative action. The open-ended text of 85(1) gives considerable leeway for interpretation and enforcement purposes. It has, for example, been interpreted to cover nonbinding "gentlemen's agreements." *ACF Chemiefarma v. Commission* (1970) Eur.Comm.Rep. 661. Trade association "recommendations" influencing competition are also caught. *Re ANSEAU–NAVEWA* (1983) Eur.Comm.Rep. 3369. It also generates considerable uncertainty as to the validity of many business agreements, since full market analyses of their competitive and trade impact are often required. However, Article 85(3) permits Article 85(1) to be declared inapplicable when agreements, decisions, concerted practices or classes thereof:

(1) contribute to the improvement of the production or distribution of goods, or to the promotion of technical or economic progress; while

(2) reserving to consumers an equitable share of the resulting benefits; and neither

(3) impose any restrictions not indispensable to objectives 1 and 2 (i.e., least restrictive means must be used); nor

(4) make it possible for the businesses concerned to substantially eliminate competition.

The prohibitions of Article 85(1) may be tempered by Commission "declarations of inapplicability" (exemptions) only when the circumstances of
Article 85(3) are present. As befits exemptions
from broad prohibitions, the terms of 85(3) are
more narrow and specific. Article 85(3) and 85(1)
legal issues are often considered simultaneously in
the process of analyzing the market impact of
restrictive agreements, decisions and concerted
practices. The net result is not unlike the "rule of
reason" approach found in American antitrust law.

Regulation 17—Commission Investigations, Attorney–Client Privilege

In March of 1962 the Council of Ministers
adopted Regulation 17 on the basis of proposals
from the Commission. Regulation 17 is the major
piece of secondary law under Articles 85 and 86.
It establishes the scheme of enforcement for EEC
competition law. The Commission, for the most
part its Competition Directorate–General or department, acquires a wide range of powers under
Regulation 17.

Regulation 17 confers investigatory powers in
the Commission to conduct general studies into
economic sectors and to review the affairs of individual businesses and trade associations. The
Commission may investigate in response to a com-

plaint or upon its own initiative. These powers are particularly significant because (except in the case of mergers) notification of restrictive agreements, decisions and practices to the Commission, although at times beneficial, is not mandatory. The Commission may request all information *it* considers necessary, and examine and make copies of record books and business documents.

Written communications with external EC lawyers undertaken for defense purposes are confidential and need not be disclosed. *AM & S Europe Ltd. v. Commission* (1982) Eur.Comm.Rep. 1575. Written communications with in-house lawyers are *not* exempt from disclosure, nor are communications with external *non*-EC counsel. *Id.* Thus communications with North American attorneys (who are not also EC licensed attorneys) are generally discoverable. Shortly after the *AM & S* decision, the Commission obtained in-house counsel documents from John Deere, Inc., a Belgian subsidiary of the American multinational. These documents were drafted as advice to management on how to avoid EC competition liability for export prohibition restraints. They were used by the Commission to justify the finding of an intentional Article 85 violation and a fine of 2 million ECUs. *John Deere v. Commission* (1985) 28 Off.J.Eur. Comm. L/35, 58. American attorneys have followed these developments with amazement and trepidation. Disclaimers of possible nonconfidentiality are one option to consider in dealing with clients on EC law matters. At a minimum, U.S.

attorneys ought to advise their clients that the usual rules on attorney-client privilege may not apply.

In conducting its investigations, the Commission may ask for verbal explanations on the spot and have access to premises. One author refers to these powers as "dawn raids and other nightmares." Nevertheless, the Court of Justice has affirmed this right of hostile access. *Hoechst v. Commission* (1987) Eur.Comm.Rep. 1549; *Dow Chemical Nederland BV. v. Commission* (1987) Eur. Comm.Rep. 4367. In these matters the Commission acts on its own authority. It must, however, inform member states prior to taking such steps and may request their assistance. Regulation 17 requires the member states to render assistance when businesses fail to comply with competition law investigations of the Commission.

Businesses involved in the Commission's investigatory process have limited rights to notice and hearing. See generally *Hoffmann–La Roche v. Commission* (1979) Eur.Comm.Rep. 461. They do not have access to the Commission's files. Any failure on the part of an enterprise to provide information requested by the Commission or to submit to its investigation can result in the imposition of considerable fines and penalties. For example, the Belgian and French subsidiaries of the Japanese electrical and electronic group, Matsushita, were fined 5,000 European Currency Units (ECU) by the Commission in 1982 for supplying it with false information about whether Matsushita recommended retail prices for its products. These sanctions are civil in nature and run against the corporation, not its directors or management.

The Commission has been increasing the use of its investigatory powers. Several procedural requirements for Commission investigations and hearings have been discussed by the Court of Justice. One notable Court decision upheld the authority of the Commission to conduct searches of corporate offices without notice or warrant when it has reason to believe that pertinent evidence may be lost. *Re National Panasonic* (1980) Eur.Comm. Rep. 2033. Another notable decision permitted a Swiss "whistle blower" who once worked for Hoffmann–La Roche (a defendant in EEC competition law proceedings) to sue the Community in tort for disclosure of his identity as an informant. *Adams v. Commission* (1985) Eur.Comm.Rep. 3539.

Regulation 17 envisions significant cooperation between EC and national authorities in the field of competition law. Copies of nearly all important documents and applications in the hands of the Commission must be forwarded to governmental authorities in member states before formal EC proceedings commence. Constant liaison with those authorities through the Advisory Committee on Restrictive Practices and Monopolies takes place prior to Commission enforcement decisions. The results of such consultations are not available to private parties. Attorneys from the Commission and member state governments meet at least four times a year to discuss EEC law enforcement actions, pending or planned.

As with businesses and trade associations, the Commission under Regulation 17 may obtain all necessary information from national governments and authorities. Not only must national authorities give whatever information they possess upon request, but they must also undertake new investigations considered necessary by the Commission. In 1973, for example, the results and information gathered in a Monopolies and Mergers Commission investigation into the pricing of certain pharmaceuticals in Britain were transmitted to the Commission. The Commission then began a similar inquiry under EEC competition law. However, the system of hearings, fines and penalties applicable to businesses under Regulation 17 does not apply to national governments and authorities that do not cooperate with Commission investigations. The Commission could, however, bring an Article 169 prosecution before the Court of Justice against a member state for failure to adhere to its EC competition law obligations under the Treaty of Rome. See Chapter 3.

Regulation 17—Commission Prosecutions and Sanctions

Regulation 17 also authorizes the Commission to determine when violations of the competition law provisions of Articles 85 or 86 occur. This is the source of the Commission's power to render enforcement decisions. A regulation now limits the time period in which the Commission may render a decision in competition law cases to five years. All Commission decisions, including enforcement decisions and decisions to investigate, fine or penalize must be published and are subject to judicial review. Since 1989, most of these appeals are heard by the Court of First Instance. During interim periods, the Commission has the power to order measures indispensable to its functions. *Camera Care v. Commission* (1980) Eur.Comm.Rep. 119.

Before deciding that a competition law breach has occurred, the Commission issues a statement of "objections." Regulation 99/63, Article 2(4). This statement must reveal which facts the Commission intends to rely upon in reaching a decision that a violation has occurred. *AEG v. Commission* (1983) Eur.Comm.Rep. 3151. A hearing can then be requested by the alleged violator(s) or any interested person. Id. Article 7. These hearings are conducted in private, with separate reviews of complainants and witnesses. The Commission must disclose only those non-confidential documents in its file upon which it intends to rely and are necessary to prepare an adequate defense. *VBVB and VBBB v. Commission* (1984) Eur.Comm.Rep. 19. After the hearing, the Commission consults with the Advisory Committee on Restrictive Practices and Monopolies, which is composed of one civil servant expert from each member state. The results of this consultation are not made public.

Having consulted the Committee, the Commission is then free to render an enforcement decision.

In its enforcement decision, the Commission may require businesses to "cease and desist" their infringing activities. In practice, this power has sufficed to permit the Commission to order infringing enterprises to come up with their own remedial solutions. Daily penalties may be imposed to compel adherence to the order to cease and desist. Commission decisions on violations of Articles 85 and 86 are also accompanied by a capacity to substantially fine any intentionally or negligently infringing enterprise. When appeals are lodged against Commission decisions imposing fines and penalties, payment is suspended but interest is charged and a bank guarantee for the amounts concerned must be provided. *Hasselblad v. Commission* (1982) Eur.Comm.Rep. 1555.

In the early years, Regulation 17 fines and penalties actually levied by the Commission were few, relatively small in amount and frequently reduced on appeal to the Court of Justice. As EEC competition law doctrine has become clearer, these trends have all been reversed. In its more recent decisions, the Court has upheld substantial fines and penalties imposed by the Commission in competition law proceedings and recognized their deterrent value. See *Musique Diffusion Francaise SA v. Commission* (1983) Eur.Comm.Rep. 1825. In 1991, the Commission imposed the highest EC competition law fines ever: Roughly $35 million on

Solvay of Belgium and $20 million on Imperial Chemical Industries of Britain for market division and price fixing in soda ash.

Any complete picture of the development of Article 85 must account for the Commission's informal negotiations as well as its decisions to prosecute, exempt or clear infringing activities. Business compliance with Articles 85 and 86 is often achieved short of a formal Commission decision. Word of informal file-closings is occasionally revealed. In *Re Eurofima,* for example, the Commission terminated proceedings without issuing a decision. In the process of responding to complaints from suppliers, the Commission was able to secure termination of infringing conduct from Eurofima, the most important buyer of railway rolling stock in the EC. Eurofima also undertook to continue to comply with EEC competition law. The Commission announced these results in a press release. (1973) Common Mkt.L.Rep. D217.

Regulation 17—Individual Exemptions and Negative Clearances

Regulation 17 not only sets up the investigatory and law enforcement machinery for EEC competition law, but also the means to avoid that law. Businesses may forestall enforcement action by the Commission under Article 85 by seeking an individual exemption, a negative clearance, or both. To do this, they must formally notify the Commission of the terms of any existing or proposed agreement, decision or concerted practice falling within the scope of Article 85(1). Notification suspends the possibility of fines under Regulation 17 and establishes the earliest effective date if an exemption is granted.

The Commission has developed a "comfort letter" practice in connection with requests for negative clearances and Article 85(3) exemptions. This practice avoids the delays inherent in the process of reaching formal exemption or clearance decisions. Comfort letters are issued only when the businesses concerned wish to have them and only after public notice and limited opportunity to comment. They signal that the Commission's file is closed without issuance of a negative clearance or an 85(3) exemption. Comfort letters state that the Commission sees no reason to intervene in opposition to the activities notified. The parties then typically proceed to implement their agreement. In the absence of a change of circumstances, the Commission cannot alter its position and is precluded from fining the recipient. However, national courts are not bound by the comfort letter in their determinations of Article 85 violations. *L'Oréal v. De Nieuwe AMCK* (1980) Eur.Comm.Rep. 3775.

Individual exemptions are granted by the Commission under Article 85(3) for a limited period of time and are no barrier to prosecution under Article 86. See *Tetra Pak Rausing SA v. Commission* (1990) Eur.Comm.Rep. ___ (Case T–51/89, Court of

First Instance). They are subject to review on renewal and may be conditioned upon extensive stipulations. Individual exemptions can also be revoked or altered by a subsequent Commission decision. Exempt activities may later be prohibited, under Regulation 17, when:

(1) the situation has changed with respect to a factor essential in the Commission's original decision;

(2) a stipulation is infringed;

(3) the original decision was based on false information or obtained fraudulently; or

(4) those concerned abuse the exemption.

The Commission may revoke its decision retroactively in cases (2), (3), and (4). One notable use of Article 85(3) has been Commission authorization of "crisis cartels," i.e. production restricting arrangements in industries with prolonged overcapacity.

Regulation 17 permits businesses in doubt as to the applicability of Article 85(1) to their activities to request a "negative clearance" from the Commission. The Commission grants negative clearances solely on the basis of the factual and legal information then before it. A negative clearance indicates that the Commission sees no grounds at present to intervene under Article 85(1). The Commission may find that the relevant agreement, decision or concerted practice does not perceptibly affect trade between member states, or does not perceptibly restrain competition within the Common Market as 85(1) requires. In such circumstances it issues negative clearances.

There is a critical difference under Regulation 17 between a negative clearance and an individual exemption. The latter admits an Article 85(1) violation or potential violation, but requests a declaration of inapplicability under the special terms of Article 85(3). The former denies the violation or potential violation of 85(1) because of the terms of that article and the nature of the activities involved. These lines of argument can be and often are pursued simultaneously before the Commission using Form A/B. Only the Commission (not national authorities) can grant individual exemptions and negative clearances.

When the Commission intends to grant a negative clearance or an 85(3) individual exemption, it must publish the "main content" of the decision after allowing for protection of legitimate business secrets. After publication, all interested third parties are invited to submit their observations to the Commission prior to its decision. Since important matters may be revealed to competitors and potential litigants, this publication requirement may chill business usage of the negative clearance and individual exemption procedures erected under Regulation 17.

When the Commission has issued a statement of objections and before an adverse decision is made, the applicant is entitled to a hearing. *Hoffman–La Roche*, supra. The Court of Justice has held that the Commission has discretion whether to hear oral argument on negative clearance and individual exemption applications. *FEDETAB v. Commission* (1980) Eur.Comm.Rep. 3125. Third parties may have access to the hearing process on showing a legitimate interest. As with enforcement proceedings, the hearing is private and a record is made. The Commission must give written reasons to explain whatever final decision is taken, although the Court of Justice has held that the Commission need not discuss every fact or law issue raised during the proceedings. *FEDETAB,* supra.

Individual Exemptions—Marine Paints Example

Individual exemptions granted by the Commission under Article 85(3) have stressed the projected advantages of reduced production costs, higher productivity, more effective and less costly activities, and somewhat vague notions of technical and economic progress. Exemptions denied by the Commission have stressed the likelihood of the alleged benefits occurring under competition anyway, the undesirable protection of national markets and "serious" losses of market competition. As a general rule, the Commission weighs the advantages alleged in favor of the restrictive agreement, decision or practice against the resultant loss of market competition and against the likelihood that competition itself might produce similar advantages. This balancing process is well illustrated by the following example.

In 1962 the Transocean Marine Paint Association, eighteen medium-sized marine paint manufacturers, sought to develop and market a common brand of standard quality paint. They applied for a negative clearance or, failing that, an 85(3) individual exemption for their agreement. Five of the manufacturers were domiciled in the EEC. Sales responsibility for this brand was allocated on a territorial basis with commissions payable to offset sales in another member's territory irrespective of that member's services regarding those sales. Prices for the Association's standard paint were set individually. Members of the Association could still sell paints of either higher or lower (but not standard) quality under their own trademarks. Such nonstandard paints could not be imported into the sales territory of another member without its consent.

Since the agreement fell within all the terms of Article 85(1) and was not *de minimis,* the Commission denied the request for a negative clearance. Prior to granting an 85(3) exemption, the Commission required the association to eliminate (as incompatible with Article 85(1)) certain other territorial protection, sales allocation, collective discrimination and price information exchange clauses. The Commission perceived that a common brand of paint would make the Association's product more marketable in the EC and world markets. The availability of standard brand paint in most of the world's shipyards was important because it is apparently desirable for technical reasons to reuse the same marine paints on ships. Moreover, it appears that the marine paint market is quite distinct from the market for paints in general (80 percent of marine paints cannot be used for other purposes). Without citing market shares, the Commission noted that the Association manufacturers faced strong competition within the EC from other large international marine paint companies. Hence, reasoned the Commission, the loss of real or potential competition among medium-sized Association manufacturers was outweighed by the potential increase in EC competition in the standard-quality marine paint market viewed as a whole.

The exemption was subject to conditions requiring the Association to report to the Commission any alterations in its membership, any amendments or additions to their agreement, any relevant board decisions or arbitral awards and its annual volume of sales and inter-Association deliveries. Issued in June of 1966, the Transocean Marine Paint Association exemption was effective until January of 1973. *Re Transocean Marine Paint Association* (1967) Common Mkt.L.Rep. D9.

On application in 1972 for an extension of the exemption, the Association had grown to twenty in number. Five original members had withdrawn while eight new members had been admitted. Seven of the twenty were based in the enlarged EEC. This time the market shares of the Association and its competitors were published. The Association had an expanding 5 to 10 percent of the world marine paint market, 25 percent of which was held by International Red Hand Inc., a nonassociate. From 1966 to 1972 the Association members did well by their standard quality paint. Sales rose from ⅓ to about ¾ of the total turnover of the membership. One Far Eastern member accounted for over 60 percent of the Association's turnover. In light of these facts, the Commission declared unjustifiable, in 1973, the Association's territorial consent on nonstandard paint sales and the territorial standard brand sales commission obligations described above. Recision of these terms was ordered by the Commission before it granted the exemption renewal for another six years. (1974) Common Mkt.L.Rep. D11.

The original 1967 conditions attached to the exemption were retained in 1973 while an additional requirement concerning concentration in the industry was attached. Any new links or changes in existing links by way of common directors or managers, or by way of financial participation between an Association member and another enterprise in the paints sector, were to be reported. The Association appealed the inclusion of this additional condition on procedural grounds. It claimed lack of notice and opportunity to present contrary argument. The Court of Justice agreed with the Association and subsequently annulled this part of the Commission's decision. *Transocean Marine Paint Association v. Commission* (1974) Eur.Comm.Rep. 1063. In a revised monitoring requirement, issued in accordance with proper procedures, shareholdings amounting to 25 percent or more of firms in the paint sector doing business in the EC had to be reported.

It is worth noting the extent to which the Commission was able to gradually filter out the most anticompetitive aspects of the Association's agreement. This process has continued over the years as the Commission has periodically renewed the exemption. In December of 1988 the Commission continued the exemption through 1998. *Re The Transocean Marine Paint Association* (1988) 4 Common Mkt.L.Rep. 674. Furthermore, while the exempt practices may be illegal under competition laws elsewhere (e.g. under American antitrust law), individual exemptions do grant immunity under the *Wilhelm* case (infra) from the national competition laws of EC states.

Negative Clearances—SAFCO Example

Negative clearance proceedings do not involve a full examination of market impact such as required by Article 85(3). They focus more on the terms of Article 85(1). For example, negative clearances have been granted on the grounds that trade between member states is not perceptibly affected or that competition within the Common Market is not perceptibly prevented, restrained or distorted. Very often these two legal issues are jointly considered as the *SAFCO* case illustrates. *Re SAFCO* (1972) Common Mkt.L.Rep. D83.

Seven French producers of preserved vegetables created an exclusive sales agency (SAFCO) to encourage the export of their products to West Germany. They assigned their trademarks to SAFCO for export purposes and could be expelled summarily by the SAFCO Association. Membership in the export association was limited to enterprises with less than five million French francs capital in assets and less than five hundred employees. Admissions' decisions were made secretly. The SAFCO articles of association were transmitted in 1963 to the Commission along with a request for a negative clearance.

Prior to the formation of SAFCO, some of its members had been significantly involved in exports to West Germany. The export association was quite successful and obtained about 2 percent of the German market for preserved vegetables by 1972, the time of the Commission's much delayed decision on the negative clearance request. The Commission acknowledged that while export competition between the French producers was restricted by their agreement, it was not perceptibly restricted. The SAFCO enterprises remained in competition with each other in the French market and the preserved vegetable market within the EC and Germany was characterized by numerous products similar in quality and competitive in price. Producers of greatly superior size were competitors of SAFCO. An increasingly integrated and competitive common market for preserved vegetables was apparent. The Commission issued a negative clearance to SAFCO indicating, on the facts and law before it, that there was no necessity for intervention under Article 85(1).

Unlike Article 85(3) exemptions, the Commission cannot issue negative clearances subject to conditions, review and renewal. Although it can negotiate the removal of restrictive clauses prior to issuance, the absence of these important monitoring features makes negative clearances long-term risks as regards competition policy. In SAFCO, the agreement was for ninety-nine years duration. What may not "perceptibly" restrict EC competition or trade in 1963 or 1972 may do so in the future. Suppose SAFCO, through competition or membership expansion, obtains 10 or 20 percent of the German market. Suppose membership denials or dismissals hasten the demise of competitors in the French market. Whether negative clearances are revocable, and if so under what terms and with what effects, are legal questions that remain largely unexplored. The Commission could argue that negative clearances are based strictly on the information before it and that any significant change of circumstances therefore entitles it to revoke the clearance.

Article 85—Group Exemptions and Policy Notices

The Commission received an onslaught of negative clearance requests and Article 85(3) notifications in 1962 when Regulation 17 took effect. The vast majority of the business activities involved in this deluge were in the distribution and licensing areas. As a result, the Commission sought and obtained authorization in 1965 from the Council to formulate, for limited time periods, group "declarations of inapplicability" under Article 85(3). These are commonly known as "group or block exemptions." The Council granted this authorization, noting that Article 85(3) allows "classes" of exempt agreements.

Group exemptions, and policy announcements by the Commission in areas where group exemptions have not yet been promulgated, eliminate the notification or request requirements of the negative clearance and individual exemption procedures created by Regulation 17. Businesses are invited and encouraged to conform their agreements and behavior to the terms and conditions of the Commission regulations embodying group exemptions. In other words, group exemptions rely upon confidential business self-regulation.

After a number of test enforcement decisions and definitive rulings by the Court of Justice, the Commission issued Regulation 67 in 1967. It became the first of a series of group exemptions from Article 85(1). Regulation 67/67 was replaced in 1983 by Regulation 1983/83. This regulation concerns exclusive dealing methods of distribution. Exclusive dealing agreements ordinarily involve restrictions on manufacturers and independent distributors of goods. These restraints concern who the manufacturer may supply, to whom the manu-

facturer or distributor may sell, and from whom
the distributor may acquire the goods or similar
goods.   Exclusive dealing agreements should be
distinguished from agency or consignment agreements where title and most risk remain with the
manufacturer until the goods are sold by their
retail agents to consumers.   The announced EC
policy position is that competition law will not
require a manufacturer to compete with its agents.
Exclusivity in genuine retail agency agreements is
therefore legal.   Commission Announcement on
Exclusive Agency Contracts Made with Commercial Agents, Official Journal 2921 (1962).   But see
Re Pittsburgh Corning Europe (1973) Common Mkt.
L.Rep. D2.

Regulation 1983/83 acknowledges that many exclusive dealing agreements fall within the scope of
the prohibitions of Article 85(1).   Under Article
85(2) they would be automatically void.   Regulation 1983/83 also recognizes that exclusive dealing
activities can lead to an improvement in the distribution and competition of products sold in the
Common Market.   While a manufacturer may be
reluctant to sell and compete in new territories
through nonexclusive distributors, it may be willing to do so through exclusive outlets.   These re-
tailers must often provide services, advertising or
other goodwill to back up the products.   By removing the ability of distributors to sell competing
brands, exclusive dealing creates a singular incentive to market the manufacturer's goods.   In the
context of the evolution of the Common Market,

exclusive dealing may encourage greater penetration by producers who have traditionally sold only in their national markets.

Following the Article 85(3) formula, Regulation 1983/83 states that consumers will receive a fair share of the resultant benefits from exclusive dealing agreements by virtue of their improved ability to obtain a wider range of goods. However, Article 85(3) requires that the restrictions utilized in exclusive dealing agreements be indispensable to their objectives and that they do not substantially eliminate competition in the goods concerned. Regulation 1983/83 therefore exempts only agreements or concerted practices not in any way inhibiting parallel imports of the same goods from other exclusive dealers. The concern here has been that exclusive dealing agreements are often accompanied by efforts at absolute territorial market protection, a practice considerably more restrictive of competition than mere exclusive dealing.

Regulation 67 and its successor, Regulation 1983/83, may be seen as an excellent example of Commission efforts to employ and develop EEC competition law under Article 85 to serve the goal of economic integration. The formation of absolute territorial trade barriers, similar in impact to national tariffs and quotas that existed prior to the creation of the Common Market, would negate some of the economic benefits of increased trade and economic integration. Yet to prohibit exclusive dealing entirely would deter Common Market sales by national manufacturers. Hence, under Regulation 1983/83, distributive competition among goods for sale within the Common Market is encouraged by permitting exclusive dealing agreements between manufacturers and independent distributors *and* by insuring that competition as between exclusive dealers in the same goods is also preserved. It is only *absolute* territorial exclusive dealing that precludes benefit from the group exemption. It is precluded whether achieved by the exercise of national patent, copyright or trademark rights, or simply by contractual restraints between manufacturers and their exclusive dealers.

A series of Commission regulations have followed the pattern established by Regulation 67. Test cases are initiated by the Commission before the European Court prior to creating a group exemption. Group exemptions now exist for exclusive purchasing agreements (Regulation 1984/83), patent licensing agreements (Regulation 1984/2349), motor vehicle distribution and servicing agreements (Regulation 123/85), production specialization agreements among small firms (Regulation 417/85), research and development agreements among small firms (Regulation 418/85), franchise agreements (Regulation 4087/88) and know-how licensing agreements (Regulation 556/89).

Commission competition law "notices," while not of the binding legal stature of group exemption regulations, have similar attributes. It is generally perceived that businesses may rely upon them as revocable statements of prosecutorial policy. They have, as a practical matter, the same self-regulatory impact as group exemptions. Competition law notices issued by the Commission concern agreements of "minor" importance (1986 Official Journal C231/2), various "minor" cooperation agreements (1968 Official Journal C75/3), exclusive agency contracts (supra), and technology sharing agreements among small and medium-sized businesses (1979 Official Journal C1/2).

Article 85—Undertakings and Concerted Practices

There can be no violation of Article 85(1) unless there is an agreement between "undertakings," a decision by an association of undertakings or a concerted practice among undertakings. In other words, except for trade association decisions, at least two parties must be involved. Single-firm behavior is not caught by Article 85(1). "Undertaking," as a matter of EEC law, has been interpreted to mean a functionally independent economic entity. This definition includes profit or nonprofit organizations, and partnerships or sole proprietorships. *FEDETAB v. Commission* (1980) Eur.Comm.Rep. 3125. It generally precludes finding agreements or concerted practices as between parent corporations and subsidiaries. *Centrafarm v. Sterling Drug* (1974) Eur.Comm.Rep. 1147; *Hydrotherm v. Compact* (1984) Eur.Comm.Rep. 2999.

The meaning of "concerted practices" is critical to Article 85(1). Concerted practices include any kind of informal cooperation between enterprises, and contrast with formal written or oral agreements and decisions. Without such a flexible legal concept, substantial evasion of the reach of Article 85(1) might be achieved by nonbinding but regularly followed business "understandings."

The Commission and the Court of Justice considered the concept of a concerted practice extensively in *Imperial Chemical Industries (ICI) v. Commission*. *ICI* involved nearly all the producers of aniline dyes in the EC when it had only six member states. Three industry-wide price increases between 1964 and 1967 took place over the full range of more than 6000 aniline dye products.

The Commission, acting on information furnished by trade organizations using dyestuffs, found ten producers of aniline dyes in violation of Article 85(1) by concerting on these price increases. Together they held about 80 percent of the EC aniline dyes market. Proof of the concerted practices tendered by the Commission included: (1) the near identity of the price increases in each country; (2) the uniformity of products covered by the price increases; (3) the exact timing of the increases; (4) the simultaneous dispatch to subsidiaries and representatives of price increase instructions that were nearly identical in form and content; and (5) the existence of informal contacts and occasional meetings between the enterprises concerned.

The Commission decided these circumstantial facts warranted its conclusion that a concerted price fixing practice took place. (1969) Common Mkt. L.Rep. 494.

On appeal, the Court of Justice affirmed. The Court distinguished the concept of concerted practice from an agreement or decision under Article 85(1): "A form of coordination between undertakings which, without going so far as to amount to an agreement properly so called, knowingly substitutes a practical cooperation between them for the risks of competition." The Court added that while independent parallel behavior by competitors did not fall within the concept of a concerted practice, the fact of such behavior could be taken as a strong indicator of a concerted practice where it produced market conditions, especially price equilibrium, different from those thought ordinarily to prevail under competition. The cartel's defense of "conscious parallelism" on prices was therefore another piece of evidence affirming the Commission's enforcement decision. The sum total of the evidence on which the Commission relied to find a concerted practice was explicable, in the eyes of the Court, only by convergent intentions of producers to increase prices and avoid competitive conditions in the aniline dyes market. *ICI v. Commission* (1972) Eur.Comm.Rep. 619.

The impact of the concept of concerted practice in EEC competition law depends on the evidence available to prove cooperative business behavior.

It is a legal standard rooted in fact more than law. And it has proved useful in combating other Common Market cartels. In the *Sugar Cartel* case, for example, the Court of Justice reaffirmed *ICI* and then laid down a general warning against competitor cooperation and contact. It held that EEC competition rules *inherently* require that each enterprise independently determine its activities in the Common Market. Direct or indirect contact with the object or effect of influencing the market conduct of an actual or potential competitor, the disclosure of courses of market conduct of an actual or potential competitor or the disclosure of courses of market conduct intended for adoption by others, is prohibited. *Suiker Unie UA v. Commission* (1975) Eur.Comm.Rep. 1663. The full extent to which concerted practice is a legal concept suitable for use against oligopolies in EC industry awaits future enforcement action and clarification of the Commission's power to order structural or regulatory remedies.

Article 85—Competitive Impact

Article 85(1) only applies when an agreement, decision or concerted practice has as its object *or* effect the prevention, restriction or distortion of competition within the Common Market. Distinctions can be drawn as between preventing, restraining and distorting competition, but the sweep of this language basically creates a legal and conceptual net in which most activities of competing enterprises may be examined by the Commission.

(Folsom, Eur.Comm.Law NS—11)

The manner in which the Commission has cut official holes in this net through exemptions and policy announcements has already been discussed. Nevertheless, since there is a sense in which nearly all actions by enterprises affect their competitive position in the marketplace, the language of Article 85 grants expansive administrative power. However, the Court of Justice has imposed a "rule of reason" test when evaluating competitive impact. Only those restraints which are "sufficiently deleterious" to competition in the context in which they appear are prohibited and void. *Société Technique Minière v. Maschinenbau Ulm GmbH* (1966) Eur.Comm.Rep. 235; *Nungesser v. Commission* (1982) Eur.Comm.Rep. 2015.

Restraints of competition by enterprises may take place at different levels of economic activity. Restraints involving competition among firms operating at the same level in the production or distribution process are known as horizontal restraints. Businesses operating at different levels may restrain competition between themselves and third parties (vertical restraints). In *Grundig,* the Court of Justice declined to follow the recommendations of its Advocate General and affirmed that both horizontal and vertical restraints are embraced by Article 85(1). *Consten and Grundig v. Commission* (1966) Eur.Comm.Rep. 299. This decision involved a German manufacturer of consumer electronics that established an exclusive dealing agreement with Consten, a French distributor. In other words, *Grundig* was a vertical restraints case. The agreement was made prior to the adoption of Regulation 67/67 (supra). As part of the agreement, Grundig undertook not to deliver its products directly or indirectly to anyone else in France. Grundig also contracted to similar territorial restraints with its other Common Market dealers outside of France. Consten agreed to sell only in its French territory. The result was that no dealer or wholesaler of Grundig products in the EC could sell outside its contracted territory. To strengthen this absolute pattern of territorial distribution, Grundig assigned the French trademark "GINT" to Consten. GINT was placed on all products delivered to Consten in addition to the usual "GRUNDIG" mark.

When prices in France were 20 to 25 percent above those in Germany, a French firm began competing with Consten by importing Grundig products bearing the GINT mark from a renegade German wholesaler. Consten then sued the importer in the French courts for infringement of GINT and violation of French law on unfair competition. The importer replied that the Grundig–Consten contract and the GINT assignment were void under Articles 85(1) and 85(2). Meanwhile, Grundig notified its series of exclusive dealing agreements to the Commission and sought Article 85(3) exemptions for them. The Cour d'Appel de Paris stayed the proceedings under French law. The Commission found the entire agreement prohibited by Article 85(1) and denied an 85(3) exemption. Although not restrictive of competition as between Grundig and Consten, the agreement was restrictive as between Consten and third-party sellers of Grundig products. It amounted, the Commission said, to absolute territorial protection in France from the competition of parallel imports of Grundig products. Since, in the Commission's view, the object of the agreement was to restrain competition, an extensive market analysis of its actual competitive impact was not necessary.

The Court of Justice upheld the Commission's position on coverage of vertical restraints by Article 85(1) and on the absence of need for extensive market analysis in this case. However, it partially accepted the argument that, in ascertaining whether competition was restrained under Article 85(1), the Commission ought to have considered the whole of the market for consumer electronics (where Grundig faced strong interbrand competition). Competition within the overall market, it was argued, was increased by the entry of Grundig into France through Consten's exclusive, territorially protected sales. This increase in interbrand competition, the argument continued, outweighed the restrictions on intrabrand competition in Grundig products.

The Court responded to these arguments by holding that only certain clauses of the Grundig–Consten agreement, the absolute territorial protection clause and the GINT assignment, infringed Article 85(1). Only these clauses were automatically void under Article 85(2). The remainder of the agreement, including the exclusive dealing provisions, was severable and legally binding. Thus, Grundig could enter the French market through an exclusive retailer, but that retailer could not be sheltered from other Grundig sellers in the Common Market. These principles were subsequently incorporated in Regulation 67/67 for which *Grundig* was an important test case. A modified Grundig selective distribution system has since been granted an individual exemption by the Commission. Official Journal L233 (Aug. 30, 1985).

Market Division and Intellectual Property Rights

In *Grundig,* the Court of Justice affirmed the Commission's remedial order to the parties to refrain from any measure tending to obstruct or impede the acquisition of Grundig products. To reduce the negative impact of national industrial and intellectual property rights on EC trade and competition, the Commission and the Court of Justice have relied on a number of Treaty provisions. In the *Grundig* case, the Court held that Article 85 limitations may be imposed on the exercise or use of national trademark rights. In the Court's opinion, absolute territorial distribution rights are not essential to the protection or benefit sought to be conferred by trademarks. The net result was a Court order prohibiting Consten from exercising its rights under French trademark law to use GINT as a trade and competition barrier.

When used with the object or effect of preventing, restraining or distorting Common Market competition, national industrial and intellectual property rights have generally yielded to the competition law of the European Community. In *Deutsche Grammophon*, for example, results comparable to those in *Grundig* were achieved with copyright-based territorial restraints. (1971) Eur.Comm.Rep. 487. When record imports into Germany from the French subsidiary of Deutsche Grammophon caused competition for the parent company, then enjoying lawful resale price maintenance in Germany, it sought infringement protection under German copyright law. Competition law restraints on the exercise (as opposed to the existence) of national copyright rights denied infringement protection. Deutsche Grammophon's German copyright rights were said to be "exhausted" by the sales to its French subsidiary. Dividing up the Common Market was not perceived to be essential to the financial reward and other purposes of German copyright. On the other hand, increased intrabrand Deutsche Grammophon sales and price competition was completely compatible with the Treaty of Rome.

Much of the litigation surrounding intellectual property rights in the Common Market has been undertaken in connection with Article 36 and the free movement of goods. As in the competition law area, such rights have generally given way to the Treaty of Rome. See Chapter 4.

Articles 85 and 86—Trade Impact

To come within the prohibition of Article 85, an agreement, decision or concerted practice must raise a probability that it will affect trade between member states. *Remia v. Commission* (1985) Eur. Comm.Rep. 2545. Because of this requirement, it is insufficient to consider the object of restrictive agreements under EEC law without also considering their potential trade effects. While in certain cases, such as *Grundig,* it is possible to avoid an extensive market analysis of the competitive impact of restrictive agreements because an intent to restrain competition is clear, analysis of an agreement's *trade* impact is always required. This is doubly true because agreements that affect trade or competition between member states in a *de minimis* fashion are not subject to Article 85(1).

In *Völk v. Vervaecke,* a German manufacturer of washing machines contracted with a Dutch exclusive dealer, Vervaecke. The contract was similar to that of Consten–Grundig and provided for absolute territorial protection. Völk's share of the German washing machine market ranged between 0.2 and 0.05 percent. This time the Court of Justice, on voluntary reference from the Oberlandesgericht in Munich, emphasized the overall product market effect of the restrictive agreement. From that interbrand perspective, the Court advised that the agreement "affect[ed] the market insignificantly" and therefore escaped Article 85(1). (1969) Eur.Comm.Rep. 295. This *de minimis* doctrine has been developed more fully in subsequent decisions and the Commission's Notice on Agreements of Minor Importance. Official Journal C231/2 (1986).

In theory, agreements, decisions and concerted practices of a purely national character not affecting trade between member states are outside the scope of Article 85. In practice, however, few national activities of any significance are likely to escape its reach. For example, in the *VCH* case, an entirely national cartel of cement merchants in Holland held a steadily declining two-thirds share of the Dutch retail cement market. The cartel maintained certain fixed and recommended prices and resale conditions as well as a variety of other restraints on competition among its members. Prior to 1967 the merchants' cartel had been exclusively allied with a German, Dutch and Belgian manufacturers' cartel for its supplies. The Commission noted that about one-third of the total sales of cement in Holland were of cheaper products imported from Belgium and West Germany. It held that the merchants' agreement therefore restricted competition within the Common Market and affected trade between member states. In the Commission's view, the agreement inhibited German and Belgian producers from increasing their share of the Dutch cement market. The Commission denied an Article 85(3) individual exemption and a negative clearance for the agreement.

On appeal, the Court of Justice upheld the Commission. *VCH v. Commission* (1972) Eur.Comm.

Rep. 977. It issued a broad opinion aimed at all restrictive national cartels even when imported products are not involved:

"A restrictive agreement extending to the whole territory of a member state by its very nature consolidates the national boundaries thus hindering the economic interpenetration desired by the Treaty and so protecting national production."

The expansive approach of the Court of Justice to trade impact analysis under Article 85 is also relevant to Article 86 which contains the same language.

Article 86

Article 86 of the Treaty of Rome prohibits abuses by one or more undertakings of a dominant position within a substantial part of the Common Market insofar as the abuses may affect trade between member states. The existence of a dominant position is not prohibited by EEC law. Only its abuse is proscribed.

Article 86 proceeds to list certain examples of what constitute abuses by dominant enterprises:

(1) the imposition of unfair prices or other trading conditions;

(2) the limitation of production, markets or technical development which prejudices consumers;

(3) the application of dissimilar conditions to equivalent transactions thereby engendering competitive disadvantages; and

(4) the subjection of contracts to commercially unrelated supplementary obligations.

These examples are remarkably, although not exactly, similar to the examples of anticompetitive agreements, decisions and concerted practices provided in Article 85(1). Indeed, insofar as two or more enterprises are abusing their dominant market position under Article 86 they may well be simultaneously engaging in an Article 85(1) infringement. However, fines for the same conduct under both Articles 85 and 86 will not be permitted by the Court of Justice. *ACF Chemiefarma v. Commission* (1970) Eur.Comm.Rep. 661.

Article 86 differs fundamentally from Article 85. There are no provisions to declare abuses by dominant enterprise(s) automatically void, nor to permit any exemptions from its prohibitions. Article 86 might well be viewed as a *per se* rule of law. Thus, under the administrative framework of Regulation 17, no individual or group exemptions can be granted by the Commission for Article 86. The absence of exemptions from Article 86 means that there is little incentive for dominant firms to notify their abuses to the Commission. Negative clearances are obtainable, however, indicating that the Commission sees no grounds for intervention on the facts and law before it. Quite understandably, few requests for Article 86 clearances have been made. Regulation 17 grants the Commission the same powers with reference to Article 86 as it possesses under Article 85 to obtain information, investigate corporate affairs, render infringement decisions, and fine or penalize offenders.

A few Commission decisions concerning Article 86 have their origins in complaints to the Commission from competitors or those abused. Generally, however, the Commission has acted *sua sponte* in Article 86 proceedings. Some of the Commission's decisions have been the subject of appeal to the Court of Justice, which occasionally has received Article 86 issues on reference from national courts under the Article 177 preliminary ruling procedure. A limited number of Article 86 cases have been resolved informally through Commission negotiations. To highlight the more important developments in the interpretation of the language and scope of Article 86, a selection of cases and issues follows.

Article 86—Dominant Positions

Unless an enterprise or group of enterprises possesses a dominant position within a substantial part of the Common Market, no questions of abuse can arise. A dominant position may exist on either the supply or demand side of the market. *Re Eurofima* (1973) Common Mkt.L.Rep. D217 (dominant buyer).

In establishing the existence of dominant positions, the Commission has tended to look at commercial realities, not technical legal distinctions. For example, the only two producers of sugar in Holland were legally and financially independent of each other. In practice they systematically co-operated in the joint purchase of raw materials, the adoption of production quotas, the use of by-products, the pooling of research, advertising and sales promotion, and the unification of prices and terms of sales. To other enterprises they appeared as if a single firm. They were involved in over 85 percent of the sales of sugar in Holland. The Commission and the Court of Justice held them to be a single enterprise for the purpose of assessing the existence of a dominant position under Article 86. *Re European Sugar Cartel* (1973) Common Mkt.L.Rep. D65 (Commission); (1975) Eur.Comm. Rep. 1663 (Court of Justice).

A celebrated mergers case involved Continental Can, a large American corporation. *Europemballage Corporation and Continental Can Co., Inc. v. Commission* (1972) Common Mkt.L.Rep. D11 (Commission); (1973) Eur.Comm.Rep. 215 (Court of Justice). It is a leading case on the existence of a dominant position under Article 86 law. Evidence of Continental Can's worldwide and German national market strength in the supply of certain metal containers and tops, a concentrated market characterized by ineffective consumers and competitors, and strong technical and financial barriers to entry were sufficient for the Commission to find the existence of a dominant position in certain areas of Germany. In so doing, the Commission stressed that enterprises are in a dominant position

> "when they have the power to behave independently, which puts them in a position to act without taking into account their competitors, purchasers or suppliers ...   This power does not necessarily have to derive from an absolute domination ... it is enough that they be strong enough as a whole to ensure to those enterprises an overall independence of behavior, even if there are differences in intensity in their influence on different partial markets."

Power to behave independently of competitors, purchasers or suppliers amounting to a dominant position must be exercisable with reference to the supply or acquisition of particular goods or services, i.e. a market. In *Continental Can* the Commission distinguished between that enterprise's powerful position around the world and in the EC with reference to the generic market for light metal containers, and its dominant position in Germany with reference to the particular markets for preserved meat and shellfish tins and metal caps for glass jars. Thus, initial Commission selection of the appropriate geographic and product market is the key to its analysis of whether a dominant position exists or not. It is also the key to the utility of its dominant position formula as set out in the *Continental Can* opinion. On such selection hinges the determination of the market power of the enterprise concerned. The broader the market for goods or services is defined (light metal cans versus cans for preserved meat, etc.) the less likely there will be overall independence of behavior from competitors, purchasers or suppliers. The same is true for broader geographic markets selected by the Commission (e.g. the EC versus Germany or parts thereof).

On appeal to the Court of Justice, the Commission's guiding principles for determining the existence of a dominant position under Article 86 were not seriously questioned. The Court did challenge the Commission's delineation of the relevant *product* market and its failure to explain in full how Continental Can had the power to behave independently in the preserved meat, shellfish, and metal top markets. Its German market shares were, by the Commission's calculation, 75, 85 and 55 percent respectively. Regarding the first criticism the Court said:

> "The products in question have a special market only if they can be individualized not only by the mere fact that they are used for packaging certain products but also by special production characteristics which give them a specific suitability for this purpose."

In other words the Commission failed to make clear, for the purpose of assessing the existence of a dominant position, why the markets for preserved meat tins, preserved fish tins, and metal tops for glass jars should be treated separately and independently of the general market for light metal containers.

The Commission's failure here overlapped with the Court's second point:

> "A dominant position in the market for light metal containers for canned meat and fish cannot be decisive insofar as it is not proved that competitors in other fields but not in the market for light metal containers cannot, by mere adaptation, enter this market with sufficient strength to form a serious counterweight."

The Court felt that the existence or lack of competition from substitute materials such as plastic or glass as well as potential competition from new entrants to the metal container industry or purchasers who might produce their own tins were also aspects of market power insufficiently explored by the Commission. Under the Commission's own formula for establishing a dominant position, the Court annulled the decision because it did not "sufficiently explain the facts and appraisals of which it [was] based."

The Court's emphasis in *Continental Can* on "special production characteristics," entry barriers and potential competition amounted to instructions to the Commission to do its homework a little better in future market power analyses under Article 86. Evaluating potential competition, of course, involves hypothetical calculations with which even an expert Commission would have difficulty. Yet these factors, as well as those considered by the Commission, made up the commercial realities of the German marketplace for canned meat and fish tins and metal tops for glass jars. What is clear from the Court's *Continental Can* opinion is that dominance can be found under Article 86 in sub-product markets such as these, provided the Commission is exhaustive in its research and analysis.

Subsequent opinions of the Court have elaborated upon the product market analysis presented in *Continental Can.* The "interchangeability" of products for specific uses is a critical factor in determining the relevant product market under Article 86. *Hoffmann–La Roche v. Commission* (1979) Eur.Comm.Rep. 461. Thus bananas were a proper product market since their interchangeability with other fresh fruits was limited. *United Brands Co. v. Commission* (1978) Eur.Comm.Rep. 207. And the replacement market for tires (as distinct from original equipment) is another submarket capable of sustaining a dominant position. *Michelin NV v. Commission* (1983) Eur.Comm.Rep. 3461. In exceptional circumstances, even a brand name product may be the relevant sub-market. *General Motors Continental NV v. Commission* (1975) Eur.Comm.Rep. 1367 (legal monopoly over import certificates for which excessive prices were charged); *Hugin Cash Registers Ltd. v. Commission* (1979) Eur.Comm.Rep. 1869 (spare parts for brand name product must be supplied to service competitor.)

Partial *geographic* markets can also be relevant to Article 86 market power analyses. A dominant position must exist within a "substantial" part of the Common Market. The Commission discussed geographic markets amounting to the whole of Germany in its opinion concerning tins and metal tops. Yet each of these products has different transport costs. The geographic commercial realities of competition in metal tops, given their relatively low level of transport costs, are likely to be much broader than that for tins. The same comparison can be made as between small and large tins. The Court held that the Commission's geographic delineation of the markets for large and small tins in *Continental Can* was at odds with some of its own evidence on their relative transport costs. The commercial realities of potential competition in small tins appeared to go beyond the national boundaries of Germany. Thus the Commission's delineation of the particular geographic markets in *Continental Can* was insufficiently explained and appraised. Later decisions have deferred to the Commission's expertise and discretion in selecting relevant geographic markets. Belgium, Holland and Southern Germany, for example, have been held substantial parts of the Common Market for Article 86 purposes. *Re Sugar Cartel,* supra.

When exclusive intellectual property rights are conferred by national states, the question of the existence of a dominant position remains vital. A patent, copyright or trademark for an individual product does not necessarily give an enterprise independent market power. *Parke, Davis v. Probel and Centrafärm* (1968) Eur.Comm.Rep. 55; *Sirena v. Eda GmbH* (1971) Eur.Comm.Rep. 69. Other patented or nonpatented products of a similar nature may provide effective market competition and thereby protect suppliers and purchasers from abuse. The full market power analysis required in *Continental Can* must be undertaken. Similarly, the absence of patent rights is no barrier to finding a dominant position where know-how and costly and complex technology give former patentholders complete market power. *Commercial Solvents Corp. v. Commission* (1973) 12 Common Mkt.L.Rep. D50 (Commission); (1974) Eur.Comm.Rep. 223 (Court of Justice).

Article 86—Abuse

If the existence of a dominant position in the supply or acquisition of certain goods or services within a substantial part of the Common Market has been established, the next issue under Article 86 is whether an abuse or exploitation of that position has occurred. In *Commercial Solvents,* the Commission and the Court of Justice found abuse in the activities of the only producer in the world of aminobutanol, a chemical used in the making of the drug ethambutol. Commercial Solvents, a U.S. corporation, sold the chemical in Italy to its subsidiary, Istituto Chemioterapico, which in turn sold it to Zoja, an Italian firm making the drug. After merger negotiations between Istituto and Zoja broke off, Zoja sought but failed to get supplies of the chemical from Istituto.

After receiving a complaint from Zoja, the Commission commenced Article 86 infringement proceedings. It eventually held that the refusal to deal of Commercial Solvents and Istituto (viewed as one enterprise) amounted to an abuse. Commercial Solvents, through its Italian subsidiary, was ordered to promptly and in the future make supplies of aminobutanol available to Zoja at a price no higher than the maximum which it normally charged. *Commercial Solvents Corp. v. Commission,* supra.

In Re GEMA, the only German authors' and composers' rights licensing society was in possession of a dominant position within a substantial part of the European Community. This dominant position was reinforced by agreements with other societies in the EC granting exclusive rights to the various national markets. The societies were extremely advantageous and profitable to recording artists who otherwise faced formidable, if not impossible, tasks of distributing rights to their copyrighted goods on an individual basis to record manufacturers and other users. These commercial realities reinforced the Commission's conclusion that GEMA's market position was a dominant one.

The Commission instituted Article 86 infringement proceedings *sua sponte.* (1971) Common Mkt. L.Rep. D35; (1972) Common Mkt.L.Rep. 694. It decided that the imposition of higher license fees on importers of records and tape recorders, compared with fees imposed on German manufacturers, was restrictive of competition between them and therefore an abuse of GEMA's dominant position relative to its purchasers. GEMA similarly abused its dominant position by extending its members' copyrights to noncopyrighted works through a system of package license fees that failed to distinguish between copyrighted and noncopyrighted works. By discriminating through loyalty rebates between German users and users from different EC states, GEMA abusively helped to prevent the establishment of a single common market for the supply of recording services. In other words, it also abused its market power concerning potential EC competitors.

GEMA's discrimination against foreign members regarding management positions and a supplementary benefits scheme also constituted abuses of its dominant position. Requirements imposed on members to assign their rights to GEMA for the whole world and all marketing categories were deemed unnecessary to its operation and fell into the same category. GEMA members were also abusively excluded by their contract terms from recourse to the courts in the event of disputes as to distribution of GEMA funds. By requiring a six-year term, by obliging assignment of all future works during that six-year period, and by establishing a lengthy period of waiting to be eligible for certain payments, GEMA abused its dominant position through agreements with its supplier-members. By generally curtailing their mobility to join other societies in the Common Market, GEMA inhibited the process of economic integration and the creation of a single market for music publishers.

Many of the abuses found in *GEMA* do not fall under the examples provided by the Treaty terms of Article 86. From this survey of some of the abuses found, it should be apparent that once a dominant position is established the Commission feels free to roam the whole of the behavior of the dominant enterprise. Anticompetitive aspects of contractual and noncontractual relations between GEMA and its members, GEMA's constitution, its general commercial practices, and its relations with record manufacturers and users of rights were reviewed and ordered stopped or altered by the Commission. Regarding a French society of musical composers' rights, see *Greenwich Film Production, Paris v. SACEM* (1979) Eur.Comm.Rep. 3275.

Hoffmann–La Roche, the large multinational Swiss firm, was fined for abusing its dominant position in seven vitamin markets in the EC. It used a network of exclusive or preferential supply contracts, along with loyalty rebates, to reinforce its dominance by cornering retail markets. *Hoffmann–La Roche v. Commission* (1979) Eur.Comm. Rep. 461. United Brands, an American multinational, abused its dominant position in bananas through discriminatory, predatory and excessive pricing in various EC countries. Its abuses also extended to refusals to deal with important past customers and prohibiting the resale of bananas. Excessive pricing occurred when its banana prices bore little relation to the economic value of the bananas supplied. *United Brands v. Commission* (1978) Eur.Comm.Rep. 207. Abuse is thus a legal concept that allows the Commission to review business profits. Taking into account the "high profits" involved, the Commission fined United Brands 1,000,000 ECUs. In the Commission's opinion, this was a "moderate" fine under the circumstances.

Articles 85 and 86—Mergers and Acquisitions

In 1965 the Commission announced in a memorandum to the member states that EC concentration ought to be encouraged to achieve efficiency and economies of scale, and to combat competition from large American and Japanese multinational firms. These rationales have supported a long line of merger approvals by the Commission under its coal and steel concentration controls (supra). It was not until a European merger boom was in progress and extensive studies revealed increasing trends toward industrial concentration that the Commission took action against a merger in *Continental Can.* (1972) Common Mkt.L.Rep. D11.

The Commission decided Continental Can abused its dominant positions in the manufacture of meat and fish tins and metal caps in Germany in only one fashion: By announcing an 80 percent control bid for the only Dutch meat and fish tin company. The Commission reasoned that Continental Can would strengthen its dominant German market position through this Dutch acquisition, to the detriment of consumers, and that this amounted to an abuse. The Commission emphasized that potential competition between companies located within the EC was to be eliminated. Acting quickly before the merger was a *fait accompli,* the Commission underscored its inability to block proposed mergers. Continental Can was given six months to submit proposals for remedying its Article 86 infringement.

On appeal to the Court of Justice, Continental Can argued that the Commission was acting beyond its powers in attempting to control mergers under Article 86. (1973) Eur.Comm.Rep. 215. The Advocate General to the Court concurred. Nevertheless, the Court chose to go beyond the limits of the language of Articles 85 and 86 and interpret them in light of Articles 2 and 3 of the Treaty of Rome. These Articles set out the basic tasks and activities of the Community. Article 3(f) calls for the erection of a system of nondistorted competition in the Common Market.

The Court reasoned teleologically that both Articles 85 and 86 were intended to assist in the maintenance of nondistorted competition. If businesses could freely merge and eliminate competition (whereas Article 85 agreements, decisions or concerted practices merely restrict competition), a "breach in the whole system of competition law that could jeopardize the proper functioning of the common market" would be opened.

"There may therefore be abusive behavior if an enterprise in a dominant position strengthens that position so that the degree of control achieved substantially obstructs competition, i.e. so that the only enterprises left in the market are those which are dependent on the dominant enterprise with regard to their market behavior."

One problem with relying on Article 86 for control of mergers and acquisitions was the absence of any pre-merger notification system. Once a merger is a *fait accompli,* it is always difficult to persuade a court or tribunal that dissolution is desirable or even possible. The key to effective mergers regulation, as the United States has learned under its Hart–Scott–Rodino pre-merger notification rules (15 U.S.C. § 18A), is advance warning and sufficient time to block anticompetitive mergers before they are implemented.

The possibility of using Article 85 against selected mergers was surprisingly dismissed by the Commission in an early 1966 competition policy report. Commission Competition Series No. 3, *The Problem of Industrial Concentration in the Common Market* (1966). Article 85(3) notifications seeking individual exemptions (supra) could conceivably have been used for pre-merger regulatory purposes. One explanation for the Commission's early dismissal of this possibility is the contrast between the Treaty of Rome's complete absence of specific coverage of mergers and the Treaty of Paris' detailed grant of authority to the Commission of control over coal and steel concentrations. See Article 66 of Treaty of Paris. By the 1980s, with industrial concentration continuing to increase in the Community, the Commission reversed its position on the applicability of Article 85 to mergers and acquisitions. It challenged a tobacco industry acquisition as an unlawful restraint under Article 85(1). The Court of Justice held that Article 85 could be applied to the acquisition by one firm of shares in a competitor if that acquisition could influence the behavior in the marketplace of the companies involved. *British American Tobacco Co. Ltd. and R.J. Reynolds Industries, Inc. v. Commission* (1987) Eur. Comm.Rep. 4487. Likewise, Article 86 could apply if the acquisition resulted in effective control of the target company. Id.

After the ruling of the Court of Justice in *Continental Can,* the Commission submitted a comprehensive mergers' control regulation to the Council for its approval. Nearly twenty years later, a regulation on mergers was finally implemented.

Commission Regulation of Concentrations

In December of 1989, the Council of Ministers unanimously adopted Regulation 4064/89 on the Control of Concentrations Between Undertakings

("Mergers Regulation"). This regulation became effective Sept. 21, 1990. It vests in the Commission the power to oppose large-scale mergers and acquisitions of competitive consequence to the Common Market. For these purposes, a "concentration" includes almost any means by which control over another firm is acquired. This could be by a merger agreement, stock or asset purchases, contractual relationships or other actions. Most "joint ventures" between independent competitors, however, are excluded from the Mergers Regulation. See Article 3(2).

The control process established by the Mergers Regulation commences when a concentration must be notified to the Commission. The duty to notify applies within one week of the signing of a merger agreement, the acquisition of a controlling interest or the announcement of a takeover bid. Article 4(1). The Commission can fine any company failing to notify it as required. Article 14(1). The duty to notify is triggered only when the concentration involves enterprises with a combined worldwide turnover of at least 5 billion ECUs (approximately $6 billion) *and* two of them have an aggregate Community-wide turnover of 250 million ECUs (approximately $300 million). Article 1(2). These thresholds may be revised by qualified majority vote in the Council starting in 1994. Article 1(3).

As a general rule, concentrations meeting these criteria cannot be put into effect and fall exclusively within the Commission's domain. The effort here is to create a "one-stop" regulatory system. However, certain exceptions apply so as to allow national authorities to challenge some mergers. For example, this may occur under national law when two-thirds of the activities of each of the companies involved take place in the *same* member state. Article 1(2). The member states can also oppose mergers when their public security is at stake, to preserve plurality in media ownership, when financial institutions are involved or other legitimate interests are at risk. Article 21(3). If the threshold criteria of the Mergers Regulation are not met, member states can ask the Commission to investigate mergers that create or strengthen a dominant position in that state. Article 22(3). States that lack national mergers' controls seem likely to do this.

Once a concentration is notified to the Commission, it has one month to decide to investigate the merger. If a formal investigation is commenced, the Commission ordinarily then has four months to challenge or approve the merger. Article 10. During these months, in most cases, the concentration cannot be put into effect. It is on hold.

The Commission evaluates mergers in terms of their "compatibility" with the Common Market. Article 2(1). Using language reminiscent of *Continental Can* (supra), the Mergers Regulation states that if the concentration creates or strengthens a dominant position such that competition is "signifi-

cantly impeded," it is incompatible.   Article 2(2).
The Commission is authorized to consider in its
evaluation the interests of consumers and the "development of technical and economic progress."
Article 2(1)(b).   These considerations suggest an
analysis like that followed under Article 85(3) (supra).

During a mergers investigation, the Commission
can obtain information and records from the parties, and request member states to help with the
investigation.   Fines and penalties back up the
Commission's powers to obtain records and information from the parties.   Articles 11–15.   If the
concentration has already taken effect, the Commission can issue a "hold-separate" order.   Articles 7 and 10.   This requires the corporations or
assets acquired to be separated and not, operationally speaking, merged.   Approval of the merger
may involve modifications of its terms or promises
by the parties aimed at diminishing its anticompetitive potential.   Initial signs are that negotiations
with the Commission to obtain such approvals follow the pattern of negotiations associated with
negative clearances and individual exemptions under Article 85 (supra).   If the Commission ultimately decides to oppose the merger in a timely
manner, it can order its termination by whatever
means are appropriate to restore conditions of effective competition.   Such decisions can be appealed to the Court of First Instance.

*Articles 85 and 86—Application to Public Enter-
prises*

It is important to keep in mind that the provisions of Articles 85 and 86 apply to both public and
private business activities. Nationalized industries
and, to a lesser extent, state trading corporations
are relatively common phenomena in the EC. In
Italy and France, for example, the state owns businesses that account for one-third of the GDP of
those countries. In Article 90(1), the member
states agree that they shall neither enact nor
maintain any measure contrary to (*inter alia*) Article 85 or 86 for the benefit of public enterprises
or businesses granted special or exclusive rights.
The Commission can issue directives and decisions
addressed to member states to ensure compliance
with Article 90(1). See e.g. Commission Directive
80/723 (disclosure of financial relations between
member states and public enterprises) upheld in
*France, Italy and the United Kingdom v. Commis-
sion* (1982) Eur.Comm.Rep. 2545.

Under Article 90(2), any enterprise "entrusted
with the operation of services of a general economic interest" or having the character of a "revenue-
producing monopoly" is made subject to EEC competition law *but only* to the extent that the application of such law does not obstruct the de jure or de
facto fulfillment of its tasks. This "exemption"
does *not* apply if its impact on the development of
trade is contrary to the interests of the Community. The Commission may enforce EEC competition

law against Article 90(2) enterprises by appropriate directives or decisions addressed to member states. In 1989, for example, the Commission issued a directive requiring member states to increase competition in the market for telecommunications terminal equipment, including telephones, modems and telex terminals. Commission Directive 88/301. Once again the Court of Justice upheld the Commission's authority to issue directives of this type. *France v. Commission* (1991) Eur.Comm.Rep. ___ (Case C–202/88). A controversial feature of Article 90 directives is that they bypass the Community's normal legislative procedures, including Parliamentary consultation and cooperation as well as Council enactment.

The line between public and private enterprise in EEC competition law has yet to be fully clarified. GEMA, the only German authors' rights society in existence, lacked a formal state charter and was operated for profit. *Re GEMA* (1971) Common Mkt.L.Rep. D35. Consequently, it was not treated as an enterprise charged with the management of services of a general economic interest under Article 90(2). RAI, the former Italian national cablevision and television monopoly, was a public enterprise for the purposes of Article 90(1) and (2). Because many public enterprises often hold monopoly or near monopoly market positions, they are more frequently involved with Article 86 than Article 85. In *State v. Sacchi,* the Tribunale di Biella criminally prosecuted the owner-manager of a private television cable relay station operating

TV sets for the public without payment of the viewers license fee. The defendant argued that the Italian state broadcasting monopoly (RAI) was the recipient of these fees in violation of Article 86 and other treaty provisions. The Tribunale di Biella stayed its proceedings and referred these issues under Article 177 to the Court of Justice for preliminary ruling. The Italian government had strong doubts as to the necessity of such a reference to enable the judge to reach a decision.

The Court of Justice noted that there was nothing in the Treaty of Rome that prohibited member states from granting special or exclusive rights to certain public enterprises. *State v. Sacchi* (1974) Eur.Comm.Rep. 409. When these enterprises deal in goods but not, as here, in services, they remain subject to Article 37 prohibitions against discriminatory behavior on the part of state commercial monopolies. In addition, they could come under the scope of Article 86 via Article 90(2). Thus, RAI was charged with the operation of services of a general economic interest whose tasks might be obstructed by an application of EEC competition law. Since the prohibitions of Article 86 were of direct effect, the Court of Justice reasoned that they created rights for individual citizens—rights that national courts must safeguard against the activities of public enterprises.

In particular, it was for the Tribunale di Biella to ascertain whether any abuses of RAI's dominant position in commercial television services had taken place. Whether its tasks would then be obstructed by the application of Article 86 and whether this obstruction could be overridden as contrary to the interests of the Community in developing trade was a matter (like Article 85(3), the Court implied) best determined by the Commission. An abuse decision was subsequently avoided in this case by a judgment of Corte Costituzionale indicating RAI's monopoly did not extend to private cablevision enterprises. An obstruction of tasks "exemption" under Article 90(2) was therefore not necessary. The defendant was not criminally liable to the state for nonpayment of license fees used to finance RAI, but any lingering doubts about the ability of national courts or authorities and the Commission to apply Article 86 to dominant public enterprises were removed.

Generally speaking, an enterprise is "public" whenever a member state exerts a controlling influence over it. *Commission v. Italy* (1987) Eur. Comm.Rep. 2599. The source of the influence can be shareholdings, financial participation or legal provisions. Id. Thus the influence of government through subsidies, licensing or regulatory procedures can be important in determining the "public" versus "private" nature of any EC enterprise.

The distinction has legal significance. An enterprise deemed private falls directly in the path of Article 86 and Regulation 17. An enterprise deemed public may also be subject to Article 90(1) or 90(2) which involve additional considerations.

Article 90(2), for example, has its own exempting (and exception to the exemption) language and interpretive difficulties, most of which still await full development. See *Ministère Public Luxembourgeois v. Muller* (1971) Eur.Comm.Rep. 723 (Article 90(2) not directly effective); *CBEM SA v. Compagnie Luxembourgeoise de Télédiffusion SA* (1985) Eur.Comm.Rep. 3261 (national courts may entertain Article 90(2) inquiries). Despite the uncertainties of the public versus private enterprise distinction drawn in the Treaty of Rome, the attempt at placing all businesses under the rule of competition is nothing less than fundamental.

Articles 85 and 86—Directly Effective Community Law

Articles 85 and 86 are directly effective Treaty provisions. *Bosch v. deGeus* (1962) Common Mkt. L.Rep. 1; *Belgische Radio en Televisie v. SABAM* (1974) Eur.Comm.Rep. 51. All EC regulations, e.g. Council Regulation 17 of 1962, are directly applicable law in member states. Directly effective Treaty provisions and directly applicable EC regulations give individuals within member states (including enterprises) the immediate right to rely on Community law. This means that they may raise competition law issues in private litigation before national courts and tribunals. See Chapter 3. Indeed, under the supremacy doctrine, they may rely on such law to challenge contradictory national law. See Chapter 2. The directly effective nature of Articles 85 and 86 helps to explain the pervasive impact that competition law has had in European Community business life.

Article 85(2) renders offending agreements (or parts thereof) null and void. Since this is a directly effective Treaty provision, the national courts ordinarily enjoin such agreements. This assumes of course that the agreement is not exempted by the Commission under Article 85(3). Thus the national courts must assess the possibility that a business agreement is exempt or might be negatively cleared by the Commission. In making this assessment, they can avail themselves of the guidance of the Court of Justice under the Article 177 preliminary ruling procedure. See Chapter 3. Or they may simply rely upon their own analysis of the various block exemption regulations (supra) issued by the Commission under Article 85(3). Still another possibility is that the agreement will be notified by one party to the Commission for an individual exemption or negative clearance decision while national litigation is pending. In many such cases, the national courts will suspend their proceedings pending the outcome at the Commission. It is clear, however, that they need not do so as a matter of law. *SABAM,* supra. Their ability to act is derived from the directly effective nature of Articles 85 and 86.

If the agreement violates Community competition law, it is up to the national courts to determine the consequences of the nullification of agreements by Article 85(2). *Société de vente de Ciments Bétons v. Kerpen + Kerpen* (1983) Eur.Comm.Rep. 4173. This could possibly include an award of damages. Article 86 does not contain a provision that is comparable to Article 85(2). Thus the private legal remedies available when a dominant firm abuses its position must be determined strictly under national law. In Britain, the House of Lords has suggested that Article 86 creates "statutory duties," the breach of which permits the recovery of damages under torts principles. *Garden Cottage Foods Ltd. v. Milk Marketing Board* (1983) 2 All Eng.Rep. 770, 1984 A.C. 130.

The Extraterritorial Reach of Articles 85 and 86

There is a question about the extent to which the competition rules of the EEC extend to activity anywhere in the world, including activity occurring entirely or partly within the territorial limits of the United States or Canada. Decisions by the Commission and the Court of Justice suggest that the territorial reach of Articles 85 and 86 is expanding and may extend to almost any international business transaction.

For an agreement to be incompatible with the Common Market and prohibited under Article 85(1), it must be "likely to affect trade between Member States" and have the object or effect of impairing "competition within the Common Market." Taken together, these requirements amount to an "effects test" for extraterritorial application of Article 85. This test is similar to that which operates under the Sherman Act of the United States.

The Court has repeatedly held that the fact that one of the parties to an agreement is domiciled in a third country does not preclude the applicability of Article 85(1). Swiss and British chemical companies, for example, argued that the Commission was not competent to impose competition law fines for acts committed in Switzerland and Britain (before joining the EC) by enterprises domiciled outside the Community even if the acts had effects within the Common Market. See *ICI v. Commission* (1972) Eur.Comm.Rep. 619. Nevertheless, the Court held those companies in violation of Article 85 because they owned subsidiary companies within the Community and controlled their behavior. The foreign parent and its EC subsidiaries were treated as a "single enterprise" for purposes of service of process, judgment and collection of fines and penalties. In doing so, the Court observed that the fact that a subsidiary company has its own legal personality does not rule out the possibility that its conduct is attributable to the parent company.

The Court has extended its reasoning to the extraterritorial application of Article 86. An American parent company, for example, was held potentially liable for acquisitions by its EC subsidiary which affected market conditions within the Community. See *Europemballage Corp. and Conti-*

nental Can Co., Inc. v. Commission (1973) Eur. Comm.Rep. 215. In another decision, the Court held that a Maryland company's refusal to sell its product to a competitor of its affiliate company within the Community was a result of united "single enterprise" action. See *Commercial Solvents Corp. v. Commission* (1974) Eur.Comm.Rep. 223. It proceeded to state that extraterritorial conduct merely having "repercussions on competitive structures" in the Common Market fell within the parameters of Article 86. The Court ordered Commercial Solvents, through its Italian affiliate, to supply the competitor at reasonable prices.

In 1988, the Court of Justice widened the extraterritorial reach of Article 85 in a case where wood pulp producers from the U.S., Canada, Sweden and Finland were fined for price fixing activities affecting EC trade and competition. These firms did not have substantial operations within the EC. They were primarily exporters to the Common Market. This decision's reliance upon a place of implementation "effects test" is quite similar to that used under the Sherman Act. *Woodpulp Producers v. Commission* (1988) Eur.Comm.Rep. 5193. The Court has also affirmed the extraterritorial reach of Articles 85 and 86 to airfares in and out of the Community. *Ahmed Saeed Flugreisen v. Zentrale zur Bekämpfung unlauteren Wettbewerbs* (1989) Eur.Comm.Rep. 838.

Conflicts of Competition Law

Conflicts between EEC and national laws governing business competition occur. National competition laws are not per se preempted by the Treaty of Rome, whereas they appear to be preempted by the Treaty of Paris on coal and steel. The basis for the latter opinion is the absence of a requirement that infringing activities under the Treaty of Paris affect trade between member states.

In *Wilhelm v. Bundeskartellamt,* a conflict of competition laws emerged succinctly before the Court of Justice. (1969) Eur.Comm.Rep. 1. Four German producers of dyes were fined by the Bundeskartellamt authorities for price fixing activities under the German Law against Restraints of Competition. The dye producers appealed to the Kartellsenat of the Kammergericht in Berlin. The same 1967 price fixing activities of the four German firms were, *inter alia,* the subject of parallel competition law proceedings initiated by the Commission under Article 85. Before the Commission rendered its decision, defendants argued that in the light of the possibility of a conflict between EEC and German competition law, the Kammergericht could not continue its proceedings. The Kammergericht stayed its proceedings and requested a preliminary ruling on that issue from the Court of Justice.

The European Court reviewed Article 87(2)(e) of the Treaty of Rome. This article authorizes the Council to define, by regulation or directive, the relationship between national laws and EEC law on business competition. Such Council action has yet to take place, but it is worth noting that the Council could preempt national competition law entirely under this authority. The Court went on to read Article 87 in conjunction with Article 2, which enumerates certain fundamental EEC tasks including the promotion of the harmonious development of economic activities within the Community. Reading Articles 87 and 2 together, while acknowledging that the EC has instituted its own legal order which is integrated into that of its member states, the Court came to the following conclusions:

> "In principle the national authorities in competition matters may take proceedings also with regard to situations liable to be the object of the decision of the Commission ... conflicts between the Community rule and the national rules on competition should be resolved by the application of the principle of the primacy of the Community rule ... the application of national law may not prejudice the full and uniform application of the Community law or the effect of acts in implementation of it."

Insofar as EEC and national laws are in harmony, their simultaneous application can result in multiple liability. In this particular case, the four German firms were fined by the Commission and ordered to cease and desist their price fixing activities. The Kammergericht in Berlin continued to hold its proceedings in abeyance and eventually, after the Commission's decision was rendered, annulled the violations and fines imposed under German competition law on constitutional and evidentiary grounds.

The *Wilhelm* principles extend to American antitrust and EEC competition law conflicts. For example, one European member of an international price fixing quinine cartel was fined under EC law. *Re Quinine Cartel* (1969) Common Mkt.L.Rep. D41. Subsequently, that firm was fined for the same activities by U.S. authorities under American antitrust law. The price fixer then requested a credit against the EC fines in the amount of the U.S. fines. The Commission denied this request, noting that it had always been aware of the parallel American proceedings. *Re Boehringer Mannheim* (1972) Eur.Comm.Rep. 1281.

The *Wilhelm* decision reaffirms the supremacy of EC law in the event of a conflict with national competition law. In such circumstances, litigants can ordinarily invoke EEC competition law to nullify national proceedings and liability. An Article 85(3) exemption, for example, could convey immunity at the national level, but a comfort letter does not. *L'Oreal v. De Nieuwe AMCK* (1980) Eur. Comm.Rep. 3775. Since EEC competition law is very extensive, the *Wilhelm* rule of supremacy in the event of conflicts of competition law has wide repercussions.

EFTA–EEC Competition Law

The substance of EEC business competition law has already expanded its jurisdictional horizons beyond the Community's borders. In all the bilateral free trade treaties adopted in 1973 between the enlarged Community and the six remaining EFTA states, plus Finland, public and private business competition rules nearly identical to those of the Treaty of Rome were incorporated. The EFTA–EEC competition rules are intended to preserve the "proper functioning" of those treaties. Intergovernmental remedies are provided. Either the EEC or any of the EFTA states may refer incompatible business behavior for mutual consideration and acceptable solution. Sanctions lie with the administrative and legal powers of the EFTA state or the EEC wherein the offending enterprises rest. Failure to assist in the elimination of business behavior jointly objected to or about which no agreement can be reached after three months gives the party that first raised the objection the prerogative of retaliatory measures, including the withdrawal of tariff concessions.

These EFTA–EEC procedures could work as follows. Any EEC-based business or consumer group could raise the question of distortionary competitive behavior taking place in an EFTA nation with the Commission. The Commission must decide to pursue the matter and then consult with representatives of the EFTA nation. In so doing, it would undoubtedly rely on substantive developments in

competition law within the EEC to give meaning to
the similar terms that govern industrial competition as between the EEC and EFTA nations. In
one case involving a Swiss multinational defendant, the Commission relied on the competition
law of Articles 23–26 of the EEC–Switzerland Free
Trade Treaty. Here, however, the Commission by-
passed the intergovernmental procedures and acted directly against the multinational, an enterprise
that was doing business within the Community.
Commission v. Hoffmann–LaRoche (1976) Common
Mkt.L.Rep. D25.

In another case, a Swedish firm relied on the
EEC–Sweden Free Trade Treaty competition rules
in its defense to private litigation before the Nar-
ingsfrihetsombudsman (the Swedish Antitrust
Commissioner). *Hans Hauenschild Chemische Fa-
brik KG v. AB Kemiska Byggnads Produkter* (1976)
Common Mkt.L.Rep. D9. Whenever the EFTA–
EEC competition rules are interpreted as "directly
effective" law in EEC and EFTA states, as appears
to have been assumed in this Swedish case, then
there is no need to go through the Commission or
EFTA national governments to seek redress. See
Hauptzollamt Mainz v. C.A. Kupferberg Ge KG
(1982) Eur.Comm.Rep. 3641 (Portugal–EEC Free
Trade Treaty directly effective). Private action
raising EFTA–EEC competition law issues in any
national court or tribunal would suffice, just as it
does under EEC competition law.

The EFTA–EEC competition law provisions are
procedurally and substantively similar to those

that have existed and to a limited degree been applied as between EFTA states since 1959. The EFTA Treaty requires that expected "benefits" of the treaties be frustrated before the competition rules come into effect. This difficult criterion has inhibited the application of internal EFTA competition law. Nevertheless, the EFTA countries have agreed to investigate business activities whenever there is *prima facie* evidence of an infringement. This agreement removes the need for instigation of formal intergovernmental complaint procedures under the EFTA Treaty. A similar agreement as between EFTA states and the EEC would provide another means for fast action on individual complaints under EFTA–EEC competition rules.

The net result substantively of the EEC Treaty, the EFTA Treaty and the bilateral 1973 EFTA–EEC treaties is a coherent body of business competition law for most of Western Europe. Only the enforcement systems differ, differences that do not significantly impede legal integration in this field. Indeed, early signs in the current negotiations over the linkage of EFTA and the EC in a European Economic Area (EEA) suggest that EEC competition law rules will be applied within the scope of that agreement. Enforcement will apparently be undertaken by an equivalent of the Commission composed of EFTA and EC officials.

CHAPTER 8

BEYOND 1992

President Mitterand of France has said that European history is accelerating. European Community law reflects this truth. This final chapter briefly and provocatively considers what lies beyond 1992.

Enlargement

The European Community is like a magnet. The larger its size, the greater its force. If the 1992 campaign is fully or even just mostly realized, as seems likely, the attraction of the EC to other European nations will be overwhelming. Doubly so if a single currency and an economic union materialize by the turn of the millennium. The Community will temporize on new admissions and create interim arrangements like the European Economic Area with EFTA. Eventually, however, it will open up out of self-interest, political pressure and moral imperatives. Austria, Sweden, Norway, Malta, Iceland and perhaps even Switzerland are likely to lead the way. Finland, Hungary, Poland and Czechoslovakia could be the second wave. And the third wave would bring in the rest, maybe with parts of the Soviet Union.

In time, the pressure to admit other European nations to the European Community will prevail. An EC with as many as 30 member states is not inconceivable. This prospect makes study of the law of the EC the study of much of the future of Europe.

Economic and Monetary Union

The legal basis for the European Monetary System and ECUs was substantially advanced by the addition to the Treaty of Rome of Article 102A by the Single European Act of 1987. This article commits the Member States to further development of the EMS and ECU, recognizes the cooperation of the central banks in management of the system, but specifically requires further amendment of the Treaty if "institutional changes" are required. In other words, a common currency managed by an EC central bank system is *not* a part of the 1992 campaign. In 1990, however, draft plans for such developments surfaced in the Commission using the U.S. Federal Reserve Board as a model. Britain, always concerned about losses of economic sovereignty (what greater loss is there than the power to print money?), proposed an alternative known as the "hard ECU." This proposal retains the national currencies but adds the hard ECU as competitor of each, letting the marketplace in most instances decide which currency it prefers.

In December of 1989, the European Council (out-voting Britain) approved a three stage approach to economic and monetary union (EMU) of the Community. Stage One began July 1, 1990. Its focus is on expanding the power and influence of the Committee of Central Bank Governors over monetary affairs. This Committee is a kind of EuroFed in embryo. It is primarily engaged in "multilateral surveillance." Stage One also seeks greater economic policy coordination and convergence among the member states. Stage Two envisions the creation of a Community central banking system (EuroFed), which will function with national currencies in the context of the EMS and ERM. Stage Two is a learning and transition period. In October of 1990, it was agreed (save Britain) that Stage Two will commence January 1, 1994. Stage Three involves the replacement of the national currencies with a single currency, the ECU managed by the EuroFed. No date has been fixed for implementation of Stage Three, but many predict it will occur prior to the year 2000. Negotiations are underway within an intergovernmental conference on Treaty of Rome amendments to achieve economic and monetary union.

Political Union

How long can governance of the Community postpone its rendezvous with democracy? The predominance of the Council will become increasingly embarrassing and intolerable. Negotiations within

an intergovernmental conference on "political union" amendments to the Treaty of Rome are underway. Incremental changes, as in the past, will
prevail. But what is the end result? One vision of
the future has the Council of Ministers becoming
an "upper house" like the American Senate to the
House of Representatives, though most probably
with more power. In this scenario, the Commission becomes the Executive Branch of EC government. It could have a directly elected President
who then appoints a Cabinet with Parliamentary
or Council approval. The variations on these
themes are endless.

Another vision of the future was adopted, way
before its time, in 1984 by the Parliament. In its
"Draft Treaty establishing European Union" (Spin-
nelli Report), the Parliament showed strong feder-
alist proclivities. This Treaty would have totally
replaced the Treaty of Rome. The law-making
powers of the Council would be shifted to the
Parliament and Commission with limited member
state ability to block new policy initiatives. There
would also be serious sanctions on member states
who persistently breach their EC duties. The
Court of Justice would get the power to appeal
decisions of national courts. A common monetary
system, a common citizenship and effective protection of fundamental human rights were also part
of Parliament's vision of European Union.

Foreign Policy (Political Cooperation)

The Foreign Ministers of the member states regularly meet and seek to coordinate EC foreign policy matters. These ministers have their own secretariat in Brussels to monitor and implement common foreign policy positions. Junior staff members supervise much of this work through what is called the European Political Committee. The EC Commission is represented at all meetings of this Committee and the Foreign Ministers. The EC Parliament, however, is merely briefed after the fact about these meetings and is for the most part limited to asking questions of the Foreign Ministers.

The heads of state and government also meet twice a year in what is called "The European Council," as distinct from the Council of Ministers. The President of the Commission participates in meetings of the European Council. These meetings have increased the degree of foreign policy cooperation (known as "political cooperation") within the Community, but not without criticism. The European Council and the Foreign Ministers' meetings function outside the Treaty of Rome and its various policy making mandates and voting procedures, including consultation or cooperation with Parliament. Hence, foreign policy coordination is purely intergovernmental in nature, and does not involve supranational EC mandates. Foreign policy cooperation has been a part of Community affairs since 1970 and was formally recognized in Article 30 of the Single European Act of 1987. Unlike most SEA provisions, this article does not amend the Treaty of Rome. It stands on its own as a separate international agreement and, to a large extent, codifies the existing foreign policy cooperation procedures.

The net result is that the European Community increasingly speaks with a single voice on foreign affairs. This has been very evident regarding political developments in Eastern Europe, the Middle East (less so on the Gulf War), Cyprus, South Africa, Namibia, Angola, Iran (especially to condemn the threats against Salman Rushdie), Cambodia, Afghanistan, and Central America. But the increasing involvement of the European Community in world politics makes it more difficult for traditionally neutral nations like Austria, Sweden and Switzerland to join the EC, not to mention the discomfort that neutral Ireland feels on the inside. Already there are arguments over whether it is possible to segregate the Community's economic and political spheres for membership purposes.

Defense

In the early years of the Coal and Steel Community, a European Defense Community (EDC) treaty was drafted and nearly adopted. It failed when the French National Assembly refused to ratify it in 1954. Under this proposal, a European army would have been placed under the control of a European Ministry of Defense functioning within the North Atlantic Treaty Organization (NATO) alliance. The institutional structure of the EDC would have been similar to that employed in the Coal and Steel Community. The rejection by the French National Assembly was led by the Gaullists who quite simply did not want to surrender sovereignty over the French army, even if this meant that the West Germans could re-arm on their own. Following a British initiative, however, a looser confederation for military purposes was established, the Western European Union (WEU). It was under this Union that West Germany and Italy re-armed and were integrated into the NATO alliance.

The Western European Union presently includes nine of the twelve EC member states. Denmark, Ireland and Greece are not members. In April of 1990, in the middle of a European Council summit meeting, a short WEU meeting of foreign ministers was held. The purpose of this meeting was to organize the airlift to the Kurds that the summit had just agreed upon. Some observers see this meeting as an historic first step towards making the WEU the defense arm of the European Community.

The integration of Europe's defense may be the ultimate in politically sensitive issues. Neutrality, the NATO alliance and a host of national interests stand in the way of a Common Defense Policy for the European Community. Transfers of sovereignty over war, peace, military forces, military weap-

ons, and military command are momentous issues
not only for the member states, but the world.

APPENDIX A

1992 AT A GLANCE

By 1992, the European Community intends to have
implemented 282 regulations to create a single
internal market. The following specific
changes represent the major part of the 1992
program. The EC's intended dates of implementation follow each subject area. The status of these regulations is coded as follows: (1)
Adopted (2) Mostly Adopted (3) Proposed (4)
Proposal Due, NA—Not Applicable, TBA—To
Be Announced.

In standards, testing and certification

Harmonization of standards for:

Simple pressure vessels (1) 7/92

Toys (1) 6/89

Construction products (1) 6/90

Machine safety (1) 12/92

Agricultural & forestry tractors (1) 9/88–1/91

Cosmetics (1) 12/89

Quick frozen foods (1) 7/90

Flavorings (1) 7/90

Food emulsifiers (1) 1/85

Food preservatives (1) 12/86

Jams (1) 12/89

Fruit juices (1) 5/91

Food inspection (1) 6/91

Definition of spirited beverages & aromatised wines (1) 12/89

Coffee extracts & chicory extracts (1) 7/88

Food additives (1) 6/90

Materials & articles in contact with food (1) 7/90–1/92

Tower cranes (noise) (1) 6/89

Household appliances (noise) (1) 12/89

Tire pressure gauges (1) 11/87

Hydraulic diggers (noise) (1) 1/90

Detergents (1) 1/90

Law mower (noise) (1) 7/91

Radio interferences (1) 1/92

Automobiles, trucks, motorcycles and emissions (1) 7/88

Liquid fertilizers & secondary fertilizers (1) 1989, 90, 91, 92

Lifting and loading equipment (1) NA

Measuring instruments (1) 1/92

Gas appliances (1) 1/92

Telecommunications (2) 7/24–12/94

Earthmoving equipment (2) 1/89–12/93

Medicinal products & medical specialties (2) 1/92

Personal protection equipment (2) 1991, 1992

Global Approach to Testing & Certification (3) 1/93

Medical devices (3) 1/92

Infant formula (3) NA

New rules for harmonizing packing, labelling and processing requirements

Ingredients for food & beverages (1) 5/89

Irradiation (1) NA

Nutritional labelling (1) 4/92

Classification, packaging, & labelling of dangerous preparations (1) 6/89–6/91

Extraction solvents (3) NA

Harmonization of regulations for the health industry

Medical specialties (1) 7/87 *

High technology medicines (1) 7/87

Veterinary medicinal products (1) 7/87

Implantable electromedical devices (1) 7/92

Pharmaceuticals (2) 12/89–12/92

Non implantable, active medical devices (4) NA

Non active medical devices (4) NA

In-vitro diagnostics (4) NA

Changes in government procurement regulations

Coordination of procedures on the award of public works & supply contracts (1) 7/90 **

Extension of E.C. law to telecommunications, utilities, transport (3) services (1) 7/92

Harmonization of regulation of services

Mutual Funds (1) 10/89

Broadcasting (1) 10/91

Tourism (1) 10/85, 12/92

Air transport (1) 1988, 1992

Electronic payment cards (1) 1/89

Information services (2) NA

Life & nonlife insurance (2) 1/90

Banking (2) 12/90–1/93

Securities (2) 2/87–1/93

Maritime transport (2) 7/87

Road passenger transport (2) 1/88–7/90

Railways (3) NA

Liberalization of capital movements

Long-term capital, stocks (1) 2/87 ***

Short-term capital (1) 7/90

Consumer protection regulations

Misleading definitions of products (1) 10/88

Indication of prices (1) 6/90

Harmonization of taxation

Value added taxes (3) 1/86–12/92

Excise taxes on alcohol, tobacco, and other (3) 12/92

Harmonization of laws regulating company behavior

Trademarks (2) 12/91

Accounting operations across borders (2) 1/90

Protection of computer programs (3) TBA

Transaction taxes (3) TBA

Company law (3) TBA

Mergers & acquisitions (2) 9/90

Copyrights (3) TBA

Cross border mergers (3) 9/90

Bankruptcy (4) NA

Harmonization of veterinary & phytosanitary controls

Harmonization of an extensive list of rules covering items such as:

Antibiotic residues (1) 4/87–12/87

Bovine animals and meat (1) 1/88

Porcine animals and meat (1) 3/87

Plant health (1) 1/85

Fish & fish products (3) 1/93

Live poultry, poultry meat and hatching eggs (3) 9/89

Pesticide residues in fruit & vegetables (3) 12/89

Elimination and simplification of national transit documents and procedures for intra-EC trade

Introduction of the Single Administrative Document (SAD) (1) 1/88

Abolition of customs presentation charges (1) 1/88

Elimination of customs formalities & the introduction of common border posts (1) 7/87

Harmonization of rules pertaining to the free movement of labor and the professions within the EC

Mutual recognition of higher educational diplomas (1) 1/91

Comparability of vocational training qualifications (1) 7/87

Specific training in general medical practice (1) 1/95

Training of engineers (1) 12/92

Activities in the field of pharmacy (1) 10/87

Activities related to commercial agents (1) 1/90–1/94

Income taxation provisions (3) 7/90

Elimination of burdensome requirements related to residence permits (4) NA

---

* Portugal must comply by 1/91

** Spain, Portugal, Greece by 3/92

*** Portugal 1/90, Spain 1/92

Source: Business America, February 25, 1991

APPENDIX B

THE COMMUNITY'S AGREEMENTS WITH MEDITERRANEAN AND ACP COUNTRIES

Entry into force		Industry	Agriculture	Other measures: a) social b) econ. and tech. cooperation c) financial pro- tocol
Maghred Algeria Tunisia Morocco	1977	duty-free access to EEC market ex-cept for cork and refined petroleum products	30–100% tariff pref-erences, special rules for wine, vege-tables, olive oil	a + b + c
Mashrek Egypt Jordan Syria Lebanon	1976	duty-free access to EEC market with import ceilings for certain woven cot-ton fabrics, refined petroleum prod-ucts, phosphate fertilizers and alu-minums	tariff preferences of 40–100% on some products	b + c
Malta	1971	70% tariff prefer-ences, except for textile products	tariff preferences of 40–75% for particu-lar periods and products	b + c
Cyprus	1973	70% tariff prefer-ences	tariff preferences, special rules for po-tatoes and grapes	b + c
Israel	1975	duty-free access to EEC market	20–80% tariff pref-erences, special rules for certain products	b + c
Yugoslavia	1980	duty-free access to EEC market, tariff ceilings on 29 prod-ucts	tariff preferences coupled with ceil-ings on wine, tobac-co, beef and veal	a + b
Turkey	1964	duty-free access to EEC market, ex-cept for petroleum and textile prod-ucts	tariff preferences on certain products	a + b + c

ACP States	1976	duty-free access to EEC market	tariff preferences, sugar protocol for guaranteed purchase of 1.4 million tons	b + c

Stabilization of export earnings (Stabex)

Source: Guth and Aeikens, Implications of The Second Enlargement for the Mediterranean and 'ACP' Policies of the European Community, Europe Information (1980).

Appendix C

EC LEGISLATION FROM
START TO FINISH

(Directives and Regulations)

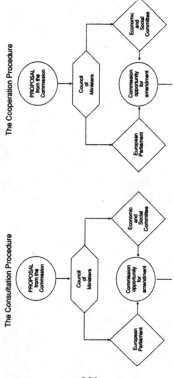

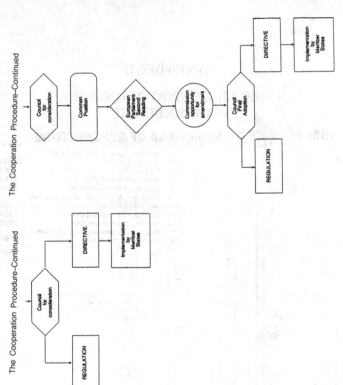

Source: COMPLETING THE INTERNAL MARKET (EC Official Publications, 1989)

APPENDIX D

EC 1989 BUDGET BY MAIN AREA
OF EXPENDITURE

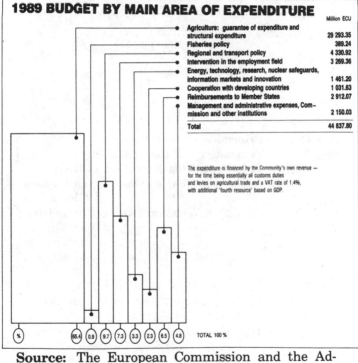

1989 BUDGET BY MAIN AREA OF EXPENDITURE

Million ECU

Agriculture: guarantee of expenditure and structural expenditure	29 293.35
Fisheries policy	389.24
Regional and transport policy	4 330.92
Intervention in the employment field	3 269.36
Energy, technology, research, nuclear safeguards, information markets and innovation	1 461.20
Cooperation with developing countries	1 031.63
Reimbursements to Member States	2 912.07
Management and administrative expenses, Commission and other institutions	2 150.03
Total	**44 837.80**

The expenditure is financed by the Community's own revenue — for the time being essentially all customs duties and levies on agricultural trade and a VAT rate of 1.4%, with additional 'fourth resource' based on GDP.

% (65.4) (0.9) (9.7) (7.3) (3.3) (2.3) (6.5) (4.8)   TOTAL 100 %

Source: The European Commission and the Administration of the Community (EC Official Publications, 1989).

331

APPENDIX E

TREATY ESTABLISHING THE EUROPEAN ECONOMIC COMMUNITY
(Treaty of Rome 1957, as amended through 1990) (1987 Single European Act Amendments identified by SEA in brackets.) *
(Selected Provisions)

Summary Table of Contents

* Courtesy of European Community Information Service, Washington, D.C. The "Merger Treaty" is the Treaty Establishing A Single Council and A Single Commission of the European Communities, July 1, 1967.

PART ONE. PRINCIPLES

Article 1

By this Treaty, the High Contracting Parties establish among themselves a EUROPEAN ECONOMIC COMMUNITY.

Article 2

The Community shall have as its task, by establishing a common market and progressively approximating the economic policies of Member States, to promote throughout the Community a harmonious development of economic activities, a continuous and balanced expansion, an increase in stability, an accelerated raising of the standard of living and closer relations between the States belonging to it.

Article 3

For the purposes set out in Article 2, the activities of the Community shall include, as provided in this Treaty and in accordance with the timetable set out therein

(a) the elimination, as between Member States, of customs duties and of quantitative restrictions on the import and export of goods, and of all other measures having equivalent effect;

(b) the establishment of a common customs tariff and of a common commercial policy towards third countries;

(c) the abolition, as between Member States, of obstacles to freedom of movement for persons, services and capital;

(d) the adoption of a common policy in the sphere of agriculture;

(e) the adoption of a common policy in the sphere of transport;

(f) the institution of a system ensuring that competition in the common market is not distorted;

(g) the application of procedures by which the economic policies of Member States can be coordinated and disequilibria in their balances of payments remedied;

(h) the approximation of the laws of Member States to the extent required for the proper functioning of the common market;

(i) the creation of a European Social Fund in order to improve employment opportunities for workers and to contribute to the raising of their standard of living;

(j) the establishment of a European Investment Bank to facilitate the economic expansion of the Community by opening up fresh resources;

(k) the association of the overseas countries and territories in order to increase trade and to promote jointly economic and social development.

Article 4

1. The tasks entrusted to the Community shall be carried out by the following institutions:

an ASSEMBLY,

a COUNCIL,

a COMMISSION,

a COURT OF JUSTICE.

Each institution shall act within the limits of the powers conferred upon it by this Treaty.

2. The Council and the Commission shall be assisted by an Economic and Social Committee acting in an advisory capacity.

3. The audit shall be carried out by a Court of Auditors acting within the limits of the powers conferred upon it by this Treaty.

Article 5

Member States shall take all appropriate measures, whether general or particular, to ensure fulfilment of the obligations arising out of this Treaty or resulting from action taken by the institutions of the Community. They shall facilitate the achievement of the Community's tasks.

They shall abstain from any measure which could jeopardise the attainment of the objectives of this Treaty.

Article 6

1. Member States shall, in close cooperation with the institutions of the Community, coordinate their respec-

tive economic policies to the extent necessary to attain the objectives of this Treaty.

2. The institutions of the Community shall take care not to prejudice the internal and external financial stability of the Member States.

Article 7

Within the scope of application of this Treaty, and without prejudice to any special provisions contained therein, any discrimination on grounds of nationality shall be prohibited.

The Council may, on a proposal from the Commission and in cooperation with the European Parliament, adopt, by a qualified majority, rules designed to prohibit such discrimination.

Article 8

1. The common market shall be progressively established during a transitional period of twelve years.

This transitional period shall be divided into three stages of four years each; the length of each stage may be altered in accordance with the provisions set out below.

* * *

6. Nothing in the preceding paragraphs shall cause the transitional period to last more than fifteen years after the entry into force of this Treaty.

7. Save for the exceptions or derogations provided for in this Treaty, the expiry of the transitional period shall constitute the latest date by which all the rules laid down must enter into force and all the measures required for establishing the common market must be implemented.

Article 8 A

[SEA]

The Community shall adopt measures with the aim of progressively establishing the internal market over a period expiring on 31 December 1992, in accordance with the provisions of this Article and of Articles 8 D, 8 C, 28, 57(2), 59, 70(1), 83, 99, 100 A and 100 B and without prejudice to the other provisions of this Treaty.

The internal market shall comprise an area without internal frontiers in which the free movement of goods, persons, services and capital is ensured in accordance with the provisions of this Treaty.

* * *

Article 8 C

[SEA]

When drawing up its proposals with a view to achieving the objectives set out in Article 8 A, the Commission shall take into account the extent of the effort that certain economies showing differences in development will have to sustain during the period of establishment of the internal market and it may propose appropriate provisions.

If these provisions take the form of derogations, they must be of a temporary nature and must cause the least possible disturbance to the functioning of the common market.

PART TWO. FOUNDATIONS OF THE COMMUNITY

TITLE I. FREE MOVEMENT OF GOODS

Article 9

1. The Community shall be based upon a customs union which shall cover all trade in goods and which shall involve the prohibition between Member States of customs duties on imports and exports and of all charges having equivalent effect, and the adoption of a common customs tariff in their relations with third countries.

2. The provisions of Chapter 1, Section 1, and of Chapter 2 of this Title shall apply to products originating in Member States and to products coming from third countries which are in free circulation in Member States.

Article 10

1. Products coming from a third country shall be considered to be in free circulation in a Member State if the import formalities have been complied with and any customs duties or charges having equivalent effect which are payable have been levied in that Member State, and if they have not benefited from a total or partial drawback of such duties or charges.

*   *   *

CHAPTER 1.   THE CUSTOMS UNION

Section 1

Elimination of Customs Duties Between Member States

Article 12

Member States shall refrain from introducing between themselves any new customs duties on imports or exports or any charges having equivalent effect, and from increasing those which they already apply in their trade with each other.

Article 13

1.   Customs duties on imports in force between Member States shall be progressively abolished by them during the transitional period in accordance with Articles 14 and 15.

2.   Charges having an effect equivalent to customs duties on imports, in force between Member States, shall be progressively abolished by them during the transitional period.   *   *   *

*   *   *

Article 16

Member States shall abolish between themselves customs duties on exports and charges having equivalent effect by the end of the first stage at the latest.

*   *   *

Section 2

Setting up of the Common Customs Tariff

Article 18

The Member States declare their readiness to contribute to the development of international trade and the lowering of barriers to trade by entering into agreements designed, on a basis of reciprocity and mutual advantage, to reduce customs duties below the general level of which they could avail themselves as a result of the establishment of a customs union between them.

Article 19

1. Subject to the conditions and within the limits provided for hereinafter, duties in the common customs tariff shall be at the level of the arithmetical average of the duties applied in the four customs territories comprised in the Community.

* * *

Article 27

Before the end of the first stage, Member States shall, in so far as may be necessary, take steps to approximate their provisions laid down by law, regulation or administrative action in respect of customs matters. To this end, the Commission shall make all appropriate recommendations to Member States.

* * *

Article 28

[SEA]

Any autonomous alteration or suspension of duties in the common customs tariff shall be decided by the Council acting by a qualified majority on a proposal from the Commission.

CHAPTER 2. ELIMINATION OF QUANTITATIVE RESTRICTIONS BETWEEN MEMBER STATES

Article 30

Quantitative restrictions on imports and all measures having equivalent effect shall, without prejudice to the following provisions, be prohibited between Member States.

Article 31

Member States shall refrain from introducing between themselves any new quantitative restrictions or measures having equivalent effect.

* * *

Article 32

In their trade with one another, Member States shall refrain from making more restrictive the quotas and measures having equivalent effect existing at the date of the entry into force of this Treaty.

These quotas shall be abolished by the end of the transitional period at the latest. During that period, they shall be progressively abolished * * *

* * *

Article 34

1. Quantitative restrictions on exports, and all measures having equivalent effect, shall be prohibited between Member States.

2. Member States shall, by the end of the first stage at the latest, abolish all quantitative restrictions on exports and any measures having equivalent effect which are in existence when this Treaty enters into force.

* * *

Article 36

The provisions of Articles 30 to 34 shall not preclude prohibitions or restrictions on imports, exports or goods in transit justified on grounds of public morality, public policy or public security; the protection of health and life of humans, animals or plants; the protection of national treasures possessing artistic, historic or archaeological value; or the protection of industrial and commercial property. Such prohibitions or restrictions shall not, however, constitute a means of arbitrary discrimination or a disguised restriction on trade between Member States.

Article 37

1. Member States shall progressively adjust any State monopolies of a commercial character so as to ensure that when the transitional period has ended no discrimination regarding the conditions under which goods are procured and marketed exists between nationals of Member States.

The provisions of this Article shall apply to any body through which a Member State, in law or in fact, either directly or indirectly supervises, determines or appreciably influences imports or exports between Member States. These provisions shall likewise apply to monopolies delegated by the State to others.

2. Member States shall refrain from introducing any new measure which is contrary to the principles laid down in paragraph 1 or which restricts the scope of the Articles dealing with the abolition of customs duties and quantitative restrictions between Member States.

3. The timetable for the measures referred to in paragraph 1 shall be harmonised with the abolition of

quantitative restrictions on the same products provided for in Articles 30 to 34.

If a product is subject to a State monopoly of a commercial character in only one or some Member States, the Commission may authorise the other Member States to apply protective measures until the adjustment provided for in paragraph 1 has been effected; the Commission shall determine the conditions and details of such measures.

4. If a State monopoly of a commercial character has rules which are designed to make it easier to dispose of agricultural products or obtain for them the best return, steps should be taken in applying the rules contained in this Article to ensure equivalent safeguards for the employment and standard of living of the producers concerned, account being taken of the adjustments that will be possible and the specialisation that will be needed with the passage of time.

5. The obligations on Member States shall be binding only in so far as they are compatible with existing international agreements.

6. With effect from the first stage the Commission shall make recommendations as to the manner in which and the timetable according to which the adjustment provided for in this Article shall be carried out.

TITLE II. AGRICULTURE

Article 38

1. The common market shall extend to agriculture and trade in agricultural products. "Agricultural products" means the products of the soil, of stockfarming and of fisheries and products of first-stage processing directly related to these products.

* * *

4. The operation and development of the common market for agricultural products must be accompanied by the establishment of a common agricultural policy among the Member States.

Article 39

1. The objectives of the common agricultural policy shall be:

(a) to increase agricultural productivity by promoting technical progress and by ensuring the rational development of agricultural production and the optimum utilisation of the factors of production, in particular labour;

(b) thus to ensure a fair standard of living for the agricultural community, in particular by increasing the individual earnings of persons engaged in agriculture;

(c) to stabilise markets;

(d) to assure the availability of supplies;

(e) to ensure that supplies reach consumers at reasonable prices.

2. In working out the common agricultural policy and the special methods for its application, account shall be taken of:

(a) the particular nature of agricultural activity, which results from the social structure of agriculture and from structural and natural disparities between the various agricultural regions;

(b) the need to effect the appropriate adjustments by degrees;

(c) the fact that in the Member States agriculture constitutes a sector closely linked with the economy as a whole.

Article 40

1. Member States shall develop the common agricultural policy by degrees during the transitional period and shall bring it into force by the end of that period at the latest.

2. In order to attain the objectives set out in Article 39 a common organisation of agricultural markets shall be established.

This organisation shall take one of the following forms, depending on the product concerned:

(a) common rules on competition;

(b) compulsory coordination of the various national market organisations;

(c) a European market organisation.

3. The common organisation established in accordance with paragraph 2 may include all measures required to attain the objectives set out in Article 39, in particular regulation of prices, aids for the production and marketing of the various products, storage and carryover arrangements and common machinery for stabilising imports or exports.

The common organisation shall be limited to pursuit of the objectives set out in Article 39 and shall exclude any discrimination between producers or consumers within the Community.

Any common price policy shall be based on common criteria and uniform methods of calculation.

4. In order to enable the common organisation referred to in paragraph 2 to attain its objectives, one or more agricultural guidance and guarantee funds may be set up.

Article 41

To enable the objectives set out in Article 39 to be attained, provision may be made within the framework of the common agricultural policy for measures such as:

(a) an effective coordination of efforts in the spheres of vocational training, of research and of the dissemination of agricultural knowledge; this may include joint financing of projects or institutions;

(b) joint measures to promote consumption of certain products.

Article 42

The provisions of the Chapter relating to rules on competition shall apply to production of and trade in agricultural products only to the extent determined by the Council within the framework of Article 43(2) and (3) and in accordance with the procedure laid down therein, account being taken of the objectives set out in Article 39.

The Council may, in particular, authorise the granting of aid:

(a) for the protection of enterprises handicapped by structural or natural conditions;

(b) within the framework of economic development programmes.

*   *   *

TITLE III. FREE MOVEMENT OF PERSONS, SERVICES, CAPITAL

CHAPTER 1. WORKERS

Article 48

1. Freedom of movement for workers shall be secured within the Community by the end of the transitional period at the latest.

2. Such freedom of movement shall entail the abolition of any discrimination based on nationality between workers of the Member States as regards employment, remuneration and other conditions of work and employment.

3. It shall entail the right, subject to limitations justified on grounds of public policy, public security or public health:

(a) to accept offers of employment actually made;

(b) to move freely within the territory of Member States for this purpose;

(c) to stay in a Member State for the purpose of employment in accordance with the provisions governing the employment of nationals of that State laid down by law, regulation or administrative action;

(d) to remain in the territory of a Member State after having been employed in that State, subject to conditions which shall be embodied in implementing regulations to be drawn up by the Commission.

4. The provisions of this Article shall not apply to employment in the public service.

Article 49

As soon as this Treaty enters into force, the Council shall, acting by a qualified majority on a proposal from the Commission, in cooperation with the European Parliament and after consulting the Economic and Social Committee, issue directives or make regulations setting out the measures required to bring about, by progressive stages, freedom of movement for workers, as defined in Article 48, in particular:

(a) by ensuring close cooperation between national employment services;

(b) by systematically and progressively abolishing those administrative procedures and practices and those qualifying periods in respect of eligibility for available employment, whether resulting from national legislation or from agreements previously concluded between Member States, the maintenance of which would form an obstacle to liberalisation of the movement of workers;

(c) by systematically and progressively abolishing all such qualifying periods and other restrictions provided for either under national legislation or under agreements previously concluded between Member States as imposed on workers of other Member States conditions regarding the free choice of employment other than those imposed on workers of the State concerned;

(d) by setting up appropriate machinery to bring offers of employment into touch with applications for employment and to facilitate the achievement of a balance between supply and demand in the employment market in such a way as to avoid serious threats to the standard of living and level of employment in the various regions and industries.

Article 50

Member States shall, within the framework of a joint programme, encourage the exchange of young workers.

Article 51

The Council shall, acting unanimously on a proposal from the Commission, adopt such measures in the field of social security as are necessary to provide freedom of movement for workers; to this end, it shall make arrangements to secure for migrant workers and their dependents:

(a) aggregation, for the purpose of acquiring and retaining the right to benefit and of calculating the amount of benefit, of all periods taken into account under the laws of the several countries;

(b) payment of benefits to persons resident in the territories of Member States.

CHAPTER 2.   RIGHT OF ESTABLISHMENT

Article 52

Within the framework of the provisions set out below, restrictions on the freedom of establishment of nationals of a Member State in the territory of another Member State shall be abolished by progressive stages in the course of the transitional period. Such progressive abolition shall also apply to restrictions on the setting up of agencies, branches or subsidiaries by nationals of any Member State established in the territory of any Member State.

Freedom of establishment shall include the right to take up and pursue activities as self-employed persons and to set up and manage undertakings, in particular companies or firms within the meaning of the second paragraph of Article 58, under the conditions laid down for its own nationals by the law of the country where such establishment is effected, subject to the provisions of the Chapter relating to capital.

Article 53

Member States shall not introduce any new restrictions on the right of establishment in their territories of nationals of other Member States, save as otherwise provided in this Treaty.

Article 54

1. Before the end of the first stage, the Council shall, acting unanimously on a proposal from the Commission and after consulting the Economic and Social Committee and the Assembly, draw up a general programme for the abolition of existing restrictions on freedom of establishment within the Community. The Commission shall submit its proposal to the Council during the first two years of the first stage.

The programme shall set out the general conditions under which freedom of establishment is to be attained in the case of each type of activity and in particular the stages by which it is to be attained.

2. In order to implement this general programme or, in the absence of such programme, in order to achieve a stage in attaining freedom of establishment as regards a particular activity, the Council shall, on a proposal from the Commission in cooperation with the European Parliament and after consulting the Economic and Social Committee and the Assembly, issue directives, acting unanimously until the end of the first stage and by a qualified majority thereafter.

* * *

Article 55

The provisions of this Chapter shall not apply, so far as any given Member State is concerned, to activities which in that State are connected, even occasionally, with the exercise of official authority.

The Council may, acting by a qualified majority on a proposal from the Commission, rule that the provisions of this Chapter shall not apply to certain activities.

Article 56

1.　The provisions of this Chapter and measures taken in pursuance thereof shall not prejudice the applicability of provisions laid down by law, regulation or administrative action providing for special treatment for foreign nationals on grounds of public policy, public security or public health.

2.　Before the end of the transitional period, the Council shall, acting unanimously on a proposal from the Commission and after consulting the Assembly, issue directives for the coordination of the aforementioned provisions laid down by law, regulation or administrative action.　After the end of the second stage, however, the Council shall, acting by a qualified majority on a proposal from the Commission in cooperation with the European Parliament, issue directives for the coordination of such provisions as, in each Member State, are a matter for regulation or administrative action.

Article 57

1.　In order to make it easier for persons to take up and pursue activities as self-employed persons, the Council shall, on a proposal from the Commission and in cooperation with the European Parliament, acting unanimously during the first stage and by a qualified majority thereafter, issue directives for the mutual recognition of diplomas, certificates and other evidence of formal qualifications.

2.　For the same purpose, the Council shall, before the end of the transitional period, acting on a proposal from the Commission and after consulting the Assembly, issue directives for the coordination of the provisions laid down by law, regulation or administrative action in Member States concerning the taking up and pursuit of activities as self-employed persons. Unanimity shall be required for directives the implementation of which involves, in at least one Member State, amendment of the existing principles laid down by law governing the professions with respect to training and conditions of access for natural persons. In other cases, the Council shall act by a qualified majority, in cooperation with the European Parliament. [SEA]

3. In the case of the medical and allied and pharmaceutical professions, the progressive abolition of restrictions shall be dependent upon coordination of the conditions for their exercise in the various Member States.

Article 58

Companies or firms formed in accordance with the law of a Member State and having their registered office, central administration or principal place of business within the Community shall, for the purposes of this Chapter, be treated in the same way as natural persons who are nationals of Member States.

"Companies or firms" means companies or firms constituted under civil or commercial law, including cooperative societies, and other legal persons governed by public or private law, save for those which are non-profitmaking.

CHAPTER 3.   SERVICES

Article 59

Within the framework of the provisions set out below, restrictions on freedom to provide services within the Community shall be progressively abolished during the transitional period in respect of nationals of Member States who are established in a State of the Community other than that of the person for whom the services are intended.

The Council may, acting by a qualified majority on a proposal from the Commission, extend the provisions of this Chapter to nationals of a third country who provide services and who are established within the Community.

Article 60

Services shall be considered to be "services" within the meaning of this Treaty where they are normally provided for remuneration, in so far as they are not governed by the provisions relating to freedom of movement for goods, capital and persons.

"Services" shall in particular include:

    (a) activities of an industrial character;

    (b) activities of a commercial character;

    (c) activities of craftsmen;

    (d) activities of the professions.

Without prejudice to the provisions of the Chapter relating to the right of establishment, the person providing a service may, in order to do so, temporarily pursue his activity in the State where the service is provided, under the same conditions as are imposed by that State on its own nationals.

Article 61

1. Freedom to provide services in the field of transport shall be governed by the provisions of the Title relating to transport.

2. The liberalisation of banking and insurance services connected with movements of capital shall be effected in step with the progressive liberalisation of movement of capital.

Article 62

Save as otherwise provided in this Treaty, Member States shall not introduce any new restrictions on the freedom to provide services which have in fact been attained at the date of the entry into force of this Treaty.

Article 63

1. Before the end of the first stage, the Council shall, acting unanimously on a proposal from the Commission and after consulting the Economic and Social Committee and the Assembly, draw up a general programme for the abolition of existing restrictions on freedom to provide services within the Community. The Commission shall submit its proposal to the Council during the first two years of the first stage.

The programme shall set out the general conditions under which and the stages by which each type of service is to be liberalised.

2. In order to implement this general programme or, in the absence of such programme, in order to achieve a stage in the liberalisation of a specific service, the Council shall, on a proposal from the Commission and after consulting the Economic and Social Committee and the Assembly, issue directives acting unanimously until the end of the first stage and by a qualified majority thereafter.

3. As regards the proposals and decisions referred to in paragraphs 1 and 2, priority shall as a general rule be given to those services which directly affect production costs or the liberalisation of which helps to promote trade in goods.

Article 64

The Member States declare their readiness to undertake the liberalisation of services beyond the extent required by the directives issued pursuant to Article 63(2), if their general economic situation and the situation of the economic sector concerned so permit.

To this end, the Commission shall make recommendations to the Member States concerned.

Article 65

As long as restrictions on freedom to provide services have not been abolished, each Member State shall apply such restrictions without distinction on grounds of nationality or residence to all persons providing services within the meaning of the first paragraph of Article 59.

Article 66

The provisions of Articles 55 to 58 shall apply to the matters covered by this Chapter.

CHAPTER 4. CAPITAL

Article 67

1. During the transitional period and to the extent necessary to ensure the proper functioning of the common market, Member States shall progressively abolish between themselves all restrictions on the movement of capital belonging to persons resident in Member States and any discrimination based on the nationality or on the place of residence of the parties or on the place where such capital is invested.

2. Current payments connected with the movement of capital between Member States shall be freed from all restrictions by the end of the first stage at the latest.

Article 68

1.   Member States shall, as regards the matters dealt with in this Chapter, be as liberal as possible in granting such exchange authorisations as are still necessary after the entry into force of this Treaty.

2.   Where a Member State applies to the movements of capital liberalised in accordance with the provisions of this Chapter the domestic rules governing the capital market and the credit system, it shall do so in a non-discriminatory manner.

* * *

Article 70

1.   The Commission shall propose to the Council measures for the progressive coordination of the exchange policies of Member States in respect of the movement of capital between those States and third countries.   For this purpose the Council shall issue directives, acting by a qualified majority.   It shall endeavour to attain the highest possible degree of liberalization.   Unanimity shall be required for measures which constitute a step back as regards the liberalization of capital movements.

2.   Where the measures taken in accordance with paragraph 1 do not permit the elimination of differences between the exchange rules of Member States and where such differences could lead persons resident in one of the Member States to use the freer transfer facilities within the Community which are provided for in Article 67 in order to evade the rules of one of the Member States concerning the movement of capital to or from third countries, that State may, after consulting the other Member States and the Commission, take appropriate measures to overcome these difficulties.

Should the Council find that these measures are restricting the free movement of capital within the Community to a greater extent than is required for the purpose of overcoming the difficulties, it may, acting by a qualified majority on a proposal from the Commission, decide that the State concerned shall amend or abolish these measures.

CHAPTER 5. TRANSPORT

Article 74

The objectives of this Treaty shall, in matters governed by this Title, be pursued by Member States within the framework of a common transport policy.

* * *

PART THREE. POLICY OF THE COMMUNITY

TITLE I. COMMON RULES

CHAPTER 1. RULES ON COMPETITION

Section 1

Rules Applying to Undertakings

Article 85

1.   The following shall be prohibited as incompatible with the common market: all agreements between undertakings, decision by associations of undertakings and concerted practices which may affect trade between Member States and which have as their object or effect the prevention, restriction or distortion of competition within the common market, and in particular those which:

(a) directly or indirectly fix purchase or selling prices or any other trading conditions;

(b) limit or control production, markets, technical development, or investment;

(c) share markets or sources of supply;

(d) apply dissimilar conditions to equivalent transactions with other trading parties, thereby placing them at a competitive disadvantage;

(e) make the conclusion of contracts subject to acceptance by the other parties of supplementary obligations which, by their nature or according to commercial usage, have no connection with the subject of such contracts.

2. Any agreements or decisions prohibited pursuant to this Article shall be automatically void.

3. The provisions of paragraph 1 may, however, be declared inapplicable in the case of:

—any agreement or category of agreements between undertakings;

—any decision or category of decisions by associations of undertakings;

—any concerted practice or category of concerted practices;

which contributes to improving the production or distribution of goods or to promoting technical or economic progress, while allowing consumers a fair share of the resulting benefit, and which does not:

(a) impose on the undertakings concerned restrictions which are not indispensable to the attainment of these objectives;

(b) afford such undertakings the possibility of eliminating competition in respect of a substantial part of the products in question.

Article 86

Any abuse by one or more undertakings of a dominant position within the common market or in a substantial part of it shall be prohibited as incompatible with the common market in so far as it may affect trade between Member States.

Such abuse may, in particular, consist in:

(a) directly or indirectly imposing unfair purchase or selling prices or other unfair trading conditions;

(b) limiting production, markets or technical development to the prejudice of consumers;

(c) applying dissimilar conditions to equivalent transactions with other trading parties, thereby placing them at a competitive disadvantage;

(d) making the conclusion of contracts subject to acceptance by the other parties of supplementary obligations which, by their nature or according to commercial usage, have no connection with the subject of such contracts.

Article 87

1. Within three years of the entry into force of this Treaty the Council shall, acting unanimously on a proposal from the Commission and after consulting the Assembly, adopt any appropriate regulations or directives to give effect to the principles set out in Articles 85 and 86.

If such provisions have not been adopted within the period mentioned, they shall be laid down by the Council, acting by a qualified majority on a proposal from the Commission and after consulting the Assembly.

2. The regulations or directives referred to in paragraph 1 shall be designed in particular:

(a) to ensure compliance with the prohibitions laid down in Article 85(1) and in Article 86 by making provisions for fines and periodic penalty payments;

(b) to lay down detailed rules for the application of Article 85(3), taking into account the need to ensure effective supervision on the one hand, and to simplify administration to the greatest possible extent on the other;

(c) to define, if need be, in the various branches of the economy, the scope of the provisions of Articles 85 and 86;

(d) to define the respective functions of the Commission and of the Court of Justice in applying the provisions laid down in this paragraph;

(e) to determine the relationship between national laws and the provisions contained in this Section or adopted pursuant to this Article.

Article 88

Until the entry into force of the provisions adopted in pursuance of Article 87, the authorities in Member States shall rule on the admissibility of agreements, decisions and concerted practices and on abuse of a dominant position in the common market in accordance with the law of their country and with the provisions of Article 85, in particular paragraph 3, and of Article 86.

Article 89

1. Without prejudice to Article 88, the Commission shall, as soon as it takes up its duties, ensure the application of the principles laid down in Articles 85 and 86. On application by a Member State or on its own initiative, and in cooperation with the competent authorities in the Member States, who shall give it their assistance, the Commission shall investigate cases of suspected infringement of these principles. If it finds that there has been an infringement, it shall propose appropriate measures to bring it to an end.

2. If the infringement is not brought to an end, the Commission shall record such infringement of the principles in a reasoned decision. The Commission may publish its decision and authorise Member States to take the measures, the conditions and details of which it shall determine, needed to remedy the situation.

Article 90

1. In the case of public undertakings and undertakings to which Member States grant special or exclusive rights, Member States shall neither enact nor maintain in force any measure contrary to the rules contained in this Treaty, in particular to those rules provided for in Article 7 and Articles 85 to 94.

2. Undertakings entrusted with the operation of services of general economic interest or having the character of a revenue-producing monopoly shall be subject to the rules contained in this Treaty, in particular to the rules on competition, in so far as the application of such rules does not obstruct the performance, in law or in fact, of the particular tasks assigned to them. The development of trade must not be affected to such an extent as would be contrary to the interests of the Community.

3. The Commission shall ensure the application of the provisions of this Article and shall, where necessary, address appropriate directives or decisions to Member States.

Section 2

Dumping

Article 91

1. If, during the transitional period, the Commission, on application by a Member State or by any other interested party, finds that dumping is being practised within the common market, it shall address recommendations to the person or persons with whom such practices originate for the purpose of putting an end to them.

Should the practices continue, the Commission shall authorise the injured Member State to take protective measures, the conditions and details of which the Commission shall determine.

2. As soon as this Treaty enters into force, products which originate in or are in free circulation in one Member State and which have been exported to another Member State shall, on reimportation, be admitted into the territory of the first-mentioned State free of all customs duties, quantitative restrictions or measures having equivalent effect. The Commission shall lay down appropriate rules for the application of this paragraph.

Section 3

Aids Granted by States

Article 92

1. Save as otherwise provided in this Treaty, any aid granted by a Member State or through State resources in any form whatsoever which distorts or threatens to distort competition by favouring certain undertakings or the production of certain goods shall, in so far as it affects trade between Member States, be incompatible with the common market.

2. The following shall be compatible with the common market:

(a) aid having a social character, granted to individual consumers, provided that such aid is granted without discrimination related to the origin of the products concerned;

(b) aid to make good the damage caused by natural disasters or exceptional occurrences;

(c) aid granted to the economy of certain areas of the Federal Republic of Germany affected by the division of Germany, in so far as such aid is required in order to compensate for the economic disadvantages caused by that division.

3. The following may be considered to be compatible with the common market:

(a) aid to promote the economic development of areas where the standard of living is abnormally low or where there is serious underemployment;

(b) aid to promote the execution of an important project of common European interest or to remedy a serious disturbance in the economy of a Member State;

(c) aid to facilitate the development of certain economic activities or of certain economic areas, where such aid does not adversely affect trading conditions to an extent contrary to the common interest. However, the aids granted to shipbuilding as of 1 January 1957 shall, in so far as they serve only to compensate for the absence of customs protection, be progressively reduced under the same conditions as apply to the elimination of customs duties, subject to the provisions of this Treaty concerning common commercial policy towards third countries;

(d) such other categories of aid as may be specified by decision of the Council acting by a qualified majority on a proposal from the Commission.

Article 93

1. The Commission shall, in cooperation with Member States, keep under constant review all systems of aid existing in those States. It shall propose to the latter any appropriate measures required by the progressive development or by the functioning of the common market.

2. If, after giving notice to the parties concerned to submit their comments, the Commission finds that aid granted by a State or through State resources is not compatible with the common market having regard to Article 92, or that such aid is being misused, it shall decide that the State concerned shall abolish or alter

such aid within a period of time to be determined by the Commission.

If the State concerned does not comply with this decision within the prescribed time, the Commission or any other interested State may, in derogation from the provisions of Articles 169 and 170, refer the matter to the Court of Justice direct.

On application by a Member State, the Council, may, acting unanimously, decide that aid which that State is granting or intends to grant shall be considered to be compatible with the common market, in derogation from the provisions of Article 92 or from the regulations provided for in Article 94, if such a decision is justified by exceptional circumstances. If, as regards the aid in question, the Commission has already initiated the procedure provided for in the first subparagraph of this paragraph, the fact that the State concerned has made its application to the Council shall have the effect of suspending that procedure until the Council has made its attitude known.

If, however, the Council has not made its attitude known within three months of the said application being made, the Commission shall give its decision on the case.

3. The Commission shall be informed, in sufficient time to enable it to submit its comments, of any plans to grant or alter aid. If it considers that any such plan is not compatible with the common market having regard to Article 92, it shall without delay initiate the procedure provided for in paragraph 2. The Member State concerned shall not put its proposed measures into effect until this procedure has resulted in a final decision.

Article 94

The Council may, acting by a qualified majority on a proposal from the Commission, make any appropriate regulations for the application of Articles 92 and 93 and may in particular determine the conditions in which Article 93(3) shall apply and the categories of aid exempted from this procedure.

CHAPTER 2. TAX PROVISIONS

Article 95

No Member State shall impose, directly or indirectly, on the products of other Member States any internal taxation of any kind in excess of that imposed directly or indirectly on similar domestic products.

Furthermore, no Member State shall impose on the products of other Member States any internal taxation of such a nature as to afford indirect protection to other products.

Member States shall, not later than at the beginning of the second stage, repeal or amend any provisions existing when this Treaty enters into force which conflict with the preceding rules.

Article 96

Where products are exported to the territory of any Member State, any repayment of internal taxation shall not exceed the internal taxation imposed on them whether directly or indirectly.

Article 97

Member States which levy a turnover tax calculated on a cumulative multi-stage tax system may, in the case of internal taxation imposed by them on imported products or of repayments allowed by them on exported products, establish average rates for products or groups of products, provided that there is no infringement of the principles laid down in Articles 95 and 96.

Where the average rates established by a Member State do not conform to these principles, the Commission shall address appropriate directives or decisions to the State concerned.

Article 98

In the case of charges other than turnover taxes, excise duties and other forms of indirect taxation, remissions and repayments in respect of exports to other Member States may not be granted and countervailing charges in respect of imports from Member States may not be imposed unless the measures contemplated have been previously approved for a limited period by the Council acting by a qualified majority on a proposal from the Commission.

Article 99

[SEA]

The Council shall, acting unanimously on a proposal from the Commission and after consulting the European Parliament, adopt provisions on the harmonization of legislation concerning turnover taxes, excise duties, and other forms of indirect taxation to the extent that such harmonization is necessary to ensure the establishment and the operation of the internal market within the time-limits laid down in Article 8A.

CHAPTER 3.   APPROXIMATION OF LAWS

Article 100

The Council shall, acting unanimously on a proposal from the Commission, issue directives for the approximation of such provisions laid down by law, regulation or administrative action in Member States as directly affect the establishment or functioning of the common market.

The Assembly and the Economic and Social Committee shall be consulted in the case of directives whose implementation would, in one or more Member States, involve the amendment of legislation.

Article 100 A

[SEA]

1. By way of derogation from Article 100 and save where otherwise provided in this Treaty, the following provisions shall apply for the achievement of the objectives set out in Article 8A. The Council shall, acting by a qualified majority on a proposal from the Commission in cooperation with the European Parliament and the Economic and Social Committee, adopt the measures for the approximation of the provisions laid down by law, regulation or administrative action in Member States which have as their object the establishment and functioning of the internal market.

2. Paragraph 1 shall not apply to fiscal provisions, to those relating to the free movement of persons nor to those relating to the rights and interests of employed persons.

3. The Commission, in its proposals laid down in paragraph 1 concerning health, safety, environmental protection and consumer protection, will take as a base a high level of protection.

4. If, after the adoption of a harmonization measure by the Council acting by a qualified majority, a Member State deems it necessary to apply national provisions on grounds of major needs referred to in Article 36, or relating to protection of the environment or the working environment, it shall notify the Commission of these provisions.

The Commission shall confirm the provisions involved after having verified that they are not a means of arbitrary discrimination or a disguised restriction on trade between Member States.

By way of derogation from the procedure laid down in Articles 169 and 170, the Commission or any Member State may bring the matter directly before the Court of Justice if it considers that another Member State is making improper use of the powers provided for in this Article.

5.   The harmonization measures referred to above shall, in appropriate cases, include a safeguard clause authorizing the Member States to take, for one or more of the non-economic reasons referred to in Article 36, provisional measures subject to a Community control procedure.

Article 100 B

[SEA]

1.   During 1992, the Commission shall, together with each Member State, draw up an inventory of national laws, regulations and administrative provisions which fall under Article 100 A and which have not been harmonized pursuant to that Article.

The Council, acting in accordance with the provisions of Article 100 A, may decide that the provisions in force in a Member State must be recognized as being equivalent to those applied by another Member State.

2.   The provisions of Article 100 A(4) shall apply by analogy.

3.   The Commission shall draw up the inventory referred to in the first subparagraph of paragraph 1 and shall submit appropriate proposals in good time to allow the Council to act before the end of 1992.

Article 101

Where the Commission finds that a difference between the provisions laid down by law, regulation or administrative action in Member States is distorting the conditions of competition in the common market and that the resultant distortion needs to be eliminated, it shall consult the Member States concerned.

If such consultation does not result in an agreement eliminating the distortion in question, the Council shall, on a proposal from the Commission, acting unanimously during the first stage and by a qualified majority thereafter, issue the necessary directives. The Commission and the Council may take any other appropriate measures provided for in this Treaty.

Article 102

1. Where there is reason to fear that the adoption or amendment of a provision laid down by law, regulation or administrative action may cause distortion within the meaning of Article 101, a Member State desiring to proceed therewith shall consult the Commission. After consulting the Member States, the Commission shall recommend to the States concerned such measures as may be appropriate to avoid the distortion in question.

2. If a State desiring to introduce or amend its own provisions does not comply with the recommendation addressed to it by the Commission, other Member States shall not be required, in pursuance of Article 101, to amend their own provisions in order to eliminate such distortion. If the Member State which has ignored the recommendation of the Commission causes distortion detrimental only to itself, the provisions of Article 101 shall not apply.

TITLE II. ECONOMIC POLICY

* * *

CHAPTER 1. COOPERATION IN ECONOMIC AND MONETARY POLICY (ECONOMIC AND MONETARY UNION)

Article 102 A

[SEA]

(1) In order to ensure the convergency of economic and monetary policy which is necessary for the further development of the Community, Member States shall cooperate in accordance with the objectives of Article 104. In doing so, they shall take account of the experience acquired in cooperation in the framework of the European Monetary System and in developing the ECU, and shall respect existing powers in this field.

(2) Insofar as further development in the field of economic and monetary policy necessitates institutional changes, the procedure laid down in Article 236 shall be applicable. The Commission, the Monetary Committee and the Committee of Governors of the Central Banks shall be consulted regarding institutional changes in the monetary area.

* * *

CHAPTER 3. BALANCE OF PAYMENTS

Article 104

Each Member State shall pursue the economic policy needed to ensure the equilibrium of its overall balance of payments and to maintain confidence in its currency, while taking care to ensure a high level of employment and a stable level of prices.

* * *

Article 107

1. Each Member State shall treat its policy with regard to rates of exchange as a matter of common concern.

* * *

Article 109

1. Where a sudden crisis in the balance of payments occurs and a decision within the meaning of Article 108(2) is not immediately taken, the Member State concerned may, as a precaution, take the necessary protective measures. Such measures must cause the least possible disturbance in the functioning of the common market and must not be wider in scope than is strictly necessary to remedy the sudden difficulties which have arisen.

2. The Commission and the other Member States shall be informed of such protective measures not later than when they enter into force. The Commission may recommend to the Council the granting of mutual assistance under Article 108.

3. After the Commission has delivered an opinion and the Monetary Committee has been consulted, the Council may, acting by a qualified majority, decide that the State concerned shall amend, suspend or abolish the protective measures referred to above.

CHAPTER 4. COMMERCIAL POLICY

Article 110

By establishing a customs union between themselves Member States aim to contribute, in the common interest, to the harmonious development of world trade, the progressive abolition of restrictions on international trade and the lowering of customs barriers.

The common commercial policy shall take into account the favourable effect which the abolition of customs duties between Member States may have on the increase in the competitive strength of undertakings in those States. * * *

* * *

Article 113

1. After the transitional period has ended, the common commercial policy shall be based on uniform principles, particularly in regard to changes in tariff rates, the conclusion of tariff and trade agreements, the achievement of uniformity in measures of liberalisation, export policy and measures to protect trade such as those to be taken in case of dumping or subsidies.

2. The Commission shall submit proposals to the Council for implementing the common commercial policy.

3. Where agreements with third countries need to be negotiated, the Commission shall make recommendations to the Council, which shall authorise the Commission to open the necessary negotiations.

The Commission shall conduct these negotiations in consultation with a special committee appointed by the Council to assist the Commission in this task and within the framework of such directives as the Council may issue to it.

4. In exercising the powers conferred upon it by this Article, the Council shall act by a qualified majority.

Article 114

The agreements referred to in Article 111(2) and in Article 113 shall be concluded by the Council on behalf of the Community, acting unanimously during the first two stages and by a qualified majority thereafter.

* * *

Article 115

In order to ensure that the execution of measures of commercial policy taken in accordance with this Treaty by any Member State is not obstructed by deflection of trade, or where differences between such measures lead to economic difficulties in one or more of the Member States, the Commission shall recommend the methods for the requisite cooperation between Member States. Failing this, the Commission shall authorise Member States to take the necessary protective measures, the conditions and details of which it shall determine.

In case of urgency during the transitional period, Member States may themselves take the necessary measures and shall notify them to the other Member States and to the Commission, which may decide that the States concerned shall amend or abolish such measures.

In the selection of such measures, priority shall be given to those which cause the least disturbance to the functioning of the common market and which take into account the need to expedite, as far as possible, the introduction of the common customs tariff.

Article 116

From the end of the transitional period onwards, Member States shall, in respect of all matters of particular interest to the common market, proceed within the framework of international organisations of an economic character only by common action. To this end, the Commission shall submit to the Council, which shall act by a qualified majority, proposals concerning the scope and implementation of such common action.

During the transitional period, Member States shall consult each other for the purpose of concerting the action they take and adopting as far as possible a uniform attitude.

TITLE III. SOCIAL POLICY

CHAPTER 1. SOCIAL PROVISIONS

Article 117

Member States agree upon the need to promote improved working conditions and an improved standard of living for workers, so as to make possible their harmonisation while the improvement is being maintained.

They believe that such a development will ensue not only from the functioning of the common market, which will favour the harmonisation of social systems, but also from the procedures provided for in this Treaty and from the approximation of provisions laid down by law, regulation or administrative action.

Article 118

Without prejudice to the other provisions of this Treaty and in conformity with its general objectives, the Commission shall have the task of promoting close cooperation between Member States in the social field, particularly in matters relating to:

—employment;

—labour law and working conditions;

—basic and advanced vocational training;

—social security;

—prevention of occupational accidents and diseases;

—occupational hygiene;

—the right of association, and collective bargaining between employers and workers.

To this end, the Commission shall act in close contact with Member States by making studies, delivering opinions and arranging consultations both on problems arising at national level and on those of concern to international organisations.

Before delivering the opinions provided for in this Article, the Commission shall consult the Economic and Social Committee.

The Council may, acting unanimously at the request of the Court of Justice and after consulting the Commission and the European Parliament, amend the provisions of Title III of the Statute. [SEA]

Article 118 A

[SEA]

1.　Member States shall pay particular attention to encouraging improvements, especially in the working environment, as regards the health and safety of workers, and shall set as their objective the harmonization of conditions in this area, while maintaining the improvements made.

2.　In order to help achieve the objective laid down in the first paragraph, the Council, acting by a qualified majority on a proposal from the Commission, in cooperation with the European Parliament and after consulting the Economic and Social Committee, shall adopt, by means of directives, minimum requirements for gradual implementation, having regard to the conditions and technical rules obtaining in each of the Member States.

Such directives shall avoid imposing administrative, financial and legal constraints in a way which would hold back the creation and development of small and medium-sized undertakings.

3.　The provisions adopted pursuant to this Article shall not prevent any Member State from maintaining or introducing more stringent measures for the protection of working conditions compatible with this Treaty.

Article 118 B

[SEA]

The Commission shall endeavour to develop the dialogue between management and labour at European level which could, if the two sides consider it desirable, lead to relations based on agreement.

Article 119

Each Member State shall during the first stage ensure and subsequently maintain the application of the principle that men and women should receive equal pay for equal work.

For the purpose of this Article, "pay" means the ordinary basic or minimum wage or salary and any other consideration, whether in cash or in kind, which the worker receives, directly or indirectly, in respect of his employment from his employer.

Equal pay without discrimination based on sex means:

(a) that pay for the same work at piece rates shall be calculated on the basis of the same unit of measurement;

(b) that pay for work at time rates shall be the same for the same job.

* * *

CHAPTER 2. THE EUROPEAN SOCIAL FUND

Article 123

In order to improve employment opportunities for workers in the common market and to contribute thereby to raising the standard of living, a European Social Fund is hereby established in accordance with the provisions set out below; it shall have the task of rendering the employment of workers easier and of increasing their geographical and occupational mobility within the Community.

* * *

Article 125

1. On application by a Member State the Fund shall, within the framework of the rules provided for in Article 127, meet 50% of the expenditure incurred after the entry into force of this Treaty by that State or by a body governed by public law for the purposes of:

(a) ensuring productive re-employment of workers by means of:

—vocational retraining;

—resettlement allowances;

(b) granting aid for the benefit of workers whose employment is reduced or temporarily suspended, in whole or in part, as a result of the conversion of an undertaking to other production, in order that they may retain the same wage level pending their full re-employment.

* * *

TITLE IV. THE EUROPEAN INVESTMENT BANK

Article 129

A European Investment Bank is hereby established; it shall have legal personality.

The members of the European Investment Bank shall be the Member States.

The Statute of the European Investment Bank is laid down in a Protocol annexed to this Treaty.

Article 130

The task of the European Investment Bank shall be to contribute, by having recourse to the capital market and utilising its own resources, to the balanced and steady development of the common market in the interest of the Community. For this purpose the Bank shall, operating on a non-profit-making basis, grant loans and give guarantees which facilitate the financing of the following projects in all sectors of the economy:

(a) projects for developing less developed regions;

(b) projects for modernising or converting undertakings or for developing fresh activities called for by the progressive establishment of the common market, where these projects are of such a size or nature that they cannot be entirely financed by the various means available in the individual Member States;

(c) projects of common interest to several Member States which are of such a size or nature that they cannot be entirely financed by the various means available in the individual Member States.

TITLE V. ECONOMIC AND SOCIAL COHESION

[SEA]

Article 130 A

In order to promote its overall harmonious development, the Community shall develop and pursue its actions leading to the strengthening of its economic and social cohesion.

In particular the Community shall aim at reducing disparities between the various regions and the backwardness of the least-favoured regions.

Article 130 B

Member States shall conduct their economic policies, and shall coordinate them, in such a way as, in addition, to attain the objectives set out in Article 130 A. The implementation of the common policies and of the internal market shall take into account the objectives set out in Article 130 A and in Article 130 C and shall contribute to their achievement. The Community shall support the achievement of these objectives by the action it takes through the structural Funds (European Agricultural Guidance and Guarantee Fund, Guidance Section, European Social Fund, European Regional Development Fund), the European Investment Bank and the other existing financial instruments.

Article 130 C

The European Regional Development fund is intended to help redress the principal regional imbalances in the Community through participating in the development and structural adjustment of regions whose development is lagging behind and in the conversion of declining industrial regions.

* * *

TITLE VI. RESEARCH AND TECHNOLOGICAL DEVELOPMENT

[SEA]

Article 130 F

1. The Community's aim shall be to strengthen the scientific and technological basis of European industry and to encourage it to become more competitive at the international level.

2. In order to achieve this, it shall encourage undertakings including small and medium-sized undertakings,

research centres and universities in their research and technological development activities; it shall support their efforts to cooperate with one another, aiming, in particular, at enabling undertakings to exploit the Community's internal market potential to the full, in particular through the opening up of national public contracts, the definition of common standards and the removal of legal and fiscal barriers to that cooperation.

3. In the achievement of these aims, particular account shall be taken of the connection between the common research and technological development effort, the establishment of the internal market and the implementation of common policies, particularly as regards competition and trade.

Article 130 G

In pursuing these objectives the Community shall carry out the following activities, complementing the activities carried out in the Member States:

(a) implementation of research, technological development and demonstration programmes, by promoting cooperation with undertakings, research centres and universities;

(b) promotion of cooperation with third countries and international organizations in the field of Community research, technological development, and demonstration;

(c) dissemination and optimization of the results of activities in Community research, technological development, and demonstration;

(d) stimulation of the training and mobility of researchers in the Community.

* * *

TITLE VII. ENVIRONMENT

[SEA]

Article 130 R

1. Action by the Community relating to the environment shall have the following objectives:

(i) to preserve, protect and improve the quality of the environment;

(ii) to contribute towards protecting human health;

(iii) to ensure a prudent and rational utilization of natural resources.

2. Action by the Community relating to the environment shall be based on the principles that preventive action should be taken, that environmental damage should as a priority be rectified at source, and that the polluter should pay. Environmental protection requirements shall be a component of the Community's other policies.

3. In preparing its action relating to the environment, the Community shall take account of:

(i) available scientific and technical data;

(ii) environmental conditions in the various regions of the Community;

(iii) the potential benefits and costs of action or of lack of action;

(iv) the economic and social development of the Community as a whole and the balanced development of its regions.

4. The Community shall take action relating to the environment to the extent to which the objectives referred to in paragraph 1 can be attained better at Community level than at the level of the individual Member States. Without prejudice to certain measures of a Com-

munity nature, the Member States shall finance and implement the other measures.

5. Within their respective spheres of competence, the Community and the Member States shall cooperate with third countries and with the relevant international organizations. The arrangements for Community cooperation may be the subject of agreements between the Community and the third parties concerned, which shall be negotiated and concluded in accordance with Article 228.

The previous paragraph shall be without prejudice to Member States' competence to negotiate in international bodies and to conclude international agreements.

Article 130 S

The Council, acting unanimously on a proposal from the Commission and after consulting the European Parliament and the Economic and Social Committee, shall decide what action is to be taken by the Community.

The Council shall, under the conditions laid down in the preceding subparagraph, define those matters on which decisions are to be taken by a qualified majority.

Article 130 T

The protective measures adopted in common pursuant to Article 130 S shall not prevent any Member State from maintaining or introducing more stringent protective measures compatible with this Treaty.

PART FOUR. ASSOCIATION OF THE OVERSEAS TERRITORIES AND COUNTRIES

Article 131

The Member States agree to associate with the Community the non-European countries and territories which have special relations with Belgium, France, Italy, the Netherlands, Portugal, Spain and the United Kingdom. These countries and territories (hereinafter called the "countries and territories") are listed in Annex IV to this Treaty.

The purpose of association shall be to promote the economic and social development of the countries and territories and to establish close economic relations between them and the Community as a whole.

In accordance with the principles set out in the Preamble to this Treaty, association shall serve primarily to further the interests and prosperity of the inhabitants of these countries and territories in order to lead them to the economic, social and cultural development to which they aspire.

* * *

Article 133

1.   Customs duties on imports into the Member States of goods originating in the countries and territories shall be completely abolished in conformity with the progressive abolition of customs duties between Member States in accordance with the provisions of this Treaty.

* * *

PART FIVE. INSTITUTIONS OF THE COMMUNITY

TITLE I. PROVISIONS GOVERNING THE INSTITUTIONS

CHAPTER 1. THE INSTITUTIONS

Section 1

The Assembly

Article 137

The Assembly, which shall consist of representatives of the peoples of the States brought together in the Community, shall exercise the advisory and supervisory powers which are conferred upon it by this Treaty.

Article 138

1. The representatives in the Assembly of the peoples of the States brought together in the Community shall be elected by direct universal suffrage.

2. The number of representatives elected in each Member State shall be as follows.

Belgium 24
Denmark 16
Germany 81
Greece 24
France... 81
Ireland 15
Italy.. 81
Luxembourg 6
Netherlands...................................... 25
Portugal 24
Spain.. 60
United Kingdom 81

*   *   *

Article 140

The Assembly shall elect its President and its officers from among its members.

Members of the Commission may attend all meetings and shall, at their request, be heard on behalf of the Commission.

The Commission shall reply orally or in writing to questions put to it by the Assembly or by its members.

The Council shall be heard by the Assembly in accordance with the conditions laid down by the Council in its rules of procedure.

Article 141

Save as otherwise provided in this Treaty the Assembly shall act by an absolute majority of the votes cast.

The rules of procedure shall determine the quorum.

* * *

Article 144

If a motion of censure on the activities of the Commission is tabled before it, the Assembly shall not vote thereon until at least three days after the motion has been tabled and only by open vote.

If the motion of censure is carried by a two-thirds majority of the votes cast, representing a majority of the members of the Assembly, the members of the Commission shall resign as a body. They shall continue to deal with current business until they are replaced in accordance with Article 158.

Section 2

The Council

Article 145

[SEA]

To ensure that the objectives set out in this Treaty are attained, the Council shall, in accordance with the provisions of this Treaty:

    —ensure coordination of the general economic policies of the Member States;

    —have power to take decisions;

    —confer on the Commission, in the acts it adopts, powers for the implementation of the rules the Council lays down. The Council may impose certain requirements in respect of the exercise of those powers. The Council may also reserve the right, in specific cases, to exercise directly implementing powers itself.

The procedures referred to above must be consonant with principles and rules to be laid down in advance by the Council, acting unanimously on a proposal from the Commission and after obtaining the Opinion of the European Parliament.

Article 146 (Article 2 of the Merger Treaty)

The Council shall consist of Representatives of the Member States. Each Government shall delegate to it one of its members.

The office of the President shall be held for a term of six months by each member of the Council in turn, in the following order of Member States: Belgium, Denmark, Germany, Greece, France, Ireland, Italy, Luxembourg, Netherlands, Portugal, Spain, United Kingdom.

* * *

Article 148

1. Save as otherwise provided in this Treaty, the Council shall act by a majority of its members.

2. Where the Council is required to act by a qualified majority, the votes of its members shall be weighted as follows:

Belgium 5
Denmark 3
Germany 10
Greece 5
France 10
Ireland 3
Italy 10
Luxembourg 2
Netherlands 5
Portugal 5
Spain 8
United Kingdom 10

For their adoption, acts of the Council shall require at least:

　　—54 votes in favour where this Treaty requires them to be adopted on a proposal from the Commission.

　　—54 votes in favour, cast by at least eight members, in other cases.

3. Abstentions by members present in person or represented shall not prevent the adoption by the Council of acts which require unanimity.

Article 149

[SEA]

1. Where, in pursuance of this Treaty, the Council acts on a proposal from the Commission, unanimity shall

be required for an act constituting an amendment to that proposal.

2. Where, in pursuance of this Treaty, the Council acts in cooperation with the European Parliament, the following procedure shall apply:

(a) The Council, acting by a qualified majority under the conditions of paragraph 1, on a proposal from the Commission and after obtaining the Opinion of the European Parliament, shall adopt a common position.

(b) The Council's common position shall be communicated to the European Parliament. The Council and the Commission shall inform the European Parliament fully of the reasons which led the Council to adopt its common position and also of the Commission's position.

If, within three months of such communication, the European Parliament approves this common position or has not taken a decision within that period, the Council shall definitively adopt the act in question in accordance with the common position.

(c) The European Parliament may within the period of three months referred to in point (b), by an absolute majority of its component members, propose amendments to the Council's common position. The European Parliament may also, by the same majority, reject the Council's common position. The result of the proceedings shall be transmitted to the Council and the Commission.

If the European Parliament has rejected the Council's common position, unanimity shall be required for the Council to act on a second reading.

(d) The Commission shall, within a period of one month, re-examine the proposal on the basis of which the Council adopted its common position, by taking into account the amendments proposed by the European Parliament.

The Commission shall forward to the Council, at the same time as its re-examined proposal, the amendments of the European Parliament which it has not accepted, and shall express its opinion on them. The Council may adopt these amendments unanimously.

(e) The Council, acting by a qualified majority, shall adopt the proposal as re-examined by the Commission.

Unanimity shall be required for the Council to amend the proposal as re-examined by the Commission.

(f) In the cases referred to in points (c), (d) and (e), the Council shall be required to act within a period of three months. If no decision is taken within this period, the Commission proposal shall be deemed not to have been adopted.

(g) The periods referred to in points (b) and (f) may be extended by a maximum of one month by common accord between the Council and the European Parliament.

3. As long as the Council has not acted, the Commission may alter its proposal at any time during the procedures mentioned in paragraphs 1 and 2.

* * *

Article 152

The Council may request the Commission to undertake any studies which the Council considers desirable for the attainment of the common objectives, and to submit to it any appropriate proposals.

* * *

Section 3

The Commission

Article 155

In order to ensure the proper functioning and development of the common market, the Commission shall:

—ensure that the provisions of this Treaty and the measures taken by the institutions pursuant thereto are applied;

—formulate recommendations or deliver opinions on matters dealt with in this Treaty, if it expressly so provides or if the Commission considers it necessary;

—have its own power of decision and participate in the shaping of measures taken by the Council and by the Assembly in the manner provided for in this Treaty;

—exercise the powers conferred on it by the Council for the implementation of the rules laid down by the latter.

* * *

Article 157 (Article 10 of the Merger Treaty)

1. The Commission shall consist of 17 members, who shall be chosen on the grounds of their general competence and whose independence is beyond doubt.

The number of members of the Commission may be altered by the Council, acting unanimously.

Only nationals of Member States may be members of the Commission.

The Commission must include at least one national of each of the Member States, but may not include more than two members having the nationality of the same State.

2. The members of the Commission shall, in the general interest of the Communities, be completely independent in the performance of their duties.

In the performance of these duties, they shall neither seek nor take instructions from any Government or from any other body. They shall refrain from any action incompatible with their duties. Each Member State undertakes to respect this principle and not to seek to influence the members of the Commission in the performance of their tasks. The members of the Commission may not, during their term of office, engage in any other occupation, whether gainful or not. When entering upon their duties they shall give a solemn undertaking that, both during and after their term of office, they will respect the obligations arising therefrom and in particular their duty to behave with integrity and discretion as regards the acceptance, after they have ceased to hold office, of certain appointments or benefits. In the event of any breach of these obligations, the Court of Justice may, on application by the Council or the Commission, rule that the member concerned be, according to the circumstances, either compulsorily retired in accordance with the provisions of Article 13 or deprived of his right to a pension or other benefits in its stead.

Article 158 (Article 11 of the Merger Treaty)

The members of the Commission shall be appointed by common accord of the Governments of the Member States.

Their term of office shall be four years. It shall be renewable.

* * *

Article 160 (Article 13 of the Merger Treaty)

If any member of the Commission no longer fulfils the conditions required for the performance of his duties or if he has been guilty of serious misconduct, the Court of Justice may, on application by the Council or the Commission, compulsorily retire him.

* * *

Section 4

The Court of Justice

Article 164

The Court of Justice shall ensure that in the interpretation and application of this Treaty the law is observed.

Article 165

The Court of Justice shall consist of 13 Judges.

The Court of Justice shall sit in plenary session. It may, however, form chambers, each consisting of three or five Judges, either to undertake certain preparatory inquiries or to adjudicate on particular categories of cases in accordance with rules laid down for these purposes.

Whenever the Court of Justice hears cases brought before it by a Member State or by one of the institutions of the Community or, to the extent that the chambers of the Court do not have the requisite jurisdiction under the Rules of Procedure as to give preliminary rulings on questions submitted to it pursuant to Article 177, it shall sit in plenary session.

Should the Court of Justice so request, the Council may, acting unanimously, increase the number of Judges and make the necessary adjustments to the second and third paragraphs of this Article and to the second paragraph of Article 167.

Article 166

The Court of Justice shall be assisted by six Advocates-General.

It shall be the duty of the Advocate-General, acting with complete impartiality and independence, to make, in open court, reasoned submissions on cases brought before the Court of Justice, in order to assist the Court in the performance of the task assigned to it in Article 164.

Should the Court of Justice so request, the Council may, acting unanimously, increase the number of Advocates-General and make the necessary adjustments to the third paragraph of Article 167.

Article 167

The Judges and Advocates-General shall be chosen from persons whose independence is beyond doubt and who possess the qualifications required for appointment to the highest judicial offices in their respective countries or who are jurisconsults of recognised competence; they shall be appointed by common accord of the Governments of the Member States for a term of six years.

Every three years there shall be a partial replacement of the Judges. Six and seven Judges shall be replaced alternately.

Every three years there shall be a partial replacement of the Advocates-General. Three Advocates-General shall be replaced alternately.

Retiring Judges and Advocates-General shall be eligible for reappointment.

The Judges shall elect the President of the Court of Justice from among their number for a term of three years. He may be reelected.

* * *

Article 168 A

[SEA]

1. At the request of the Court of Justice and after consulting the Commission and the European Parliament, the Council may, acting unanimously, attach to the Court of Justice a court with jurisdiction to hear and determine at first instance, subject to a right of appeal to

the Court of Justice on points of law only and in accordance with the conditions laid down by the Statute, certain classes of action or proceeding brought by natural or legal persons. That court shall not be competent to hear and determine actions brought by Member States or by Community Institutions or questions referred for a preliminary ruling under Article 177.

2. The Council, following the procedure laid down in paragraph 1, shall determine the composition of that court and adopt the necessary adjustments and additional provisions to the Statute of the Court of Justice. Unless the Council decides otherwise, the provisions of this Treaty relating to the Court of Justice, in particular the provisions of the Protocol on the Statute of the Court of Justice, shall apply to that court.

3. The members of that court shall be chosen from persons whose independence is beyond doubt and who possess the ability required for appointment to judicial office; they shall be appointed by common accord of the Governments of the Member States for a term of six years. The membership shall be partially renewed every three years. Retiring members shall be eligible for reappointment.

4. That court shall establish its rules of procedure in agreement with the Court of Justice. Those rules shall require the unanimous approval of the Council.

Article 169

If the Commission considers that a Member State has failed to fulfil an obligation under this Treaty, it shall deliver a reasoned opinion on the matter after giving the State concerned the opportunity to submit its observations.

If the State concerned does not comply with the opinion within the period laid down by the Commission, the latter may bring the matter before the Court of Justice.

Article 170

A Member State which considers that another Member State has failed to fulfil an obligation under this Treaty may bring the matter before the Court of Justice.

Before a Member State brings an action against another Member State for an alleged infringement of an obligation under this Treaty, it shall bring the matter before the Commission.

The Commission shall deliver a reasoned opinion after each of the States concerned has been given the opportunity to submit its own case and its observations on the other party's case both orally and in writing.

If the Commission has not delivered an opinion within three months of the date on which the matter was brought before it, the absence of such opinion shall not prevent the matter from being brought before the Court of Justice.

Article 171

If the Court of Justice finds that a Member State has failed to fulfil an obligation under this Treaty, the State shall be required to take the necessary measures to comply with the judgment of the Court of Justice.

Article 172

Regulations made by the Council pursuant to the provisions of this Treaty may give the Court of Justice unlimited jurisdiction in regard to the penalties provided for in such regulations.

Article 173

The Court of Justice shall review the legality of acts of the Council and the Commission other than recommendations or opinions. It shall for this purpose have jurisdiction in actions brought by a Member State, the Council or the Commission on grounds of lack of competence, infringement of an essential procedural requirement, infringement of this Treaty or of any rule of law relating to its application, or misuse of powers.

Any natural or legal person may, under the same conditions, institute proceedings against a decision addressed to that person or against a decision which, although in the form of a regulation or a decision addressed to another person, is of direct and individual concern to the former.

The proceedings provided for in this Article shall be instituted within two months of the publication of the measure, or of its notification to the plaintiff, or, in the absence thereof, of the day on which it came to the knowledge of the latter, as the case may be.

Article 174

If the action is well founded, the Court of Justice shall declare the act concerned to be void.

In the case of a regulation, however, the Court of Justice shall, if it considers this necessary, state which of the effects of the regulation which it has declared void shall be considered as definitive.

Article 175

Should the Council or the Commission, in infringement of this Treaty, fail to act, the Member States and the other institutions of the Community may bring an action before the Court of Justice to have the infringement established.

The action shall be admissible only if the institution concerned has first been called upon to act. If, within two months of being so called upon, the institution concerned has not defined its position, the action may be brought within a further period of two months.

Any natural or legal person may, under the conditions laid down in the preceding paragraphs, complain to the Court of Justice that an institution of the Community has failed to address to that person any act other than a recommendation or an opinion.

Article 176

The institution whose act has been declared void or whose failure to act has been declared contrary to this Treaty shall be required to take the necessary measures to comply with the judgment of the Court of Justice.

This obligation shall not affect any obligation which may result from the application of the second paragraph of Article 215.

Article 177

The Court of Justice shall have jurisdiction to give preliminary rulings concerning:

(a) the interpretation of this Treaty;

(b) the validity and interpretation of acts of the institutions of the Community;

(c) the interpretation of the statutes of bodies established by an act of the Council where those statutes so provide.

Where such a question is raised before any court or tribunal of a Member State, that court or tribunal may, if it considers that a decision on the question is necessary to enable it to give judgment, request the Court of Justice to give a ruling thereon.

Where any such question is raised in a case pending before a court or tribunal of a Member State, against whose decisions there is no judicial remedy under national law, that court or tribunal shall bring the matter before the Court of Justice.

Article 178

The Court of Justice shall have jurisdiction in disputes relating to compensation for damage provided for in the second paragraph of Article 215.

Article 179

The Court of Justice shall have jurisdiction in any dispute between the Community and its servants within the limits and under the conditions laid down in the Staff Regulations or the Conditions of Employment.

Article 180

The Court of Justice shall, within the limits hereinafter laid down, have jurisdiction in disputes concerning:

(a) the fulfilment by Member States of obligations under the Statute of the European Investment Bank. In this connection, the Board of Directors of the Bank shall enjoy the powers conferred upon the Commission by Article 169;

(b) measures adopted by the Board of Governors of the Bank. In this connection, any Member State, the Commission or the Board of Directors of the Bank may institute proceedings under the conditions laid down in Article 173;

(c) measures adopted by the Board of Directors of the Bank. Proceedings against such measures may be instituted only by a Member State or by the Commission, under the conditions laid down in Article 173, and solely on the grounds of non-compliance with the procedure provided for in Article 21(2), (5), (6) and (7) of the Statute of the Bank.

Article 181

The Court of Justice shall have jurisdiction to give judgment pursuant to any arbitration clause contained in the contract concluded by or on behalf of the Community, whether that contract be governed by public or private law.

Article 182

The Court of Justice shall have jurisdiction in the dispute between Member States which relates to the subject matter of this Treaty if the dispute is submitted to it under a special agreement between the parties.

Article 183

Save where jurisdiction is conferred on the Court of Justice by this Treaty, disputes to which the Community is a party shall not on that ground be excluded from the jurisdiction of the courts or tribunals of the Member States.

Article 184

Notwithstanding the expiry of the period laid down in the third paragraph of Article 173, any party may, in proceedings in which a regulation of the Council or of the Commission is in issue, plead the grounds specified in the first paragraph of Article 173, in order to invoke before the Court of Justice the inapplicability of that regulation.

Article 185

Actions brought before the Court of Justice shall not have suspensory effect. The Court of Justice may, however, if it considers that circumstances so require, order that application of the contested act be suspended.

Article 186

The Court of Justice may in any cases before it prescribe any necessary interim measures.

Article 187

The judgments of the Court of Justice shall be enforceable under the conditions laid down in Article 192.

* * *

CHAPTER 2. PROVISIONS COMMON TO SEVERAL INSTITUTIONS

Article 189

In order to carry out their task the Council and the Commission shall, in accordance with the provisions of this Treaty, make regulations, issue directives, take decisions, make recommendations or deliver opinions.

A regulation shall have general application. It shall be binding in its entirety and directly applicable in all Member States.

A directive shall be binding, as to the result to be achieved, upon each Member State to which it is addressed, but shall leave to the national authorities the choice of form and methods.

A decision shall be binding in its entirety upon those to whom it is addressed.

Recommendations and opinions shall have no binding force.

* * *

Article 192

Decisions of the Council or of the Commission which impose a pecuniary obligation on persons other than States shall be enforceable.

Enforcement shall be governed by the rules of civil procedure in force in the State in the territory of which it is carried out. The order for its enforcement shall be appended in the decision, without other formality than verification of the authenticity of the decision, by the national authority which the government of each Member State shall designate for this purpose and shall make known to the Commission and to the Court of Justice.

When these formalities have been completed on application by the party concerned, the latter may proceed to enforcement in accordance with the national law, by bringing the matter directly before the competent authority.

Enforcement may be suspended only by a decision of the Court of Justice. However, the courts of the country concerned shall have jurisdiction over complaints that enforcement is being carried out in an irregular manner.

CHAPTER 3. THE ECONOMIC AND SOCIAL COMMITTEE

Article 193

An Economic and Social Committee is hereby established. It shall have advisory status.

The Committee shall consist of representatives of the various categories of economic and social activity, in particular, representatives of producers, farmers, carriers, workers, dealers, craftsmen, professional occupations and representatives of the general public.

* * *

TITLE II. FINANCIAL PROVISIONS

Article 199

All items of revenue and expenditure of the Community, including those relating to the European Social Fund, shall be included in estimates to be drawn up for each financial year and shall be shown in the budget.

The revenue and expenditure shown in the budget shall be in balance.

* * *

Article 203

1. The financial year shall run from 1 January to December.

2. Each institution of the Community shall, before 1 July, draw up estimates of its expenditure. The Commission shall consolidate these estimates in a preliminary draft budget. It shall attach thereto an opinion which may contain different estimates.

The preliminary draft budget shall contain an estimate of revenue and an estimate of expenditure.

3. The Commission shall place the preliminary draft budget before the Council not later than 1 September of the year preceding that in which the budget is to be implemented.

The Council shall consult the Commission and, where appropriate, the other institutions concerned whenever it intends to depart from the preliminary draft budget.

The Council shall, acting by a qualified majority, establish the draft budget and forward it to the Assembly.

4. The draft budget shall be placed before the Assembly not later than 5 October of the year preceding that in which the budget is to be implemented.

The Assembly shall have the right to amend the draft budget, acting by a majority of its members, and to propose to the Council, acting by an absolute majority of the votes cast, modifications to the draft budget relating to expenditure necessarily resulting from this Treaty or from acts adopted in accordance therewith.

If, within forty-five days of the draft budget being placed before it, the Assembly has given its approval, the budget shall stand as finally adopted. If within this period the Assembly has not amended the draft budget nor proposed any modifications thereto, the budget shall be deemed to be finally adopted.

If within this period the Assembly has adopted amendments or proposed modifications, the draft budget together with the amendments or proposed modifications shall be forwarded to the Council.

5. After discussing the draft budget with the Commission and, where appropriate, with the other institutions concerned, the Council shall act under the following conditions:

(a) The Council may, acting by a qualified majority, modify any of the amendments adopted by the Assembly;

(b) With regard to the proposed modifications:

—where a modification proposed by the Assembly does not have the effect of increasing the total amount of the expenditure of an institution, owing in particular to the fact that the increase in expenditure which it would involve would be expressly compensated by one or more proposed modifications correspondingly reducing expenditure, the Council may, acting by a qualified majority, reject the proposed modification. In the absence of a decision to reject it, the proposed modification shall stand as accepted;

—where a modification proposed by the Assembly has the effect of increasing the total amount of the expenditure of an institution, the Council may, acting by a qualified majority, accept this proposed modification. In the absence of a decision to accept it, the proposed modification shall stand as rejected;

—where, in pursuance of one of the two preceding subparagraphs, the Council has rejected a proposed modification, it may, acting by a qualified majority, either retain the amount shown in the draft budget or fix another amount.

The draft budget shall be modified on the basis of the proposed modifications accepted by the Council.

If, within fifteen days of the draft budget being placed before it, the Council has not modified any of the amendments adopted by the Assembly and if the modifications proposed by the latter have been accepted, the budget shall be deemed to be finally adopted. The Council shall inform the Assembly that it has not modified any of the amendments and that the proposed modifications have been accepted.

If within this period the Council has modified one or more of the amendments adopted by the Assembly or if the modifications proposed by the latter have been rejected or modified, the modified draft budget shall again be forwarded to the Assembly. The Council shall inform the Assembly of the results of its deliberations.

6. Within fifteen days of the draft budget being placed before it, the Assembly, which shall have been notified of the action taken on its proposed modifications, may, acting by a majority of its members and three-fifths of the votes cast, amend or reject the modifications to its amendments made by the Council and shall adopt the budget accordingly. If within this period the Assembly has not acted, the budget shall be deemed to be finally adopted.

7. When the procedure provided for in this Article has been completed, the President of the Assembly shall declare that the budget has been finally adopted.

8. However, the Assembly, acting by a majority of its members and two-thirds of the votes cast, may if there

are important reasons reject the draft budget and ask for a new draft to be submitted to it.

9. A maximum rate of increase in relation to the expenditure of the same type to be incurred during the current year shall be fixed annually for the total expenditure other than that necessarily resulting from this Treaty or from acts adopted in accordance therewith.

The Commission shall, after consulting the Economic Policy Committee, declare what this maximum rate is as it results from:

—the trend, in terms of volume, of the gross national product within the Community;

—the average variation in the budgets of the Member States; and

—the trend of the cost of living during the preceding financial year.

The maximum rate shall be communicated, before 1 May, to all the institutions of the Community. The latter shall be required to conform to this during the budgetary procedure, subject to the provisions of the fourth and fifth subparagraphs of this paragraph.

If, in respect of expenditure other than that necessarily resulting from this Treaty or from acts adopted in accordance therewith, the actual rate of increase in the draft budget established by the Council is over half the maximum rate, the Assembly may, exercising its right of amendment, further increase the total amount of the expenditure to the limit not exceeding half the maximum rate.

Where the Assembly, the Council or the Commission consider that the activities of the Communities require that the rate determined according to the procedure laid down in this paragraph should be exceeded, another rate may be fixed by agreement between the Council, acting by a qualified majority, and the Assembly, acting by a majority of its members and three fifths of the votes cast.

10.   Each institution shall exercise the powers conferred upon it by this Article, with due regard for the provisions of the Treaty and for acts adopted in accordance therewith, in particular those relating to the Communities' own resources and to the balance between revenue and expenditure.

* * *

PART SIX.   GENERAL AND FINAL PROVISIONS

Article 210

The Community shall have legal personality.

Article 211

In each of the Member States, the Community shall enjoy the most extensive legal capacity accorded to legal persons under their laws; it may, in particular, acquire or dispose of movable and immovable property and may be a party to legal proceedings.   To this end, the Community shall be represented by the Commission.

* * *

Article 213

The Commission may, within the limits and under the conditions laid down by the Council in accordance with the provisions of this Treaty, collect any information and carry out any checks required for the performance of the tasks entrusted to it.

Article 214

The members of the institutions of the Community, the members of committees, and the officials and other servants of the Community shall be required, even after their duties have ceased, not to disclose information of the kind covered by the obligation of professional secrecy, in particular information about undertakings, their business relations or their cost components.

Article 215

The contractual liability of the Community shall be governed by the law applicable to the contract in question.

In the case of non-contractual liability, the Community shall, in accordance with the general principles common to the laws of the Member States, make good any damage caused by its institutions or by its servants in the performance of their duties.

The personal liability of its servants towards the Community shall be governed by the provisions laid down in their Staff Regulations or in the Conditions of Employment applicable to them.

* * *

Article 219

Member States undertake not to submit a dispute concerning the interpretation or application of this Treaty to any method of settlement other than those provided for therein.

Article 220

Member States shall, so far as is necessary, enter into negotiations with each other with a view to securing for the benefit of their nationals:

—the protection of persons and the enjoyment and protection of rights under the same conditions as those accorded by each State to its own nationals;

—the abolition of double taxation within the Community;

—the mutual recognition of companies or firms within the meaning of the second paragraph of Article 58, the retention of legal personality in the event of transfer of their seat from one country to another, and the possibility of mergers between companies or firms governed by the laws of different countries;

—the simplification of formalities governing the reciprocal recognition and enforcement of judgments of courts or tribunals and of arbitration awards.

Article 221

Within three years of the entry into force of this Treaty, Member States shall accord nationals of the other Member States the same treatment as their own nationals as regards participation in the capital of companies or firms within the meaning of Article 58, without prejudice to the application of the other provisions of this Treaty.

Article 222

This Treaty shall in no way prejudice the rules in Member States governing the system of property ownership.

* * *

Article 228

1. Where this Treaty provides for the conclusion of agreements between the Community and one or more States or an international organisation, such agreements shall be negotiated by the Commission. Subject to the powers vested in the Commission in this field, such agreements shall be concluded by the Council, after consulting the Assembly where required by this Treaty.

The Council, the Commission or a Member State may obtain beforehand the opinion of the Court of Justice as to whether an agreement envisaged is compatible with the provisions of this Treaty. Where the opinion of the Court of Justice is adverse, the agreement may enter into force only in accordance with the procedure laid down in Article 236.

2. Agreements concluded under these conditions shall be binding on the institutions in the Community and on Member States.

Article 229

It shall be for the Commission to ensure the maintenance of the appropriate relations with the organs of the United Nations, of its specialised agencies and of the General Agreement on Tariffs and Trade.

The Commission shall also maintain such relations as are appropriate with all international organisations.

* * *

Article 232

1. The provisions of this Treaty shall not affect the provisions of the Treaty establishing the European Coal and Steel Community, in particular as regards the rights and obligations of Member States, the powers of the institutions of that Community and the rules laid down by that Treaty for the functioning of the common market in coal and steel.

2. The provisions of this Treaty shall not derogate from those of the Treaty establishing the European Atomic Energy Community.

Article 233

The provisions of this Treaty shall not preclude the existence or completion of the regional unions between Belgium, Luxembourg and the Netherlands, to the extent that the objectives of these regional unions are not attained by application of this Treaty.

Article 234

The rights and obligations arising from agreements concluded before the entry into force of this Treaty between one or more Member States on the one hand, and one or more third countries on the other, shall not be affected by the provisions of this Treaty.

To the extent that such agreements are not compatible with this Treaty, the Member State or States concerned shall take all appropriate steps to eliminate the incompatibilities established. Member States shall, where necessary, assist each other to this end and shall, where appropriate, adopt a common attitude.

In applying the agreements referred to in the first paragraph, Member States shall take into account the fact that the advantages accorded under this Treaty by each Member State form an integral part of the establishment of the Community and are thereby inseparably linked with the creation of common institutions, the conferring of powers upon them and the granting of the same advantages by all the other Member States.

Article 235

If action by the Community should prove necessary to attain, in the course of the operation of the common market, one of the objectives of the Community and this Treaty has not provided the necessary powers, the Council shall, acting unanimously on a proposal from the Commission and after consulting the Assembly, take the appropriate measures.

Article 236

The Government of any Member State or the Commission may submit to the Council proposals for the amendment of this Treaty.

If the Council, after consulting the Assembly and, where appropriate, the Commission, delivers an opinion in favour of calling a conference of representatives of the Governments of the Member States, the conference shall be convened by the President of the Council for the purpose of determining by common accord the amendments to be made to this Treaty.

The amendments shall enter into force after being ratified by all the Member States in accordance with their respective constitutional requirements.

Article 237

Any European State may apply to become a member of the Community. It shall address its application to the Council, which shall act unanimously after consulting the Commission and after receiving the assent of the European Parliament, which shall act by an absolute majority of its component members.

The conditions of admission and the adjustments to this Treaty necessitated thereby shall be the subject of an agreement between the Member States and the applicant State. This agreement shall be submitted for ratification by all the Contracting States in accordance with their respective constitutional requirements.

Article 238

The Community may conclude with a third State, a union of States or an international organisation agreements establishing an association involving reciprocal rights and obligations, common action and special procedures.

These agreements shall be concluded by the Council, acting unanimously and after receiving the assent of the European Parliament, which shall act by an absolute majority of its component members.

Where such agreements call for amendments to this Treaty, these amendments shall first be adopted in accordance with the procedure laid down in Article 236.

Article 239

The Protocols annexed to this Treaty by common accord of the Member States shall form an integral part thereof.

Article 240

This Treaty is concluded for an unlimited period.

INDEX

References are to Pages

---

†